P9-CMW-744

THE
WORLD

ALSO BY RICHARD HAASS

A World in Disarray
Foreign Policy Begins at Home
War of Necessity, War of Choice
The Opportunity
The Bureaucratic Entrepreneur
The Reluctant Sheriff
Intervention
Conflicts Unending
Beyond the INF Treaty
Congressional Power

EDITED VOLUMES
Honey and Vinegar
Transatlantic Tensions
Economic Sanctions and American Diplomacy
Superpower Arms Control

THE
WORLD

A Brief Introduction

o———o

RICHARD HAASS

PENGUIN PRESS
NEW YORK || 2020

PENGUIN PRESS
An imprint of Penguin Random House LLC
penguinrandomhouse.com

Copyright © 2020 by Richard Haass
Penguin supports copyright. Copyright fuels creativity, encourages diverse voices,
promotes free speech, and creates a vibrant culture. Thank you for buying an authorized
edition of this book and for complying with copyright laws by not reproducing, scanning,
or distributing any part of it in any form without permission. You are supporting
writers and allowing Penguin to continue to publish books for every reader.

Illustrations by Michael Bricknell, Joyce Chen, Will Merrow, and
Katherine Vidal © Council on Foreign Relations

LIBRARY OF CONGRESS CATALOGING-IN-PUBLICATION DATA
Names: Haass, Richard, author.
Title: The world : a brief introduction / Richard Haass.
Description: New York : Penguin Press, 2020. | Includes bibliographical
references and index.
Identifiers: LCCN 2019044618 (print) | LCCN 2019044619 (ebook) |
ISBN 9780399562396 (hardcover) | ISBN 9780399562402 (ebook)
Subjects: LCSH: International relations—History. | World politics. | History, Modern.
Classification: LCC JZ1329.5 .H33 2020 (print) | LCC JZ1329.5 (ebook) |
DDC 327.09—dc23
LC record available at https://lccn.loc.gov/2019044618
LC ebook record available at https://lccn.loc.gov/2019044619

Printed in the United States of America
5 7 9 10 8 6

BOOK DESIGN BY LUCIA BERNARD

FOR SUSAN, SAM, AND FRANCESCA

CONTENTS

PREFACE   XV

PART I: THE ESSENTIAL HISTORY   1

From the Thirty Years' War to the Outbreak of World War I
   (1618–1914)   5
From World War I Through World War II (1914–1945)   14
The Cold War (1945–1989)   29
The Post–Cold War Era (1989–Present)   43

PART II: REGIONS OF THE WORLD   59

Europe   67
East Asia and the Pacific   82
South Asia   97
The Middle East   111
Africa   131
The Americas   143

PART III: THE GLOBAL ERA   155

Globalization   159
Terrorism and Counterterrorism   166

Nuclear Proliferation   173

Climate Change   183

Migration   193

The Internet, Cyberspace, and Cybersecurity   201

Global Health   208

Trade and Investment   215

Currency and Monetary Policy   230

Development   240

PART IV: ORDER AND DISORDER   251

Sovereignty, Self-Determination, and Balance of Power   257

Alliances and Coalitions   264

International Society   270

War Between Countries   280

Internal Instability and War Within Countries   288

The Liberal World Order   296

ACKNOWLEDGMENTS   305

WHERE TO GO FOR MORE   309

NOTES   315

INDEX   371

THE
WORLD

PREFACE

Every book comes with a story that helps to explain why the author committed the time and effort to produce it. In this case, the story starts on a summer's day over a decade ago fishing with a friend in Nantucket. My friend's nephew joined us on the boat, and I asked him where he went to school. "Stanford," he told me. He was a computer science major, soon to begin his senior year. I went on to ask him a number of specific questions about what else he was studying beyond coding. Anything in economics? History? Politics? His answers revealed he had taken the minimum number of courses outside his major and those he did take had little to do with the basics. What was clear was that this intelligent young man would soon graduate from one of the best universities with little or no understanding of his own country or the world. And he would do so at a moment when the fate of his country and the world were inextricably linked and more was in flux than at any time since World War II and the years just after.

This troubled me. A search of graduation requirements at most American institutions of higher learning revealed it is possible to graduate from nearly any two- or four-year college or university in the United States, be it a community college or an Ivy League institution, without gaining even a rudimentary understanding of the world. A recent survey of over eleven hundred American colleges and universities found that only 17 percent require students to take courses in U.S. government or history, while only 3 percent require them to take coursework in economics. Don't get me wrong. Virtually every college or university offers multiple courses in international relations or American foreign policy, many of them well taught and comprehensive in what they cover. But unless a student chooses to major in these subjects, these courses are not required for graduation—and in many cases not even then for those who do choose to major in a related area. One survey of the top American colleges and universities showed less than a third required history majors to take a single course in U.S. history or government! Core courses that all students must take are an endangered species. What most institutions require is that each student take one or more courses in various designated areas, such as the natural sciences, the social sciences, and the arts. In larger institutions, there may be as many as one hundred courses to choose from in each area. Thus, it can be possible to fulfill an American history requirement without learning about the American Revolution or the Civil War, or to satisfy a world history requirement without understanding World War II or the Cold War or, more fundamentally, why the world matters and how it operates. Studying a foreign language is valuable, but it is not a substitute.

In high schools, the situation is even more pronounced, in that many schools do not even offer basic courses in international relations or global issues. My purpose is not to explain how all this came to be, although I would say high schools have increasingly given short shrift to civics and social studies because of resource limitations and pressures to satisfy mandates related to science, technology, engineering, and mathematics, also known as STEM. Another explanation is the difficulty in reaching agreement as to what should be taught.

The reluctance of institutions of higher learning to assert what they believe a graduate should know and have under his or her belt is an unfortunate development. It would be far better if they would do so, and individuals could then choose to go to the school whose requirements best met their interests and objectives.

And then there is the fact that approximately one-third of Americans who graduate from high school do not attend any college and that only some 40 percent who do achieve a degree. All this, however, is a conversation for another day. What matters here and now is that an increasing number of young people in the United States and elsewhere are essentially uninformed about the world they are entering.

That said, this book is for men and women of all ages. Many of us who attended college did not focus on these issues, or even if we did study them, we forgot much of what we were taught. What's more, what people of my generation learned decades ago is increasingly inadequate or even obsolete. A great deal of history has transpired in recent years. The Cold War, which was accepted as a permanent given when I grew up in the 1950s and 1960s and defined the world for the four decades after World War II, is over, as is the Soviet Union. China is a world power. New technologies and issues, from the internet and artificial intelligence to climate change, have emerged. The time has come to stop thinking of an education as something we receive in our youth, finish by the time we are in our early to mid-twenties, and live off for the next fifty years. We need to regularly top off our intellectual tank as we drive down the proverbial highway of life.

My aim in this book is to provide the basics of what you need to know about the world, to make you more globally literate. "Global literacy" as used here is not about the number of people around the world able to read. (In case you are interested, though, it turns out that some 85 percent of adults worldwide are able to read, a number that sounds better than it is because it still means 750 million men and women cannot.) Rather, global literacy for our purposes has everything to do with how much (or little) people know about and understand the world.

Global literacy is essential, because we live in a time in which what goes on outside a country matters a great deal. Borders are not impermeable. The United States is bordered by two oceans, but oceans are not moats. For better and for worse, the so-called Vegas rule—what happens there stays there—does not apply in today's global world.

The World is designed to help you build a foundation to better navigate the headlines and filter the flood of news coming at us all. One objective is that readers will become less vulnerable to being misled by politicians with partisan agendas and by others claiming to be authorities when in fact they are not. All of us make decisions and voice opinions—be it as voters, students, teachers, parents, friends, consumers, or investors—that affect the country's (and hence our own) relationship with the world. With a better understanding of the world and the challenges that await, you will be a more informed citizen, one better able to hold your elected representatives to account and to arrive at sound independent judgments.

Just think about some of the questions that connect to the headlines. Is free trade something to support or oppose? Are tariffs a good idea? Should the United States attack North Korea and Iran, live with their nuclear programs, or negotiate? To what extent and at what cost should the United States or any country try to promote democracy and human rights and prevent genocide? How real is climate change, and what should be done about it? Should I volunteer for the armed forces or go to work for an international agency or nongovernmental organization (NGO)? Is it patriotic to buy goods produced in my own country and not elsewhere even if it is more expensive to do so or the quality is not as good? What precautions are worth taking against pandemic disease or terrorism? What do we owe refugees and others who want to enter our country? Are China and the United States bound to become enemies and enter into a relationship reminiscent of what existed between the United States and the Soviet Union during the Cold War?

There is no limit to the number of questions that could be raised dealing with the world where the answers could have profound consequences for our lives. We exist in a moment when history is being made. The fact that we describe the present in terms of the past—for instance, that we live in the post–Cold War world—tells us where we have been, not where we are heading. The tectonic plates of international relations are moving. History did not end with the Soviet Union's collapse. This is a critical time to understand what is taking place in the world, why it is taking place, and how it will affect our lives.

A second reason for knowing about the world is that every country, and the United States in particular given its large role and responsibilities, requires citizens who are familiar with the world and can operate successfully overseas. These men and women can literally be a country's foot soldiers, or they can be involved in the worlds of diplomacy, intelligence, law enforcement, foreign aid, and homeland security. Such opportunities need not be limited to government. We are also talking about journalists, academics, and businesspeople as well as those who opt to work for one of the many NGOs involved in promoting education, health, or development.

A third rationale for global literacy stems from economic self-interest. Take the case of the United States, which accounts for only one out of twenty people in the world. While the U.S. share of global economic output is a considerably higher percentage (on the order of 25 percent), this number is coming down. Every other country accounts for a smaller share of global output, and every other country except China and India constitutes an even smaller percentage of the world's population. Understanding foreign markets is one requirement for remaining competitive, and knowing what is going on elsewhere is essential to all kinds of business and investment decisions.

Americans arguably have an additional reason to become globally literate, in that the United States has played a leading role in the world for the past three-quarters of a century. The United States has been the world's principal architect as well as its general contractor. What the country chooses to do (and not to do) in the future will have an enormous impact on others and on the world at large, which in turn will have a large impact on what goes on within the United States itself.

Notwithstanding the case for Americans becoming more knowledgeable about the world, I have endeavored to write these pages in a manner that makes them equally relevant to those from other countries. American foreign policy is uniquely American, but the world it seeks to shape is not.

The World focuses on the ideas, issues, and institutions essential for a basic understanding of the world. I also shed light on each region of the world, the major powers, the challenges associated with globalization, and the most relevant history. The book may not seem all that brief, but virtually every chapter, and in many cases parts of chapters, could sustain a book by itself. What survives includes little of the theory central to most textbooks written for introductory courses in this area for the simple reason that much of the theory that dominates the academic study of the field is too abstract and too far removed from what is happening to be of value to most of us.

If there is a parallel to what is provided here, it is the study of language. This book will not make you "fluent" in international relations, but it will make you conversant, able to make sense of developments in the world and proposals to shape them. Although the day-to-day details of what is going on will inevitably change, much of what is discussed in the coming chapters will remain relevant. The book is thus envisioned as something evergreen that will remain useful even as history continues to unfold, as it inevitably will.

The book is divided into four sections. The first emphasizes history and is global in scope. Chapters are devoted to what is essential to know about the period of several hundred years leading up to World War I, the three decades from World War I to the end of World War II, the four-plus decades of the Cold War, and the current period. History, Mark Twain is alleged to have said, does not repeat itself, but it rhymes. We need to learn history's lessons to increase the odds that the future will improve upon the past.

The second section of the book begins with an introduction to the world writ large and includes chapters on the six principal regions of the world: Europe, East Asia and the Pacific, South Asia, the Middle East, sub-Saharan Africa, and the Americas. Each chapter examines the importance of the region, provides its core history, and explains its dynamics.

The third and longest section of the book addresses global challenges, including climate change, terrorism, cybersecurity, the proliferation of weapons of mass destruction, and trade. Depending on how well these challenges are managed, they can be a source of disorder or stability. This requires examining global governance in each of these realms. Just to be clear, global governance (which is really a fancy name for international cooperation) is not to be confused with global government, the notion of a single international entity or authority that has more power than individual governments. Such an authority does not exist and most likely never will.

A fourth and final section deals with world order, the most basic concept of international relations, as well as what brings it about and what threatens it. This part of the book delves into some of the principal sources of stability in the world, including the notion and reality of sovereignty, deterrence, the balance of power, alliances and less formal coalitions, and the role of international organizations, democracy, trade, and international law. It also assesses disorder in the world and ends with a discussion of what all this means for the current international era.

The notes that begin on page 315 are extensive. They include not just details as to sources used for this book, but also suggestions for further reading. In addition, there is a short discussion titled "Where to Go for More" that begins on page 309 and covers the many ways interested readers can follow up this book and keep up with what is going on in the world.

The World can be read from start to finish, or it can be read in bits. I imagine some readers might want to begin with the last section, on world order, and work backward. Whatever route you decide to take, my goal is that you finish the book with a better grasp of how the world we live in came to be, how it works, and why it matters.

Part I

THE ESSENTIAL HISTORY

History can help explain who we are as a people, a society, or a country, where we are, and how we got here. It can also help us understand others by providing context and perspective while increasing understanding.

History also has a practical side. It can provide lessons. While it is true that no two situations are exactly alike in every detail, there are patterns. George Santayana, a late nineteenth- and early twentieth-century writer, went so far as to suggest, "Those who cannot remember the past are condemned to repeat it."

As you would expect, there is an almost unlimited amount of history that could be mined to provide background for anyone seeking to gain a better understanding of the world. In an attempt to provide history that is useful but manageable in scale, I deal with what is widely understood to constitute the modern international era, that is, the history that starts in the seventeenth century.

This start date is not arbitrary. The Thirty Years' War, a conflict that involved much of Europe and that had both political and religious dimensions, ended in 1648 with the Treaty of Westphalia, a peace agreement that is widely viewed as heralding the rise of the modern international system, one with sovereign countries accepting one another's independence and respecting the boundaries separating them.

There is admittedly a European bias in all this. There is, however, a logic behind it. In this era, Europe had an outsized role in and influence over other parts of the world, and the norms embodied in the Treaty of Westphalia continue to provide the foundation of international relations throughout the world. In fact, some of the countries (China comes to mind) that are the most "Westphalian" now and hold the most traditional views of sovereignty can be found outside Europe.

The history presented here is divided into four periods. The first covers the longest period, roughly three hundred years from the early seventeenth century to the outbreak of World War I in 1914. In addition to the rise of the modern international state system, this period spans the colonial period, the demise of several empires, the opening of Japan and the creation of Germany, the American Civil War and the subsequent rise of the United States as a great power, and the emergence of technologies that revolutionized manufacturing, transportation, and warfare.

The second period focuses on roughly three decades, from 1914 through 1945, the deadliest years in all of history. It is bookended by the two prolonged and costly world wars that dominated the first half of the twentieth century. It also includes the establishment and subsequent failure of the League of Nations, the Great Depression, the rise of nationalism and fascism, and the many errors of foreign policy and diplomacy that contributed to the outbreak of world war for the second time in a single century.

The third section is devoted to the Cold War, the four-decade period following the end of World War II that was dominated by the struggle between the United States and the Soviet Union. It looks at why the Cold War broke out, why it stayed cold, and why it ended when and how it did.

The fourth and final history chapter assesses the post–Cold War period. It began in 1989, and three decades later is still where we find ourselves. At some point, this era will better define itself and earn a new name. Too much is unsettled and uncertain for us to know what will emerge and how it will appear in the eye of the historian. Again, though, it is essential to know how this era has unfolded to this point if we are to grasp where we stand.

From the Thirty Years' War to the Outbreak of World War I (1618–1914)

The modern international system has its roots in seventeenth-century Europe. This continent was the center of the world because it had harnessed new technologies that proved critical to producing goods and crops and to transportation, publishing, and fighting wars. As is often the case, transition was marked by conflict.

The critical event was the Thirty Years' War, a war that began in 1618, contained both political and religious dimensions, and was fought both within and across borders by many of the major European powers of the era. Until then Europe was made up of a patchwork quilt of empires and small kingdoms. Religious and political authorities regularly confronted one another over territory and power. Borders were not respected; wars and lower-level forms of meddling were commonplace.

When the dust settled, countries emerged as an alternative to empires and principalities. Empires were often ruled from afar, which did not engender loyalty in citizens, and their large size made them inefficient to govern. Small principalities, in contrast, lacked the scale needed to compete for foreign markets or pool the resources necessary to wage war effectively. People proved more willing to devote themselves to governments they saw as their own. The emergence of a world composed of independent countries that respected one another's

EUROPE ON THE EVE OF THE TREATY OF WESTPHALIA, 1648

Source: Wilson, Peter H. 2009. *The Thirty Years War: Europe's Tragedy.*

independence turned out to be a major innovation, one that introduced a greater degree of stability and peace but also created a capacity to make war on a level never before seen.

The Treaty of Westphalia, which ended the Thirty Years' War in 1648, codified this new understanding. The treaty in many ways established the modern international system, one dominated by countries and the principle of sovereignty. The concept of sovereignty had three basic dimensions. First, countries should accept the borders of other countries and not use force in an attempt to change them. Second, countries should not interfere in events inside other countries. Third, governments should have a free hand to do as they please within their own borders. These three notions may not seem to amount to all that much, but they represented a major step forward, one that if honored would have dramatically reduced the instability and violence that had become relatively commonplace in the world.

European nations, however, often violated the sovereignty of their neighbors, which explains, in part, why the history of this continent has been so violent and destructive. The Treaty of Westphalia did, however, introduce a period of relative peace. Europe did not descend into another major war or, to be more precise, a series of wars until the rise of Napoleon Bonaparte, the brilliant, ambitious French general turned politician turned emperor. He came to power following a revolution in France that—like most revolutions—ended in excess and disorder. After a number of military victories that gave him control of much of Europe, Napoleon became overextended, electing to fight too many foes on too many fronts, and was finally defeated by a coalition that included Austria, Prussia, Russia, and the United Kingdom. The victors and the vanquished (minus Napoleon) came together in Vienna in 1814 and 1815 and created a settlement designed to prevent France from threatening its neighbors and to make it more difficult for revolutionary movements to overthrow the unelected governments of the day. The Congress of Vienna also made the wise choice of integrating a defeated France into the new order rather than penalizing and ostracizing it and potentially sowing the seeds of a France that would one day rise and try to overthrow the order.

The Congress of Vienna produced what became known as the Concert of Europe, a name that suggests the diplomatic equivalent of an orchestra of musicians playing together. This system was centered on Europe, but it nonetheless constituted much of the international order of its day given the dominant position of Europe and Europeans in the world at the start of the nineteenth century. In fact, by the middle of the nineteenth century, Western Europe accounted for roughly one-third of global economic output, eclipsing China and India and maintaining a substantial lead over the United States. The Concert put into practice understandings that were at the core of the Treaty of Westphalia, above all ruling out invasion of another member country or any involvement in the internal affairs of another participant in the Concert without its permission. The Concert had a decidedly conservative bias, meaning that it favored the continued rule of existing dynasties and opposed revolutionary impulses. Beyond the obvious self-interest of rulers, what also allowed the arrangement to hold for as long as it did was the balance of military power in Europe that made it unattractive for any individual country to go against its principles.

The Concert technically lasted until the eve of World War I, but it ceased to play a meaningful role decades before then. It is a matter of judgment as to when it effectively ended, but I would argue for the middle of the nineteenth century, when most of the major powers had a falling-out with Russia over Crimea. This was an early conflict over who would come to control lands then part of the declining Ottoman Empire. It was followed by wars between Prussia (the principal forerunner of modern Germany) and both Austria and France. As will be discussed below, what remained of the Concert could not survive the rise of Germany, which was unified under the Prussian minister president Otto von Bismarck in 1871 and under his successors disrupted European stability.

BEYOND EUROPE

It would be an error to limit a review of eighteenth- and nineteenth-century history to Europe, even though Europe was the part of the world where the most powerful and influential entities of this era were to be found. A great deal of the world—parts of the Middle East, South Asia, Africa, the Americas, and East Asia—was colonized, mostly by European countries (principally Britain, France, Portugal, and Spain, and to a lesser extent Germany and Italy), but also by Japan and the United States. The principal motive was economic, although matters of national pride and the pursuit of glory were not far behind.

For China, the nineteenth century began well enough; its economy was relatively large, in part because of profitable trading relations with the British and others. But the century proved to be anything but glorious. It was a time that came to be marked by unimaginative imperial rule, internal challenges to central authority, and foreign aggression against China, including the Opium Wars, in which Britain forced China to participate in an opium trade that China wanted no part of given the effect of the drug on its citizens. These conflicts were followed by a series of incursions into China on the part of Britain, France, Germany, Japan, and Russia, which in turn set off a scramble among these powers for economic concessions from China, which had fallen far behind the European powers economically, administratively, and militarily. This reality would not change until well into the second half of the twentieth century.

The period beginning with the Opium Wars and ending with Mao Zedong's proclamation of the founding of the People's Republic of China in 1949 has become known to the Chinese as the "century of humiliation" and continues to shape how China's citizens view the world. China's current government argues that a China in internal disarray invites aggression from foreign powers and that only a strong central government can hold China together. The Communist Party employs this argument to justify its dominance.

Japan began the nineteenth century the same way it had begun and ended the two previous centuries, largely isolated from the outside world. In 1853, the United States (a Pacific country looking for new markets) led the charge to open Japan to trade with the outside world. When American warships showed up uninvited to demand access to Japanese markets, Japan gave in because there was no way it could hold its own militarily. Like China, it was forced to make humiliating economic and legal concessions to outsiders. These concessions proved to be widely unpopular in Japan and helped trigger a successful political challenge to the ruling shogun (the general who was first among equals among fellow feudal lords). By 1868, the imperial order had been restored under the emperor Meiji.

Meiji (which means "the enlightened ruler") ruled Japan for nearly fifty years, until 1912, a period widely described as the Meiji Restoration in which the modern Japanese state was established. Unlike China, Japan followed a course parallel to what was taking place in Europe and the United States. A modern bureaucratic government and administrative apparatus was established in Tokyo to oversee the entire country. Japan implemented an industrial policy and built a modern military. It also followed the European imperial example in the last two decades of the century. While the British, French, Germans, and others were occupying or controlling large swaths of the Middle East, Africa, and parts of Asia, Japan was establishing control over parts of Korea, Taiwan, and China. Japan handily defeated Russia in their 1904–1905 war, marking the first time during the modern era that an Asian power was victorious over a European one. Japan, like the major European powers of the day, was caught up in a wave of nationalist pride.

In the so-called New World, there were the British colonies in North America, which by the middle of the eighteenth century had grown increasingly frustrated over being forced to pay taxes to the British crown and having little control over their own fate. What is termed the Revolutionary War (or the American War of Independence) was in fact a war of national liberation that began in 1775. It was fought by many who hailed from Britain and elsewhere in Europe against their British overseers. It proved (after more than a few setbacks) successful, and the new country, the United States of America, declared its independence in 1776.

Even a cursory history of the United States—one that tracked the political evolution of this new democracy through the Civil War, Reconstruction, the Gilded Age, and the Progressive Era—would go far beyond the limits of this book. But what is relevant for our purposes is that the country would evolve into a major agricultural, industrial, trading, financial, and military power, one whose decisions and actions (and inaction) would have a major impact on the rest of the world. Indeed, the twentieth century is often dubbed the American Century for good reason, although significant American involvement in the world only became permanent starting with World War II.

THE PATH TO WORLD WAR

Beginning in the mid-eighteenth century, one of the dominant features of European history was the ascension of Britain to a position of global primacy as a result of its strong economy, trade links, access to raw materials and markets through its colonies, and globe-spanning navy. This primacy arguably lasted until the mid- to late nineteenth century, when the costs of empire and war began to mount and Germany emerged as a serious rival. By the late nineteenth and early twentieth centuries, Europe was a venue of both the strong and the weak. The strong were the Germans and British and to a lesser extent the French. Germany was by far the most powerful, with a thriving and increasingly industrial economy and a population far larger than that of Britain or France. France had never quite recovered from its loss to Prussia in their 1870 war and was held back by its own political and social structures. Britain was also increasing in economic strength and in population but could not keep pace with Germany and in any event was more a sea than a land military power. The weak were the fading empires: Russia, the Ottoman Empire (Turkey), and Austria-Hungary. In some ways, the outbreak of World War I can be understood as the result of the interplay between these rising and declining entities and the competition among the former as to who would prevail in the coming era.

Exactly why World War I broke out and who or what was to blame are questions that have kept a good many talented historians occupied for decades. It was a war that did not need to happen. One influential history described Europe as "sleepwalking" its way to war in 1914; I have previously called it a war of choice, but a better description might be a war of carelessness.

There is no simple cause or explanation. Wars tend to break out both for underlying reasons and for immediate ones. World War I was no exception; in the words of Liddell Hart, arguably the preeminent military historian of the war, "Fifty years were spent in the process of making Europe explosive. Five days were enough to detonate it." It is thus not enough to say the war broke out because of the assassination in Sarajevo in June 1914 of Archduke Franz Ferdinand, the heir to the Austro-Hungarian throne, by a terrorist backed by Serbia, which in turn had ties to Russia. There had been similar killings before that did not trigger a conflict. Near-nonstop skirmishing between Russia and Austria-Hungary in the Balkans did, however, play a role in creating momentum toward war. Military mobilizations also contributed to the momentum toward war because leaders felt pressure to match what other leaders were doing lest they find themselves at a disadvantage. Diplomacy never found a way to keep up.

Poor statecraft also contributed to the alliances (such as those between Germany and Austria-Hungary or France and Russia) that were forged without thinking through their implications. Arguments that countries would not dare to disrupt the mutually enriching trade that had grown up among them proved incorrect. The fact that a rough balance of power existed also proved insufficient. Such rational considerations could not compete successfully with the rising nationalism of the era that produced a cavalier attitude that war was inevitable but not to be feared because it would lead to quick and relatively painless victory. And last but far from least, the rise of Germany must be a principal explanation for the war. The modern country that the great Prussian chancellor Otto von Bismarck created in the second half of the nineteenth century out of what had been literally hundreds of states and principalities became strong and ambitious, inclined to risk and aggression in the less judicious hands of those who succeeded Bismarck.

From World War I Through World War II (1914–1945)

War came in the summer of 1914. The leaders who plunged their countries into war envisioned a short contest—they famously said their soldiers would be home for the holidays—but the fighting dragged on through the fall of 1918. On one side was the Triple Entente: Britain, France, and Russia. Japan later joined them, while Russia withdrew from the war following the start of its revolution in 1917. On the other side was the Triple Alliance: Germany, Austria-Hungary, and Italy, although Italy stayed neutral in 1914 and subsequently opted to join the Entente powers.

Despite its intimate ties to Great Britain and France, the United States attempted to sit out the war. This reflected the country's longstanding avoidance of discretionary involvement abroad, above all getting enmeshed in what it viewed as the intractable conflicts of the old world. This tradition can be traced as far back as President George Washington, who in his farewell address of 1796 advised Americans to eschew entangling alliances and remain detached from the affairs of other nations. It was consistent, too, with the views of John Quincy Adams, who in 1821 as Secretary of State explained that the United States ". . . goes not abroad, in search of monsters to destroy. She is the

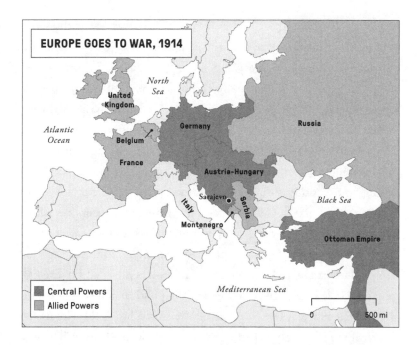

well-wisher to the freedom and independence of all. She is the champion and vindicator only of her own."

What brought the Americans into the war in April 1917 was the German decision to engage in unrestricted submarine warfare, in which Germany used submarines to target ships carrying American supplies to stop them from reaching Britain and France. Americans who were on board these ships lost their lives, and the public outcry in the United States was considerable. It is possible that the United States also entered the war in part owing to the publication in early 1917 of a secret diplomatic message (the so-called Zimmermann Telegram) in which Germany promised Mexico the territory of Texas and several other states in return for its entering an alliance with Germany should the United States enter the war on the other side. Whatever the explanation, the

U.S. entry into the war was significant, because it was on the threshold of becoming a major power, one with a population of 100 million and a growing economy and military. U.S. involvement in the fighting helped to tip the scales against Germany and bring about an end to the war sooner than would have been the case had it remained on the sidelines.

The war itself was the deadliest and most expensive conflict to date due to innovations such as modern railways, the telegraph, mass conscription, more powerful long-range weapons, and the use of airpower. Adding to the cost was the gradual ascendance of defense over offense; if there was an image of World War I, it was that of the trenches where so many fought and died. As many as 200,000 British forces were killed or wounded in a single campaign in which the British and their allies sought unsuccessfully to seize the Gallipoli peninsula from the Ottomans. (This campaign nearly ended the political career of a young government minister by the name of Winston Churchill.) The use of chemical weapons only added to the human cost of the war. The gap between the naive, even optimistic expectation of what war would bring and the horrific reality was and is breathtaking. The poetry of Wilfred Owen—"Men marched asleep. Many had lost their boots, / But limped on, blood-shod. All went lame; all blind; / Drunk with fatigue; deaf even to the hoots / Of gas-shells dropping softly behind"— captures this contrast as well as any history book.

The war's cost was immense and horrific: some nine million soldiers lost their lives. Another twenty-one million were wounded. Civilian deaths numbered in the millions or even tens of millions if those who succumbed to infectious disease made worse by the war are counted. All this was at a time when the world's population was on the order of 1.5 billion, roughly one-fifth of what it is today. You would need to multiply each of these statistics by five in order to come up with a figure that would represent proportionate costs were an event of this magnitude to happen now.

It was thus a war that was costly for combatants and civilians alike. Adding insult to injury, it was a war that resolved little. World War I and its aftermath sowed many of the seeds for the second great war of the century that came merely two decades later. It is one of history's ironies and tragedies that "The Great War" and "The War to End All Wars," as World War I was dubbed, turned out to be but a prelude to another, even greater war.

THE END OF WAR AND THE IMMEDIATE AFTERMATH

Interestingly, there was more than a little optimism in the wake of World War I, and diplomatic efforts to shape what was to be the postwar world began while fighting was still under way. Woodrow Wilson, the twenty-eighth president of the United States, prioritized the creation of a standing international organization (which became the League of Nations) that he believed would all but preclude such a war from ever happening again by eliminating what would cause countries to go to war. This was the last of his Fourteen Points, first articulated in a speech to Congress in January 1918.

President Wilson's points were for the most part generous and idealistic. He wanted all diplomatic agreements not just to be made public but also, when possible, to be negotiated in the open. There was to be freedom of navigation at sea at all times. Trade barriers were to come down. Armaments were to be collectively reduced through what we today would call arms control. Colonial arrangements would be adjusted so that the claims of the people being governed would be equal to the claims of the colonial government. (This principle of giving more voice to those governed grew into what became known as the right of self-determination.) Borders throughout Europe were to be adjusted to reflect national realities and to undo past acts of aggression.

President Wilson's belief that founding the League of Nations would be the best guarantee against future aggression by Germany—or anyone else—was not universally shared. In particular, France, led by Georges Clemenceau, the host of the Paris Peace Conference that was to bring a formal end to World War I, was preoccupied with ensuring that Germany would be sufficiently weakened so that it could not wage war again. What made the French particularly uneasy about the future was that Russia, its traditional ally in opposing Prussian and then German might, could not be counted on because it was in the throes of civil war, a development that led Russia to withdraw from the war effort. (Russia and Germany signed a separate treaty in 1918, one very much in Germany's favor.)

The revolution and subsequent Russian civil war, fought between militant Bolsheviks led by Vladimir Lenin and more moderate Mensheviks, was triggered by the cost of participation in World War I and by Russia's own economic, political, and social shortcomings. Russia's civil war would go on for years, ending in the victory of the Bolsheviks. By the end of 1922, this led to the founding of the Union of Soviet Socialist Republics (U.S.S.R.), or, as it was more widely known, the Soviet Union. It was a country nominally headed by a government but in practice dominated by its Communist Party. The Soviet Union would play a central role in two of the great struggles of the twentieth century, namely, World War II and the Cold War.

World War I ended in November 1918 after Germany, following a failed offensive during the spring of 1918, expressed its desire for peace and signed an armistice. Two months later delegates from all the protagonists (other than Germany and Russia) met in France, and by the end of June 1919 agreed to the Treaty of Versailles. Germany accepted blame for the war, agreed to pay costly financial penalties known as reparations to the governments of the countries it had fought against, and returned to France the territory of Alsace-Lorraine that it had annexed following the Franco-Prussian War half a century before. Germany also ceded smaller amounts of territory to Belgium and Poland, forfeited its overseas colonies, accepted sharp reductions in the size of its army and navy, agreed to a limited French military occupation, and ceded economic control of the coal and iron mines in its Saar region to France for fifteen years. The powers agreed to establish a League of Nations, which represented an embrace of idealism over realism, the latter holding that power considerations alone drive a country's behavior. (This is something very different from "realism" as a foreign policy orientation that seeks to shape the external behavior of other countries rather than their internal nature.) For its part, the League rested on the idea of collective security, whereby all powers would uphold the status quo and work together to turn back any challenges, and the stronger powers would not use their might to make adjustments in their favor.

A separate treaty parceled out significant parts of the Ottoman Empire to Greece, Italy, France, and Britain. A number of independent countries, including Czechoslovakia, Poland, Romania, and Yugoslavia, were established in Eastern Europe. The majority of the countries that make up today's Middle East got their start when the Ottoman Empire collapsed in the wake of the war and the region's map was redrawn by British and French officials more interested in dividing the spoils than in laying the foundation for regional stability. Self-determination was largely limited to Europe; the inhabitants of the Middle East, Asia, and Africa mostly lost out, part of the price Wilson paid to keep the major powers who wanted to maintain their colonial holdings supportive of the new League of Nations.

World War I toppled four empires, and with President Wilson's promotion of self-determination nationalism asserted itself throughout the world. Nationalism in its most basic form has to do with populations in a particular area coming to see themselves as sharing a distinct identity, the result of a common history, language, religion, ethnicity, and/or set of political beliefs. Nationalism often gains momentum when people are ruled by those they consider outsiders. Frustrated with their status as subjects or a colony, populations desire to rule themselves, to be independent, to enjoy religious freedoms and speak in their native language and shape their own destiny.

President Wilson returned home to the United States from France in mid-1919. He went on a whirlwind trip around the country in a futile effort to translate domestic political support for the League into persuading a majority of senators to vote for it. Working against Wilson were both isolationists, who did not want the United States involved in the world to any significant degree, and unilateralists, who wanted the United States to retain a free hand and not be constrained by commitments to the League. The exhausted president returned to Washington, only to suffer a stroke. Weeks later, in November 1919, the Senate defeated the proposed treaty that would have led to the United States becoming a founding member of the new organization.

The League of Nations—which was created, in part, to peacefully settle disputes that might arise between countries—never recovered from the failure of the United States to join. It also suffered from a requirement for unanimity before collective action could be taken and an inability to enforce its decisions. The truth, though, is the League failed less because of its structural shortcomings than from the fundamental reality that the countries at its core, above all Britain and France, lacked the will and the means to act on behalf of its principles. At this moment in history, the United States, Great Britain, and France were more committed to pacifism than they were to building and maintaining an international order. The Europeans were depleted after World War I, while the United States was determined to avoid being embroiled in Europe's conflicts.

THE PATH TO WAR (AGAIN)

Nothing captured the empty idealism of the age so much as the Kellogg-Briand Pact, which was initially signed by fifteen countries in 1928 and eventually included 62 signatories. The parties committed not to resort to war to settle disputes among them. It was less an act of serious foreign policy than an alternative to it—a high-minded statement without teeth. Interestingly, among the original signatories were Germany, Japan, and Italy, the three countries most responsible for triggering World War II a decade later.

Meanwhile, the major countries were fast coming undone from within. Germany for its part established a parliamentary democracy (known as the Weimar Republic) in the aftermath of World War I. The country labored under the weight of a lack of democratic experience, reparations, and hyperinflation that destroyed the value of its currency and much of Germany's middle class with it. Internal stability began to break down.

Politics everywhere were affected by the Great Depression that began in 1929. A lack of prudent regulation and reckless speculation combined to bring about a stock market crash in the United States. The crash in turn left many individuals and businesses unable to pay their debts. American gross domestic product (GDP) fell sharply, unemployment soared, and banks failed. The Federal Reserve's response was inadequate, as it did not take sufficient measures to stimulate the American economy. In addition, the Smoot-Hawley Tariff Act, which imposed tariffs to discourage imports, led other countries to retaliate in kind and is seen by many observers as having deepened the Depression everywhere by reducing international trade. One school of thought is that significant economic ties, known as economic interdependence, make war too disruptive and hence too costly to contemplate. By decreasing these economic linkages, protectionist trade policies reduced the cost of going to war and thereby increased its likelihood.

In Germany, the Depression was the final nail in the coffin of the Weimar Republic. Germany needed loans to pay its reparations, but once the Depression hit, its funding dried up and hyperinflation ensued as the government printed more money in a desperate effort to come up with the funds to repay what it owed. The collapse of the Weimar Republic was a textbook case of what happens when democracy and capitalism fail; angry, desperate people became willing to go along with a suspension of the most basic civil liberties in the hope that order and prosperity would be restored. Parties and politicians embracing fascism—a philosophy animated by extreme nationalism that called for government control of virtually all aspects of political and economic life—gained ground in Germany, Italy, Austria, and Japan. By 1932, the Nazi Party had become the largest party in the German parliament; a year later, Adolf Hitler became chancellor. He quickly consolidated power, dismantled democratic protections, formalized harsh discrimination against Jews and others, and began rearming Germany. Hitler broke through the military constraints set by the Versailles Treaty. The absence of a French or British response taught Hitler the dangerous lesson that he could assert German rights as he saw them with little to fear.

The Soviet Union by the late 1920s and early 1930s was well on its way to being transformed into a Communist country, with a centralized government that possessed even more power than a traditional authoritarian system. It controlled most facets of people's lives and oversaw most aspects of the economy. Joseph Stalin succeeded Lenin in 1924 and instituted a series of five-year plans to transform the country. Peasants were conscripted to work as free markets were abolished. Millions died of hunger as a result of the imposition of terrible policies, and millions more were imprisoned and, in many cases, executed during Stalin's effort to consolidate political control.

History was unfolding in Asia as well as Europe. In China, popular protests against the Qing dynasty, which had failed to modernize China or push back against foreign encroachments on Chinese sovereignty, led to its toppling in 1912, ending some two thousand years of imperial rule. Chinese Nationalists (a non-Communist movement inclined toward authoritarianism) gained control of important parts of the country. But in the early 1930s, Japan, then led by an extreme right-wing nationalist government, attacked and began to control parts of China, setting up a pro-Japan puppet state in Manchuria and in 1937 seizing Shanghai.

Preoccupied with their domestic challenges associated with the Great Depression, world leaders had little bandwidth for dealing with international challenges. In 1935, Italy's fascist leader, Benito Mussolini, invaded Abyssinia (Ethiopia). The emperor there appealed to the League of Nations for help. With no serious help forthcoming, Italy readily conquered the country. The League proved feckless, instituting some weak economic sanctions against Italy that were rolled back less than a year later. This demonstrated to other nations that aggression could succeed with little or no cost.

The world's willingness to accept aggression, initially in China and Ethiopia and subsequently in Europe, came to be known as appeasement. It is best understood as adopting a policy of granting concessions to an ambitious, aggressive country in the hopes its appetite can be satiated and it will then cease to be aggressive. It was subsequently adopted with respect to Germany by most members of the League of Nations and above all by successive British governments, who totally misread the nature of Hitler and the threat he posed to Europe.

Appeasement reached its height (or, some might say, depth) in Europe in the late 1930s. Hitler sought to gain living space (lebensraum) for "Aryan" Germans of European or Indo-European descent who would assert their "mastery" over "inferior" races. Breaking out of constraints imposed by the Versailles Treaty, Germany withdrew from the League of Nations in 1933, took back the Saarland in 1935, marched into the demilitarized Rhineland in 1936 (the same year it entered into alliances with Japan and Italy), and annexed Austria in early 1938. That September, at a diplomatic conference in Munich, Hitler demanded that Germany be given the Sudetenland, the part of Czechoslovakia that was home to ethnic Germans. Practicing appeasement, the British and French prime ministers went along with this demand in exchange for a pledge from Hitler that he would respect the independence of what remained of Czechoslovakia. A year later, Hitler went back on his cynical pledge and invaded Czechoslovakia, after which Britain and France extended military commitments to several still independent European countries, including Poland. On September 1, 1939, Hitler invaded Poland, and what would become World War II was under way.

Not surprisingly, these events discredited those associated with appeasement, leading to Winston Churchill's forming a new British government in May 1940 predicated on fighting Germany. On the same day that Churchill became prime minister, Germany invaded Belgium, the Netherlands, and France. By June, France was under German control. Germany followed up by launching an air campaign against Great Britain but eventually called off the operation when British resistance proved effective.

The United States stayed aloof from the fighting in Europe and Asia but tilted in the direction of the Allies and against Germany, introducing the "lend-lease" program that made war material available to the Allies in late 1940. The American president, Franklin Delano Roosevelt, tried to navigate a middle course of doing enough to keep Great Britain in the war and Germany from prevailing but not so much that he would encounter massive resistance from isolationists at home, who argued the country could and should resist involvement in Europe's conflicts. Meanwhile, the United States instituted a selective embargo against Japan in order to deny it raw materials it needed for continuing its military buildup.

Russia pursued its own path. In August 1939, the Soviet Union and Germany concluded a nonaggression pact, which among other things gave the Soviet Union pieces of Poland and the Baltic states but also bought it time to prepare for what Stalin judged to be an inevitable war with Hitler. Hitler sought the agreement so he would be free to focus his energies on conquering large areas of Europe and not have to worry about fighting a two-front war. When he had accomplished much of what he set out to do in the west, Hitler turned on the Soviet Union, invading it in June 1941. Much as Napoleon learned a century and a half before, war with a country of the Soviet Union's size was easier to begin than to win. Indeed, Hitler's strategic decision weakened Germany significantly and contributed meaningfully to the war's ultimate outcome.

WORLD WAR II

I wrote at the start of this chapter that World War I did not have to happen. It was, to borrow from the historian Barbara Tuchman, an act of folly. World War II could not have been more different. Germany and Japan embraced values and objectives that could not be accommodated within the existing order. Both had become hostages to political systems that essentially eliminated any checks and balances on those wielding power. They were free to overreach, and they did. They invested heavily in instruments of war and demonstrated no reluctance in putting those instruments to work.

This is not to say that World War II was always inevitable but rather that somewhere along the way it became so. John Maynard Keynes, the renowned economist who was part of the British delegation to the peace conference that formally ended World War I, wrote a scathing book in 1919 about the collective shortsightedness of the victors. Keynes made the case that the origins of a second world war could be found in the Treaty of Versailles that ended the first, above all in its punitive peace that penalized Germany rather than helping it to recover in a managed fashion.

Germans resented not only the terms of the treaty but also the clause that placed the responsibility for World War I on its shoulders. It was seen as an affront to the German people that needed to be rectified, and this resentment, born out of the requirement that Germany pay harsh reparations, forfeit territory it judged to be its own, and accept stringent limits on rearmament, fueled nationalist sentiment. Adolf Hitler fed off this excessive nationalism in his rise to power.

Still, there were ample opportunities to prevent what became World War II. The United States deserves a share of the responsibility. The Senate's rejection of the new League of Nations presaged a retreat into isolationism, which gained traction in America during the two decades between the two world wars. Making matters worse was a simultaneous embrace of protectionism that weakened economies and democracies around the world along with a decline in U.S. military readiness. Franklin Delano Roosevelt, the U.S. president from 1933 to nearly the end of World War II in 1945, encountered political resistance when he attempted to provide help to the Allies facing Germany, because a good many Americans feared doing so would get the United States dragged into European fighting. (The isolationist movement went by the name of America First. One of its principal representatives was Charles Lindbergh, whose solo flight across the Atlantic had made him a public hero.) The opposition to Roosevelt signaled to German and Japanese leaders that they could invade others with a degree of impunity. A balance of power requires both military capability and the political will to use it, and during the 1930s the United States possessed neither. The public and many of its elected representatives failed to appreciate how American economic and physical security was tied to events in Europe and Asia.

The European Allies also share some of the blame. As is often the case in history, it was not what the major European countries did as much as what they chose not to do. The lack of military preparation, the embrace of symbolic but toothless international pacts, the appeasement of German acts of aggression throughout the 1930s—all set the stage for World War II.

In the end, it took the Japanese attack on the U.S. fleet at Pearl Harbor in Hawaii on December 7, 1941, to bring the United States into the war. Given the alliance among Japan, Germany, and Italy, the U.S. declaration of war on Japan quickly translated into mutual declarations of war. By then, Germany was in control of most of continental Europe. It would take more than three years, but ultimately the full participation of the United States, by then a great economic and military power—alongside Britain, Russia, and others in Europe—proved decisive. Victory in Europe came in the spring of 1945.

The United States took the lead in rolling back Japan's conquests in Asia. By the summer of 1945, most of Asia had been liberated, but Japan had not been defeated. The choice was judged to be either an invasion of the Japanese home islands—something that promised to be extraordinarily difficult and costly—or using a terrible new weapon that would likely convince the Japanese that further resistance was futile. The United States, then led by Harry Truman, who had become president following Roosevelt's death in April 1945, opted for the latter, and dropped atomic weapons on the Japanese cities of Hiroshima and Nagasaki. Within days Japan surrendered, and the Pacific war (and with it World War II) was over. The nuclear age, however, had just begun.

The cost of World War II was, like its predecessor, extraordinarily high. More than 15 million soldiers died in the fighting; a far larger number of civilians also perished, including 6 million Jews in the Holocaust, the signature genocide of this or any era. France, the United Kingdom, and Italy each lost approximately half a million people, mostly soldiers. Germany lost around 7 million people, Japan almost 3 million. The Soviet Union lost as many as 24 million people, while China lost 15 million, most of whom were civilians. The costs to the United States were on the order of 400,000 soldiers killed.

If there was a saving grace, it is that (in contrast to World War I) World War II can be said to have ended with a clarity of outcome and vision. Germany and Japan were soundly defeated and knew it. But they were treated with a degree of respect. Both were transformed into robust democracies through occupations that can best be described as farsighted and benign. Both were integrated into regional and global economic, political, and security arrangements.

We can debate how much of this was because of lessons learned and how much was because of the need to enlist them as partners into what would become the Cold War. But what can be said with confidence is that the seeds of the Cold War were not sown during World War II in the way that World War II can be traced back to World War I. The Cold War was the result of its own dynamic, one that grew out of the rise of the United States and the Soviet Union with their fundamentally different political and economic systems, opposing ideologies, and no less different global interests and ambitions.

The Cold War (1945–1989)

The Cold War refers to the four-decade-long competition between the United States and the Soviet Union, the two great powers (or superpowers, as they were often called) of the post–World War II era. What makes their competition unprecedented is that it stayed "cold" and did not descend into a violent conflict fought directly between them. This stands in stark contrast to the great-power competitions that had twice led to conflict on a horrendous scale in the first half of the twentieth century.

The United States and the Soviet Union were allies in the all-out struggle against Germany and Japan in World War II. In just a matter of years, though, they were locked in their own fight for global primacy. If such an outcome was not inevitable, it was highly likely given their opposing ideologies. The United States was a democracy that in principle—if not always in practice—respected individual rights, favored a large role for free markets, and encouraged private accumulation of wealth; the U.S.S.R. was built on a large state role in the economy, collective ownership, and a dominant role for the government (rather than the individual) in political life. It was a revolutionary power that sought to export Communism to other countries around the world.

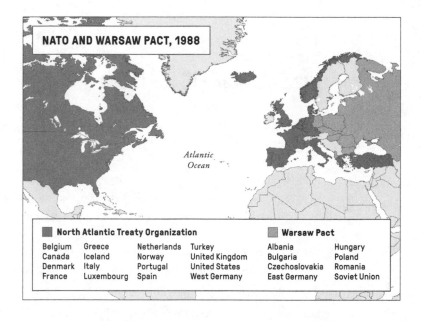

NATO AND WARSAW PACT, 1988

Atlantic Ocean

■ North Atlantic Treaty Organization				■ Warsaw Pact	
Belgium	Greece	Netherlands	Turkey	Albania	Hungary
Canada	Iceland	Norway	United Kingdom	Bulgaria	Poland
Denmark	Italy	Portugal	United States	Czechoslovakia	Romania
France	Luxembourg	Spain	West Germany	East Germany	Soviet Union

The two also differed when it came to their objectives in the world. In liberated and newly independent countries, Soviet leaders opposed both democracy and capitalism and sought fealty to their dictates. Their goal was to directly dominate all of Europe and to install pro-Soviet governments elsewhere. The United States worked to resist Soviet ambitions, promoting anti-Soviet, anti-Communist, and, where possible, pro-capitalist democracies.

Efforts to avoid such friction in the post–World War II period began while the war was still being waged. There were a series of conferences and summits, the most important of which was held at Yalta, a resort town on the Crimean Peninsula, in early 1945, and involved the leaders of the United States (Franklin Roosevelt), Great Britain (Winston Churchill), and the Soviet Union (Joseph Stalin). Roosevelt was interested in getting Stalin to commit to join the soon-to-be-launched United Nations. Even more, he wanted the Soviets to enter the war versus Japan, which would spare American lives and open up a second front against Japan. He achieved both goals, but the latter at least was meaningless, because Russia entered the Pacific war just days before Japan's surrender. Stalin made multiple commitments to respect the independence and democratic rights of countries to be liberated from Nazi rule, but his commitments turned out to be cynical because the Soviet Union sought to dominate Poland and all of Eastern Europe. The powers agreed to demilitarize Germany and divide it into zones of occupation. What was initially envisioned as a transitional arrangement turned out to be anything but as Germany remained divided for the entire duration of the Cold War. Yalta proved to be a textbook case of the propensity of American presidents to believe that on the strength of their personal relationship with a foreign leader a resolution to intractable problems could be reached, even if that leader was dictatorial and showed an unwavering devotion to what he judged to be his own national interests. Dissatisfaction with what ultimately transpired despite what was agreed to added to the momentum that brought about the Cold War.

Resistance to Soviet ambitions took many forms. The United States extended billions of dollars in economic and military assistance to countries believed to be vulnerable to external pressure from the Soviet Union or internal pressure from Soviet-backed local Communists. This was made possible in no small part because the United States emerged from World War II as an economic and military superpower. In many ways, it was the war effort that finally enabled the United States to put the Great Depression behind it.

The Truman Doctrine articulated a willingness to provide economic and military aid to Western European countries under pressure; Greece and Turkey were early recipients. The Marshall Plan, named for President Truman's secretary of state George Marshall and announced at Harvard in June 1947, in what is arguably the most significant commencement speech ever delivered, provided $13.2 billion of aid over a period of four years—equivalent to roughly $150 billion in today's dollars—to facilitate the reconstruction of European allies. As a percentage of American output, the Marshall Plan was equivalent to providing $800 billion of aid today. This initiative reflected a rejection of isolationism and an effort to keep the United States actively involved in the world's affairs on an open-ended basis. Covert help in one form or another was also provided when open assistance was judged counterproductive. In Western Europe (under the NATO umbrella) and in Asia, the United States stationed troops and provided security guarantees to its allies.

The American approach to waging the Cold War was developed in no small part by George Kennan, a State Department official and Soviet expert. In early 1946, Kennan called for the "long-term, patient but firm and vigilant containment of Russian expansive tendencies." The doctrine became known as containment. Implicit in what Kennan argued was that the United States and its allies would favor defense over offense because the latter promised to be highly risky and quite likely bound to fail. This is in fact what they did, although Kennan speculated (and, forty years later, was proven prescient) that a system committed to global domination (as was the Soviets') could not deal with repeated frustration and sooner or later would come to change its nature and ways.

The first signs that the Cold War was under way came in Eastern Europe, where the Soviet Union interfered (often covertly) so that Communist, pro-Soviet governments gained power. As the Cold War took shape, the Soviet Union formed two empires. One was an external empire, in Eastern Europe, in which countries were nominally independent but where, in fact, Soviet officials closely controlled both their domestic and their foreign policies. Seven countries—Albania, Bulgaria, Czechoslovakia, East Germany, Hungary, Poland, and Romania—

found themselves in what was tantamount to a Soviet sphere of influence. There was also an internal empire, in which officials in the capital, Moscow, ruled the Soviet Union and its fourteen other republics, which included Estonia, Georgia, and Ukraine.

MAJOR TESTS: BERLIN, KOREA, AND CUBA

Winston Churchill, speaking as a private citizen in Fulton, Missouri, in March 1946, described the Soviet Union as creating an "iron curtain" between the countries it was dominating in Eastern Europe and the rest of Europe. Matters came to a head in Germany in the summer of 1948, when the Soviet Union blockaded West Berlin, which was surrounded on all sides by Soviet-occupied East Germany. (Under the post–World War II settlement, Berlin was initially divided into four zones, overseen respectively by the United States, France, Great Britain, and the U.S.S.R. The three western zones, all part of the Federal Republic of Germany, or West Germany, were later merged.) The U.S. and Western answer was the Berlin airlift, which provided enough food, fuel, and other basic supplies to enable the city and its residents to survive until the Soviets backed down and lifted the blockade in the spring of 1949.

Competition quickly moved beyond Europe, where the United States often opposed colonialism out of concern it would provide openings for Soviet influence. Many new countries were formed and gained independence. Japan was forced to give up its positions in Korea and parts of China and Southeast Asia, an exhausted Britain let go of India and Palestine, and the United States relinquished the Philippines. In the fifteen years following World War II, as a wave of decolonization swept through the world, three dozen new countries emerged in Asia, Africa, and the Middle East.

Cold War competition grew considerably more intense in June 1950, when Soviet-supported troops from the Democratic People's Republic of Korea, more commonly known as North Korea, crossed the border that largely followed the 38th parallel and invaded South Korea (technically the Republic of Korea) in an effort to end the division of the peninsula. North Korea's motives were nationalist, but following the Communist victory in China's civil war in 1949 the Soviets might have wanted to score another Cold War win in Asia and bring about a unified Korean Peninsula that could offset the potential emergence of a reconstituted Japan in the American strategic orbit. It is possible, too, that Stalin believed North Korean aggression would not be directly countered on account of an inadvertent comment made by Secretary of State Dean Acheson in early 1950 that South Korea fell outside the U.S. defense perimeter. Whatever the calculations, it took a large, sustained, American-led military intervention carried out under UN auspices to frustrate Soviet and North Korean designs. The U.S. effort was successful in saving South Korea's independence and restoring the 38th parallel as the effective border, but only at an enormous human and economic cost, which was exacerbated by an ill-fated U.S. attempt to reunify the entire peninsula by force. This undertaking led China to send in its own troops and extended the fighting for two more years.

A third major Cold War venue was Southeast Asia, in particular Vietnam. Following the epic military defeat of France near the village of Dien Bien Phu in 1954, a diplomatic conference was convened to dismantle French Indochina (which became Cambodia, Laos, and Vietnam). Vietnam was divided into a Communist north and a non-Communist south, with an election scheduled for 1956 to decide the country's fate. National elections never took place as the governments of both North and South Vietnam consolidated power and prepared for war. The United States poured in money, arms, advisers, and, when all else failed, millions of troops to shore up a regime in South Vietnam that was challenged by an insurgency supported by North Vietnam and by North Vietnam itself, which was receiving material assistance from both the Soviet Union and China. Successive U.S. presidents hoped not just to preserve South Vietnam but to prevent Communists from taking over all of Southeast Asia. The U.S. effort ultimately failed in South Vietnam, which fell to the North in 1975, and sowed the seeds for the ensuing civil war and genocide in Cambodia. But some argue that the years of effort also bought time for several of Vietnam's neighbors to develop politically, economically, and militarily and thereby better resist Communist encroachment.

Perhaps the most dangerous episode of the Cold War came in October 1962 when the United States discovered that Soviet personnel sent to Cuba were installing missiles armed with nuclear warheads that could reach the United States in just a few minutes. This move was inconsistent with showing restraint in areas close to the other power; it was also seen by some as undermining nuclear deterrence. Nuclear war was widely viewed as a real possibility. I recall participating in duck drills at the time, literally hiding under my wooden desk in my elementary school classroom with the belief that doing so would shield me from nuclear fallout. I also remember my friend Arnie telling us with great authority that we had only ten days before the war started and our lives would end.

Fortunately, the duck drills proved unnecessary and Arnie was proved wrong. Over the thirteen days of the crisis, the United States was firm in its demand that all Soviet missiles be removed but flexible both in how it went about pressing its case (choosing a naval "quarantine" or blockade in all but name over an attack) and in quietly agreeing to remove from Turkey its own medium-range missiles that could reach the Soviet Union. The Kennedy administration also gave a public pledge not to invade Cuba, thereby giving the Soviets a face-saving way to back down. What could easily have become a nuclear war was narrowly averted.

MANAGING THE RIVALRY

Why did the Cold War stay cold? There was, to begin with, a balance of military power. The United States anchored the North Atlantic Treaty Organization, or NATO, which included much of Western Europe. The Soviet Union, for its part, established the Warsaw Pact, which included its satellite states in Eastern Europe. The two alliances made any war in Europe sure to be costly and uncertain in outcome, and therefore unlikely. This balance was based not just on military inventories but also on a willingness by the United States and other NATO members to act directly if they determined military action was called for. The basic bargain of membership in the NATO alliance, one enshrined in Article 5 of the North Atlantic Treaty, was that an attack on one constituted an attack on all.

But such a willingness to act militarily was only one aspect of what sustained the Cold War order. What also kept the Cold War cold was the shared realization on the part of both the United States and the Soviet Union that any direct clash between them could escalate into a nuclear exchange in which the costs would dwarf any conceivable gains and in which there would be no victor in any meaningful sense of the word. Nuclear weapons thus buttressed the traditional, conventional balance of power. They dampened down competition because leaders understood that a nuclear war would be disproportionately costly regardless of the interests at stake and regardless of how it started. Behind that was the sinister genius of mutually assured destruction (popularly known as MAD) and what was known as second-strike capability, namely that a country would have the ability to absorb a nuclear strike by the other side and still be in a position to retaliate on a scale that would deter (assuming rationality was at work) the other side from acting in the first place. If nuclear weapons had never been developed, one could make a plausible case that the Cold War would not have stayed cold, that history might have evolved in very different ways because calculations would have been very different. Any number of confrontations might well have triggered either local military clashes or something much larger and more geographically diffuse. It is no exaggeration to say that absent nuclear weapons and the restraint they engendered, we might now be studying World War III rather than the Cold War.

Arms control, in effect a specialized subset of diplomacy, also helped to keep the peace. The United States and the Soviet Union negotiated, signed, and entered into a number of agreements over the decades that bolstered deterrence and stability. The SALT (Strategic Arms Limitation Talks) and START (Strategic Arms Reduction Treaty) agreements did their part by placing limits on the number and type of land-based missiles, bombers, and submarines carrying nuclear warheads each side could deploy. A 1987 treaty eliminated missiles that could carry nuclear warheads distances defined as intermediate (as opposed to either short or long range). Such agreements increased both transparency and predictability when it came to knowing what the other side did and would possess, thereby helping to avoid even more costly arms races and war through miscalculation.

Deterrence was further reinforced by draconian limits set on defense. The Anti-Ballistic Missile Treaty was signed in 1972 and remained in force for the duration of the Cold War. Under the pact, the United States and the Soviet Union denied themselves the ability to deploy certain kinds of systems that could threaten the ability of the other side's missiles to reach their targets. This left both countries vulnerable to attack, bolstering deterrence and decreasing the chance of nuclear war.

Diplomacy was not limited to arms control. There was normal diplomatic interaction via embassies and consulates. The respective ambassadors had access to the most senior levels of each other's government, as did visiting ministers. There was more than a little trade, cultural exchange, and tourism. And, most dramatically, there was regular summitry involving the leaders of the two countries. In short, the United States and the Soviet Union were great-power rivals, but their rivalry was bounded.

Just as significant, the United States, while it spoke out in protest of how the Soviet Union treated its own citizens and those living in its external empire, was quite circumspect in what it actually chose to do to challenge Soviet control. This represented a triumph of realism over idealism, as the United States carried out a foreign policy that prioritized restraining Soviet behavior beyond its borders rather than trying to fundamentally alter what it did within them. To be sure, no U.S. administration ever formally accepted the so-called Brezhnev Doctrine, named for the Soviet leader Leonid Brezhnev, by which Moscow asserted the "right" to use military force to keep loyal Communist governments in power in its so-called political satellites residing in what was in effect a Soviet sphere of influence in Eastern Europe. (A sphere of influence is an area beyond the borders of a country where it asserts special rights or considerations.) At the same time, when there were domestic political uprisings against Soviet-backed governments in East Germany in 1953, Hungary in 1956, Czechoslovakia in 1968, and Poland in 1970 and again in 1981, the United States did not intervene in any meaningful way on behalf of those peoples trying to liberate themselves. Nor did the United States block the building of the Berlin Wall in 1961 that made it impossible for residents of Communist East Berlin to escape to democratic West Berlin. Again, this was a caution born out of concern that any such intervention could lead to a direct clash with the Soviet Union, which presumably would have used force to protect what it saw as interests vital to its empire and, as a result, to itself.

This is not to say that either country ignored what was going on inside the other. The United States under Presidents Jimmy Carter and Ronald Reagan (and Congress before that) condemned human rights abuses in the Soviet Union, pressing for, among other things, the freedom of high-profile political dissidents and for Soviet Jews to be able to emigrate if they wished to do so. And the Soviet Union would regularly point out shortcomings in American society. But these efforts were limited and did not assume a priority that threatened what was seen as a more basic stake in avoiding war at the nuclear level or in avoiding direct confrontation stemming from regional competition.

For its part, the Soviet Union did what it could to promote anti-American, Communist regimes around the Western Hemisphere and succeeded in Cuba and Nicaragua. It had the advantage of aiding individuals and movements who were fighting against unpopular authoritarian governments that offered little to their people. But again the Soviet help was just that—help—usually in the form of intelligence, military assistance, and subsidies. Direct Soviet military intervention for the most part did not take place in Latin America, a part of the world where the United States had declared, through the Monroe Doctrine, that it was prepared to act to protect what it judged to be its vital interests in what was essentially viewed as an American sphere of influence.

Stability during the four decades of the Cold War also benefited from the structural design of international relations at the time, namely, bipolarity. It is less difficult to manage a world with two principal centers of power than many. There are simply fewer independent actors and decision makers with real impact. This is not to say that Great Britain and France and others always did America's bidding; they did not. And China's resentment of and split from the Soviet Union in the late 1960s is a matter of record. Still, the world of the Cold War was to a significant degree a stable "duopoly" in which changes tended to take place within the structure of an international system dominated by two powers. Most countries chose or, as was often the case with the Soviet Union, were coerced into affiliating with one of the two great powers. Some, however, resisted and chose to be "nonaligned," accepting assistance in one form or another from both superpowers without affiliating themselves. This bloc of developing countries (which on occasion proved quite adept at playing the two superpowers off each other) was also described as the third world, distinct from both a capitalist, U.S.-led first world and a Communist, Soviet-led second world.

Stability was also girded by understandings about how geopolitical competition was to be waged. Both Moscow and Washington came to appreciate that when it came to support for associates, there were limits on how much change would be tolerable for the other. The Soviets learned this lesson in Berlin when they blockaded the Western sectors and again in Cuba a decade and a half later. The United States, for its part, learned this lesson the hard way in Korea, when it was not content to restore the previous status quo and, after liberating South Korea, decided to press north to try to reunify the peninsula. This outcome was too much for both the Soviet Union and China, and the Chinese dispatched hundreds of thousands of "volunteers" to push back against the U.S.-led, UN-authorized force. The result was an additional twenty thousand American dead and a prolonged war that ended roughly along the original border. And during the October 1973 Middle East war fought by Israel against Syria and Egypt, when the Americans and the Soviets backed their respective allies, both superpowers also settled for an outcome that left Israel short of a complete victory and the encircled Egyptian army intact.

The net result was that the Soviet Union and the United States, despite being in a cold war, evolved into a state of "peaceful coexistence." Two very different political and economic systems with divergent worldviews and aims could nonetheless avoid outright conflict. Over time the two superpowers took steps to increase the odds their competition would remain peaceful. This became known as "détente," from the French term referring to a relaxation of tension in a bow.

THE COOLING OF THE COLD WAR

There is no specific date when the Cold War ended (as there tends to be when "hot" wars end), but most historians place it in late 1989, when the wall separating East and West Berlin was taken down, or in 1991, when the Soviet Union along with its external empire in Eastern Europe unraveled. I was working at the White House at the time, and while I was not responsible for U.S.-Soviet relations, I distinctly remember events moving faster and further than I or anyone else predicted.

Why did the Cold War end when and how it did? The Soviet economic system was deeply and structurally flawed and brittle. In 1987, the historian Paul Kennedy published an influential book on why major powers rise and fall throughout history, arguing that a principal reason was that the burdens of empire often undermine prosperity and as a result stability at home. The burden of its overseas role and activities surely contributed to the failure of the Soviet Union, which had to support a large military budget, a far-flung set of allies that often needed financial help, the cost of occupation in Eastern Europe, and the economic and human price of imperial adventures such as its ill-fated 1979 intervention in Afghanistan. These costs exacerbated a difficult, inefficient reality brought about by decades of an economy ruled much more by political forces than by market ones.

Political decisions and diplomacy mattered too. The Soviet Union was isolated from the other major Communist power, China, as the two increasingly fell out over China's resistance to being the junior partner in the relationship, differences over which Communist model other countries in the nonaligned third world should emulate, disagreements over the proper demarcation of their shared border, and much else. By the late 1960s, fighting had broken out between the two. Beginning in the early 1970s, the United States forged a relationship with China to further add to Soviet difficulties.

Mikhail Gorbachev, who led the Soviet Union starting in 1985, played a pivotal role in the end of the Cold War. Gorbachev clearly concluded that the Soviet Union could survive and compete on the world stage only if it changed in fundamental ways at home. But his approach to change, in which political reform came before economic restructuring, mostly resulted in a loss of control over what was happening domestically and in Eastern Europe. The Soviet Union was poorly positioned to resist the demands for greater independence from nationalities within its own borders and among its satellites in Eastern Europe. It could not prevail militarily and in the end could not compete economically or adapt politically.

But some of the credit for how history unfolded surely goes to successive U.S. presidents beginning with Harry Truman and, more broadly, the sustained efforts of the United States and its allies over four decades in Europe and Asia. George H. W. Bush, the American president at the time the Berlin Wall was dismantled by German protesters in November 1989, deserves special praise for his handling of the Cold War's final chapter. Bush has been criticized for not making more of these events, but he was careful not to humiliate Communist leaders and risk provoking a situation that could have pressured them to take dramatic action or brought to power those who wanted to do just that.

That the Cold War ended peacefully and included the breakup of the Soviet Union, the unification of Germany, and its entrance into NATO is nothing short of remarkable. Much of history is often triggered by the friction caused by epochal events, and in this case such an outcome was avoided. It demonstrates the impact of individuals on history.

The Post-Cold War Era (1989-Present)

The last period of history to be covered here may appear to be somewhat odd to think of as history, because it includes where we are now and, for the time being, where we are heading. As is always the case, we are living in history. What makes it difficult to appreciate and understand is that we do not have the advantage of hindsight, the perspective that tends to come with the passage of time. People living in the Renaissance didn't think of themselves as living in the Renaissance, or the late Middle Ages for that matter; they were just living their lives. Only afterward did these eras get defined and named.

The current period is often called the post–Cold War era, an age that extends from the Cold War's end to and through the present and for an unknown time into the future. We know roughly but not precisely when this era began, because dating the end of the Cold War is necessarily subjective. Still, November 9, 1989, is as good a date as any to mark the end of the Cold War, for it was on that date that East German citizens successfully breached the wall that had divided East from West Berlin. The fact that citizens of East Germany could leave for West Germany and not be shot, as many individuals had been over the previous decades, revealed that the Communist regime in East Germany and its sponsor, the Soviet Union, had given up the fight.

With the collapse of the Soviet Union, its external empire, comprising Albania, Bulgaria, Czechoslovakia, East Germany, Hungary, Poland, and Romania, became truly independent. What had been the Soviet Union for three-quarters of a century—its internal empire—dissolved into Russia and an additional fourteen countries, including Kazakhstan and the other four countries of Central Asia as well as Estonia, Georgia, Latvia, Lithuania, Ukraine, and others. This took place peacefully, although subsequently Russia has used force against both Georgia and Ukraine and has signaled that it seeks considerable influence over the decisions of countries in its "near abroad." It is worth noting that East Germany's sense of national identity led it to join what had been West Germany in what became a unified Germany. Nationalism can bring people together as well as tear them apart.

With the end of the Cold War, and the subsequent dissolution of both the Soviet Union and the Warsaw Pact, NATO faced a conundrum. With its principal threat now gone, the alliance could have dissolved, but its members chose instead to maintain the alliance and expand it; membership went from sixteen countries in 1989 to twenty-nine over the ensuing three decades. The rationale was to preserve NATO as a hedge against future uncertainties, above all the emergence of a Russian threat, and to help new members democratize and professionalize their militaries. The downside of this adaptation is that it diluted NATO's ability to act as a unified whole, contributed to the subsequent alienation of Russia, and created new obligations for all NATO members at a time when most members were anything but keen to meet existing commitments much less additional ones.

POST-COLD WAR CRISES

Some predicted or hoped the new era following the Cold War's end would be calm and peaceful because we would no longer live with the acute risk of nuclear war or in a world dominated by two rival superpowers. The hope was that a world dominated by the victorious and surviving superpower (the United States) would come to resemble it and be mostly democratic and peaceful. No one would have the ability—and few would have the desire—to challenge the primacy of the United States given its tradition, with some exceptions, of not seeking to impose its will on others. Others were more skeptical, fearful that a world without two rivals would lack structure and discipline and would as a result be more violent and disorderly even if the level of violence would not rise to the existential threats that were at the heart of the Cold War.

Interestingly, the first full-blown international crisis of the new era proved both the pessimists and the optimists right. In August 1990, less than a year after the Berlin Wall was torn down, Iraq, then led by the ambitious authoritarian ruler Saddam Hussein, invaded and quickly conquered its smaller and weaker neighbor to the south, Kuwait, making it part of Iraq. It was the sort of naked aggression that Iraq, closely associated with and dependent in many ways on the Soviet Union, would not have been allowed by its former patron to undertake at the height of the Cold War because it could have given the United States the pretext for intervening militarily in the part of the world that hosted the lion's share of global oil and gas reserves.

It was not obvious at the time what the United States would choose to do. I was the young National Security Council staff member who met President George H. W. Bush on the South Lawn of the White House when he returned from Camp David on August 5, just after Iraq had devoured Kuwait. After I briefed him on the latest developments, he could not have been clearer in what he declared to an anxious world: "This will not stand, this aggression against Kuwait." Consistent with the president's words, the United States intervened, first with diplomacy and economic sanctions, ultimately with military force. President Bush did not want Iraq to dominate the energy-rich Middle East; nor did he want the new era to start with the terrible precedent that force could be used to unilaterally change borders. The fact that the United States worked through the United Nations and put together an international coalition that ultimately defeated Iraq, forced it to leave Kuwait, and restored Kuwaiti independence turned what had been an enormous setback for world order into a victory and a demonstration of the value of multilateralism.

The United States was decidedly less successful in dealing with the Gulf War's aftermath, when Iraqis in the north and south of the country rose up against Saddam Hussein's brutal rule. Saddam crushed this opposition and retained power because U.S. military intervention was limited to providing humanitarian support in the Kurdish north in order to avoid getting caught up in taking sides in what was seen as a civil war.

The messiness of the war's aftermath proved to be something of a harbinger of what was to unfold over the coming years. The most dramatic development that followed involved the former Yugoslavia, a multinational country kept together throughout the Cold War by authoritarian leadership and fear of Soviet intervention. The demise of both led to the country's violent breakup in 1991 and 1992, a process that caused hundreds of thousands of civilian deaths and required NATO military action to end the fighting and the prolonged presence of international peacekeepers to prevent its resumption.

It was situations such as these (and even more the Rwandan genocide in 1994, in which 800,000 men, women, and children lost their lives) that in 2005 led to a vote in the UN General Assembly to embrace the concept that sovereign governments must provide a degree of physical and economic security to their own citizens, and that when they are unwilling or unable to do so, other countries (with UN Security Council approval) gain the authority to intervene to protect those citizens and restore order.

This became known as the Responsibility to Protect, or R2P, doctrine. Events over the next decade and a half showed, though, that it made little difference in practice, because countries could not agree on whether intervention was warranted or were unwilling to intervene because of the costs. The one time the doctrine was put into practice was in Libya in 2011, when the United States, France, the United Kingdom, and other NATO members intervened to prevent what they judged to be an imminent civil war in which many civilians would be vulnerable. Once begun, the intervention evolved into a mission to topple the regime in Libya, which led to massive disorder when the United States and its allies decided not to remain involved to stabilize the situation. As a result, in the eyes of Russia and China, two permanent members of the UN Security Council with veto power, the R2P doctrine was discredited and seen as little more than a cover for imposing political outcomes. The United States and its European allies, for their part, grew warier of the costs and difficulties of employing the R2P doctrine.

A decade earlier, on September 11, 2001 (often referred to as 9/11), nineteen individuals from four Arab countries armed only with box cutters hijacked four civilian airliners in the United States. All nineteen men were members of al-Qaeda, a terrorist network based in Afghanistan that had its origins in the struggle against the Soviet occupation there. Two planes were flown into the twin towers of the World Trade Center in New York City and a third into the Pentagon, and a fourth crashed in a field in Pennsylvania when passengers fought back against the hijackers. Three thousand people, mostly Americans but also others from nearly one hundred countries, were killed.

The attack heralded the arrival of a new age of global terrorism in which people could be inspired over the internet, recruited and funded across borders, trained anywhere, and sent around the world to carry out acts designed to kill civilians for some political purpose. September 11 galvanized increased domestic and international counterterrorism efforts, but such efforts proved costly in terms of dollars spent, police, intelligence, and military assets committed, and privacy compromised. The mission to eradicate terrorism was never completely successful given the diffuse nature and scale of the problem, something that makes "defeating" or eliminating terrorism impossible.

A second crisis was economic, or to be more precise financial, triggered by years of irresponsible mortgage lending, high-risk investments, and inadequate regulation of banks and other financial institutions in the United States and Europe. These practices came home to roost in 2007 and 2008, and it was not long before the crisis grew dramatically in scope, reach, and impact, morphing into a global recession that eliminated massive amounts of wealth and caused significant unemployment. This recession placed growing economic inequality in the developed world into starker contrast and led to the accumulation of considerable public debt.

If the crisis began in the United States, so, too, did the response, one that involved substantial government intervention to buttress beleaguered financial institutions, massive fiscal and monetary stimulus to revive economic growth, and the introduction of regulatory reforms designed to make future financial crises less likely. The response was largely a success, although the crisis increased wariness of the United States and set back the pace for economic growth and development everywhere. Middle-class wages largely stagnated, upward mobility for many proved a myth, and inequality increased. The result in the United States and around the world was increased populism and growing disaffection with capitalism.

POST–COLD WAR CHALLENGES

A number of other developments and trends need to be highlighted about the post–Cold War era. One feature is the revival of friction and rivalry between major powers, most significantly between the United States and both Russia and China. The cause of the deterioration in U.S.-Russia relations is a matter of considerable debate, with some pointing to a lack of U.S. economic assistance for Russia in its early years as an independent country and to the decision to enlarge NATO, an initiative many in Russia saw as threatening and humiliating.

Others place the burden of responsibility on Russia and above all on Vladimir Putin, a former intelligence officer who has been ruling Russia as either its president or its premier since 1999. Early on, Putin seemed to conclude that he wanted no part of the U.S.-led liberal world order, seeing it as a threat to his own continued rule and to Russia's position in the world. Consistent with that conclusion, Putin undertook a number of policies at odds with the interests and values of the United States, such as using force to annex Ukraine's Crimean Peninsula and prop up the government of Bashar al-Assad in Syria. The fact that Russia used cyberattacks and a disinformation campaign to manipulate the U.S. 2016 presidential election made a bad situation worse. But whatever the cause or causes of the significant worsening of U.S.-Russia relations, the result was that economic sanctions to penalize Russia, mutual expulsions of diplomats, breakdowns of Cold War–era arms control agreements, and renewed military competition have become staples of the relationship.

The trajectory of Sino-American relations has been different, in no small part because China took a different path from Russia. Unlike Russia, China embraced integration with the global economy, emphasizing both trade and investment, although on terms consistent with its

state-led economic model and in ways that advantaged Chinese manufacturers and exporters. China also sought a good relationship with the
United States because access to the American market and to American
technologies and a stable and predictable international environment
were deemed essential for China's development. Toward that end,
China under the leadership of Deng Xiaoping avoided direct challenges
to U.S. alliances in Asia and more broadly to U.S. primacy.

By the end of the new century's second decade, though, the
U.S.-China relationship came to be characterized much more by competition than by cooperation. Hopes that China's participation in the
global economy would lead to a more market-oriented, democratic, and
restrained China were not realized. The problem was not with integrating China, but was rather with the lack of subsequent follow-up to ensure that China was meeting the obligations it had agreed to when it
was granted entry into the World Trade Organization (WTO). For example, China still designates itself as a developing country in the WTO
and continues to receive World Bank loans even though it is the world's
second-largest economy, is investing billions of dollars in advanced
technology, and is funding infrastructure projects all over the world. At
the heart of the deterioration of the relationship has been American
frustration over trade, especially Chinese theft and forced transfer of
American intellectual property as well as Chinese barriers to American
exports. There is also concern that China is forging ahead (in no small
part because of large government subsidies) in the competition to produce next-generation technologies such as artificial intelligence, quan-
tum computing, and 5G. China's more assertive foreign policy, especially
in the South China Sea, which it declares control over despite competing claims and an international tribunal's ruling to the contrary, has
also contributed to heightened tension. Finally, other policies associated
with China's president Xi Jinping, including the abolition of term limits
on his tenure, repression of the Uighur minority in western China, a

crackdown on autonomy in Hong Kong, heightened censorship of the internet, and more restrictive policies toward nongovernmental organizations, have also increased friction.

As a result, many observers now openly raise the prospect of a cold war between the two most influential countries of this era. But if such a relationship materializes, it will be different in fundamental ways from the Cold War that existed between the United States and the Soviet Union in that China, unlike the Soviet Union, is an economic powerhouse, one highly integrated into the world economy. Containing a country such as China, one that boasts many forms of power beyond its military might, will often prove impossible. It will often prove undesirable as well, because Chinese cooperation will be essential if the world is to contend successfully with global challenges such as climate change and nuclear proliferation that have the potential to affect the interests of every country, including the United States, for the worse. Developing and implementing a foreign policy that pushes back against selected Chinese practices at home and abroad but at the same time leaves open areas for cooperation will be as vital as it will be difficult.

An important characteristic of this post–Cold War era has also been the emergence of a significant number of global challenges along with a large gap between the scale of the challenges and the world's willingness and ability to meet them. The phrase "international community" is often used, but the harsh reality (with partial exceptions, such as combating terrorism) tends to be that there is little sense of community when it comes to dealing with some of the most pressing problems.

A prime example is climate change. Ambitious attempts to forge a global "cap and trade" agreement involving negotiated ceilings that would limit the amount of gases that cause the earth's temperature to rise came to naught. The same was true for taxes proposed on carbon meant to discourage the emission of carbon dioxide. Instead, governments agreed in Paris in 2015 to set a goal for how much the world's temperature should rise over the century, with each government setting a goal for its own country's output over the following five years.

The good news is that international agreement was reached. The less-than-good news is that even if the global goal were to be met, climate change would still have advanced significantly. Making matters worse, it is almost certain the target will not be met. When the United States under President Donald Trump announced its intention to withdraw from the agreement, a bad situation became even worse. Meanwhile, the effects of climate change are increasingly obvious given the rise in temperatures and sea levels and the increasing frequency of severe weather events.

Another global challenge that largely remains unmet as the post–Cold War era unfolds involves cyberspace. Virtually all domains (including the oceans and outer space) are to a degree regulated. What sets cyberspace apart is that it is largely unregulated at the same time that it is so central to the functioning of modern societies, economies, governments, and militaries. There are few rules that are widely observed, a near absence of formal arrangements, and no mechanisms for enforcement.

To the contrary, what we are witnessing is a gradual breakdown of what little order there is. Rather than an open, peaceful internet operating according to rules agreed to by scientists, technology companies, and internet users, what has emerged is an internet increasingly influenced by governments. We see a greater censoring of content deemed politically dangerous (China's "Great Firewall") or morally offensive (European governments acting to stop pornography). The internet has also been used as a weapon to slow nuclear weapons proliferation (as the United States and Israel reportedly did against Iran), to retaliate for actions deemed hostile (as North Korea did when it hacked Sony Pictures in response to a satirical film that poked fun at its leader), and to shape political outcomes (as Russia did against the United States to affect the outcome of the 2016 presidential election).

Then there is space, a domain that hosts the satellites essential for communication of all manner: the global positioning system that helps you get from one place to another, weather forecasting, and military operations. There are nearly 2,000 active satellites in orbit as well as an inordinate amount of debris that, if collided with, could render any satellite useless. There is the 1967 Outer Space Treaty, but this only prohibits weapons of mass destruction from being placed in orbit or on the moon and other celestial bodies. There is nothing that precludes the placement in space of anti-satellite weapons, which as their name implies can be used to destroy satellites. Nor is there any protocol governing potential mining of asteroids and other bodies for valuable minerals. The result is that space is another largely unregulated realm of growing economic and military competition, something underscored by the U.S. decision in 2018 to establish a Space Command as a sixth branch of the U.S. armed forces.

REGIONAL PERSPECTIVES

Progress at the regional level in this post–Cold War era has been uneven. The most successful part of the world, by most measures, has been the Asia-Pacific. This is a region characterized by high levels of economic growth and stability between and within countries. China's rise thus far has been largely peaceful. The biggest shortcoming in security for the Asia-Pacific has been the failure to prevent North Korea from developing nuclear weapons and ballistic missiles.

The least successful region has been the Middle East. It was the venue of the first challenge of the era, when Iraq invaded Kuwait.

Saddam Hussein's aggression was repelled, but he remained in power, as did autocrats in nearly every other country of the region. Efforts to promote peace between the Israelis and the Palestinians mostly failed. Iran expanded its reach and influence throughout the region as its long-term rival Iraq was weakened as a result of America's 2003 war that removed Saddam Hussein and resulted in a country at war with itself.

Starting in late 2010, the Middle East experienced the Arab Spring that, after a period of protest, left many countries in a state of prolonged civil war (often exacerbated by outsiders) or once again ruled by authoritarian regimes. The human suffering is enormous and has taken place in a region that was already lagging behind much of the world in measures of development.

Europe, for the opening decades of the post–Cold War era, appeared to be another successful region of the world: at peace, democratic, and economically developed. The European Union not only expanded (from a dozen members when the Cold War ended to more than twice that number over subsequent decades) but also introduced a shared currency (the euro) and elements of a common foreign policy.

In the second decade of this century, though, "Euro-optimism" receded. Growth rates slowed, and Europe's share of global GDP shrank. A populist nationalist party helped to form the government in Italy, illiberal parties came to power in Poland and Hungary, and a populist movement threatened the government in France. The European Central Bank made monetary policy for those countries using the euro, while governments retained control over their individual budgets, leading to unsustainable fiscal deficits in Greece, Italy, and a number of other countries. Russia reintroduced military conquest to the Continent with its annexation of Crimea. Immigration from the Middle East stimulated the rise of right-wing nationalist political parties, including in Germany. A narrow majority of the British electorate voted in favor of Brexit, which started the country on a course to leave the EU.

Traditional centrist parties that had dominated the European political landscape for more than half a century were increasingly losing out to smaller parties on both the left and the right. Europe's bright future suddenly seemed much less certain.

For Latin America, this has been an era of democratic consolidation in many countries (including Mexico) that had long been run by a single party. It has also been a time in which a number of civil conflicts have been brought to an end, most notably in Colombia. But democracy and populism remain in tension in both Brazil and Argentina. Elsewhere, a number of weak governments, in particular those of the so-called Northern Triangle (Guatemala, Honduras, and El Salvador) and Mexico, could not maintain order within their countries. In Venezuela, once the richest country in Latin America, the government's heavy hand drove millions of people out and decimated its economy. The result has been a more unsettled region. Africa, too, experienced both progress and frustration, with gains in democracy, economic growth, and life expectancy offset by civil conflicts, authoritarian rule, corruption, sizable population increases, and disease outbreaks.

South Asia has also had an uneven post–Cold War experience. There is sustained tension between India and Pakistan as both have increased their nuclear arsenals; terrorist attacks on India mounted from Pakistan have nearly brought the two nations to blows. Pakistan's support for the Taliban (a movement of Sunni fundamentalists who have used terror and waged war against the government in Afghanistan for years) added to problems in the region and at home as Pakistan itself has increasingly been the target of terrorist violence. Meanwhile, India has had some good news in its improved economic record, although it is held back by corruption, a large bureaucracy, widespread poverty, a large and still growing population, and questions surrounding the willingness of its Hindu majority to coexist with its large Muslim minority at a time of increased Hindu nationalism and heightened

Muslim identity. Central Asia for its part has been relatively quiet, a mixed blessing that reflects the near-term stability of authoritarian political systems and, in several cases, oil-dependent economies.

Meanwhile, the United States, the principal architect of the post–World War II world, the country that began the post–Cold War era with a degree of dominance rarely if ever seen in all of history, began to pull back from its role. Costly wars in Afghanistan and Iraq introduced a significant degree of fatigue that made many Americans wary of military intervention. Across the political spectrum, there are signs that the early twentieth-century aversion to a leading world role is reappearing, as calls for retrenchment become commonplace.

As we close out the second decade of the twenty-first century, we can draw some conclusions about the post–Cold War era. This has been a period in which new information and communication technologies have burst onto the world scene in forms that have made them widely available. There have also been great advances in development, including in medicine and life expectancy. Economic growth has been considerable and widespread. Wars between countries have become rare.

But this has also been an era in which the advance of democracy has slowed or even reversed. Inequality has increased significantly. The number of civil wars has increased, as has the number of displaced persons and refugees. Terrorism has become a global threat. Climate change has advanced with dire implications for both the near and the distant futures. The world has stood by amid genocide and has shown itself unable to agree on rules for cyberspace and unable to prevent the reemergence of great power rivalry. Those who maintain that things have never been better are biased by what they are focusing on and underestimate trends that could put existing progress at risk.

It is too soon to say when or how this era will end or what will succeed it. But what is clear is that a good many of the trends are worrisome. If, for example, a Sino-American cold war materializes, it is quite possible this era may come to be known as the inter–Cold War era, one bookended by the U.S.-Soviet Cold War and one between the United States and China. Such an outcome would result in lower rates of economic growth for both because trade and investment would inevitably be curtailed. It would also reduce the potential for cooperation on regional and global issues. If the liberal world order is sustained and strengthened with the United States resuming a leading role, this could continue to be an era largely characterized by stability, prosperity, and freedom. It is possible, though, that the United States will choose to largely abandon its leading role in the world. In this case, we could in principle see an era of Chinese primacy, but given China's character, internal constraints, and the nature and scale of the domestic challenges it faces, this is improbable. More likely is that this will turn out to be an era of deterioration, one in which no country or group of countries exercises effective global leadership. In that case, the future would be one of accelerating global disorder.

Part II

◦————————◦

REGIONS OF THE WORLD

The world can be approached on many levels. It needs to be treated as a whole, at the global level, but it is also essential to tackle the world at the regional level, where much of history takes place. Few countries can exert meaningful influence across the world, although more can do so now given the reach of modern technology. Geography creates constraints. A country cannot pick up and move to another region; it is either blessed or cursed by the one it is in. The most significant interactions that a country has are often with its neighbors, especially in terms of economic and political issues and matters of war and peace.

Here I have divided the world into six regions: Europe, East Asia and the Pacific, South Asia, the Middle East, sub-Saharan Africa, and the Americas. This grouping is inevitably arbitrary, because what shapes a region is more than geography. A number of countries are included in the Middle East even though they are physically located in Africa because their orientation, identities, and interactions are mostly in the Middle East. Other countries physically span more than one region (Russia, for example, is in both Europe and Asia) but are placed in the region that reflects most of their focus and activity, which in Russia's case is Europe.

When one discusses Europe, it is important to not just talk about the individual countries but also think about the European Union's role. Europe is the region that has pooled sovereignty to the greatest extent, with powerful supranational institutions that in some realms take precedence over national governments. While Europe is where much of twentieth-century history took place, it is less likely that either

Europe or European countries will occupy so central a role in this century.

East Asia and the Pacific (sometimes referred to as "Asia" here for simplicity) is the largest, wealthiest (when measured by overall output), and most populous region of the world, although the populations of both South Asia and Africa are growing at a much faster rate. Asia, like Europe, was a principal venue of World War II and the Cold War; it is likely to emerge as the principal venue of this century's history. The role of China, as well as regional powers including Japan, South Korea, and Indonesia, will be central.

South Asia is dominated by India, which will soon surpass China as the world's most populous country. As a democracy, India offers an important alternative to China in many ways. But the region is also defined by India's rivalry with Pakistan, by the long-running war in Afghanistan, and by efforts to improve living standards for hundreds of millions of people in all these countries. Bangladesh, in particular, faces the additional challenge of providing for tens of millions of people likely to be displaced by the effects of climate change.

The Middle East has received a great deal of attention in the news in recent years as a result of its conflicts, dramatic political events, and diplomatic undertakings. The region's energy resources and its terrorism affect the world in profound if fundamentally different ways. The Middle East is changing as fast as any other region, which makes it a challenge to encapsulate. That said, the changes tend to affect details more than fundamentals, so what is observed here will likely remain true for a time, which is a shame because much of what this book says about the Middle East is unavoidably downbeat.

Africa, or more precisely sub-Saharan Africa—with those African countries north of the Sahara treated as part of the Middle East—is difficult to deal with as a whole, because there is no dominant country or shared geopolitical challenge. The common thread turns out to be more one of political and economic development, or the lack of it, within countries. The same mostly holds true for Latin America, where a defining challenge is that some governments are too weak to perform the tasks that they are expected to do.

I should note at this point that two regions do not receive separate treatment. The first is the Arctic, which is only just emerging as an area of strategic competition, in part due to climate change, which has opened up new sea lanes and raised the prospect of tapping the region's natural resources. The second, Central Asia, is mentioned in the section on South Asia, but because its global impact is modest and it has largely been within the purview of Russia (and to a growing extent China) it does not have its own chapter.

One difference that continues to animate the dynamics of many regions is religion. No religion claims a majority of the world's people. Nearly a third of the world's population, or 2.3 billion people, are Christians, while close to a quarter of humanity, 1.8 billion people, are Muslims. Just over 1 billion are Hindus, nearly 500 million are Buddhists, and some 15 million are Jews. And more than 1 billion people claim no religion of any kind. The Muslim population is expected to grow twice as fast as the overall global population so that by 2050 (when there are predicted to be as many as ten billion inhabitants of the planet) there are projected to be nearly 3 billion Muslims and only slightly more Christians. The Middle East is predominantly Muslim, but most of the world's Muslims live in Indonesia, Pakistan, India, and Bangladesh.

Changing demographics will also have an impact on regional dynamics. Certain regions, including East Asia and Europe, face demographic stagnation or even contraction. Others, especially sub-Saharan Africa and South Asia, face the prospect of significant increases. What's more, age distribution across countries is wildly uneven. Some countries, including many in Africa, have a youth bulge, and in sub-Saharan

Africa more than 40 percent of the population is under fifteen years of age and roughly 3 percent is over sixty-five. This places stress on a nation to fund schooling and find jobs for those entering the workforce. By contrast, much of Western Europe and parts of Asia have an elderly bulge; in Asia, less than 25 percent of the population is under fifteen and nearly 10 percent is sixty-five and over. (Some 27 percent of Japanese people are over sixty-five.) This increases the burden on those who are of working age (because they need to care for many others) and on the society as a whole because older people often live past their savings and require more health care. Interestingly, the United States has a relatively balanced age distribution, in large part because of immigration. Approximately 20 percent of the population is under fifteen years old, and another 15 percent (including this author) is sixty-five or older.

As you might expect, no single language is spoken by a majority of the world's peoples. (It seems Esperanto has failed to catch on.) English, though, comes closest to being a common language; it is spoken by as many as one out of every seven people in the world. Nearly as many people speak Mandarin, but almost all of them live in China.

One final word about the United States. While the United States is located in the Americas, it is discussed in the regional section only in the context of its influence in Latin America and its relations with Latin American countries and Canada. The United States is truly a global power, with military forces stationed around the world, alliance relationships in Europe and Asia, and the ability to project power into any corner of the globe. As a result, the United States is discussed in every regional chapter.

In each case, I have done my best to discuss the most powerful and influential countries, relevant regional organizations, critical history, economic performance, essential demographic data, and the principal challenges confronting the region that will determine its future. The aim is to capture why each region matters and what makes it tick.

What emerges is an uneven tale in that the regions of the world are far from equal. They are distinctly different when it comes to anything and everything, including size, population, religion, language, wealth, stability, political orientation, and relationships with those outside the region. It should also be said that every region has undergone enormous changes in recent decades and will likely continue to change at a rapid rate.

Europe

Contemporary Europe stands out from much of the world because of its relative wealth, its large number of democracies, and its considerable peace and stability. Europe's economy is slightly larger than that of the United States and represents one-quarter of the global economy. Nearly all of the region's fifty countries are judged to be free or partly free. The region is largely at peace, with the important exceptions of Ukraine and Georgia, both of which are contending with aggression supported or carried out by Russia. Other parts of Europe, such as Cyprus and parts of the Balkans, still suffer from communal tensions and territorial disputes.

Overall, Europe must be considered extraordinarily successful. During the first half of the twentieth century, Europe was the principal venue of two of history's costliest wars. Intolerant political movements came to power, denying basic freedoms to hundreds of millions and setting into motion events that cost the lives of tens of millions. By contrast, since the conclusion of World War II, Europe has known unprecedented stability, prosperity, and freedom. Much of the credit goes to the two great undertakings of the post–World War II era, namely, the NATO alliance and the project of European integration.

Still, there is a question of whether Europe's best days are behind it.

The future of both NATO and the European Union (EU) is in some doubt. Support for both within many countries is diminished, and there is no consensus as to the desired structure and role of the EU. Centrist parties have lost supporters to more radical parties of both the left and the right. There are also renewed concerns over Russian intentions, and there is no broad agreement on how to deal with China. Economic growth has slowed, while economic inequality has in many countries increased. What was once the world's most successful region now finds itself facing a demanding future with less confidence and consensus.

HISTORY

What we think of as Europe (in the political sense) emerged in the mid-seventeenth century in the aftermath of the Thirty Years' War. The nineteenth century began with the wars that ultimately brought down Napoleon and his empire. A period of stability lasting several decades followed, but this came to an end amid a war involving the major European powers in Crimea. In the second half of the nineteenth century, what we think of as Italy and Germany were created when a large number of smaller entities joined together. And Europe was the principal arena of the two world wars of the twentieth century, wars with a combined cost of tens of millions of lives and trillions of dollars.

The best place, though, to begin a consideration of today's Europe is in 1945 with the end of World War II, because we are still living with the consequences of decisions made at that time. Three challenges preoccupied those concerned with the Continent. The first was how to deal with an aggressive Soviet Union that had no intention of leaving the countries that it had occupied during the war or of demobilizing its military forces, which had been pivotal in defeating Germany. In the war's aftermath, the Soviet Union maintained a sphere of influence in

Eastern Europe, where its military was just one instrument for ensuring the subservience of these countries. Soviet military forces would also threaten Western Europe as the Kremlin worked to fuel Communist revolutions across the Continent and beyond.

The ultimate answer to this predicament was to create an alliance that would keep the peace in Europe. NATO, or more formally the North Atlantic Treaty Organization, was built to maintain the security tie between the United States and Europe that was central to victory in both World War I and World War II and that continued to be necessary given Soviet strength and European weakness. By integrating West Germany into an alliance system, NATO also anchored German democracy and offered an insurance policy against the reemergence of extreme German nationalism and militarism. Ideally, this peacetime alliance would keep the Cold War cold and also keep the countries of Western Europe secure, free, and prosperous. More succinctly, NATO's purpose (according to one clever official at the time) was to "keep the Soviet Union out, the Americans in, and the Germans down." It succeeded in achieving these goals and more.

The second post–World War II challenge was to help the countries of Europe get back on their feet. Industries needed to be rebuilt. Refugees were scattered throughout the Continent. Millions of people needed assistance. The rationale for offering assistance was not just humanitarian and economic, as important as both considerations were, but also political, because Europe needed to begin a process of economic recovery if political stability was to be achieved and Communist parties aligned with the Soviet Union were not to seize control. There was also a security dimension to granting aid. European countries would not be able to contribute to the collective defense if they lacked the desire and the means to do so.

The policy that addressed this second challenge is known as the

Marshall Plan, announced by Secretary of State George Marshall in June 1947. The focus was on Europe's recovery; the aid ($150 billion in today's dollars) was extensive but transitional, with the goal of getting Europe to the point where its economic growth would be self-sustaining.

The third challenge for post–World War II Europe was averting a return of the circumstances that had led to two costly world wars. At the heart of both of these wars was the struggle between Germany and its neighbors. The question Europe faced after 1945 was how to prevent geopolitical rivalries from reemerging without keeping Germany weak, because weakness would limit its contributions to the security of the Continent and its economic recovery. Disarming Germany would also risk alienating the German populace again, as had happened in the wake of World War I, when the punitive peace imposed by the victors at Versailles helped fuel Hitler's rise.

The idea that emerged to resolve this dilemma, normally attributed to the French statesman Robert Schuman, was to knit Germany and France so closely together that another war between them would become unthinkable. To be precise, Schuman's idea applied to West Germany, because Germany was divided between a democratic, capitalist West and a Soviet-dominated, Communist East. This solution would reconstruct West Germany's economy, its society, and its political institutions in order to prevent the rise of another militaristic regime that would be a threat to its own people and its neighbors.

The initial step to realize this idea was to create the European Coal and Steel Community, consisting of France, West Germany, and Italy, as well as Belgium, the Netherlands, and Luxembourg (often referred to as the Benelux countries). This pact fully integrated the coal and steel industries of these countries so as to make their economies mutually dependent. This marked the beginning of the European project, one that over the following decades would evolve into the European

Community (EC) and later still the European Union, which over time came to broaden its membership and enhance the authority of its institutions of collective governance to extend to economic and foreign policy.

A military balance of power between NATO and the Warsaw Pact—the alliance system set up by the Soviet Union in 1955—kept the peace for four decades. The existence of nuclear weapons bred a caution born of the concern that any conflict could escalate to the nuclear level, with potentially catastrophic consequences. Stability was further reinforced by a series of arms control negotiations that succeeded in limiting nuclear forces and, at the end of the Cold War, by a formal agreement covering conventional (nonnuclear) military forces as well.

The two alliances—a U.S.-led NATO in Western Europe and a Soviet-dominated Warsaw Pact in Eastern Europe—also reached an understanding governing political order in Europe. The Final Act that emerged in 1975 in Helsinki from the Conference on Security and Cooperation in Europe declared the impermissibility of the threat or use of force, the inviolability of borders, respect for the territorial integrity of all European states, a commitment to the peaceful settlement of disputes, and acceptance of the principle of nonintervention in one another's internal affairs. Such an approach to managing competition should not be confused with a robust peace. But it did preserve the essentials of stability in an era threatened by a real risk of conventional and nuclear war. This is precisely why these four decades are called the Cold War.

Knitting together a Europe at peace with itself was one of the post–World War II era's signature successes. The region that had been at the core of so much destructive history has enjoyed a long run of stability and prosperity. This stability was due in part to successful efforts to counterbalance the Soviet Union and deter its ambitions, but much of what was achieved also reflected Western Europe's rapid economic recovery (in no small part because of the Marshall Plan), the successful democratization of West Germany, and the progress of building Europe-wide institutions. Following the end of the Cold War and the disappearance of a common threat, it has proved more difficult for Europe to maintain stability, democracy, and prosperity.

Some of the new challenges stemmed from the unraveling of the Soviet Union. As noted earlier, the Soviet Union was in fact two empires: an internal empire, dominated by Russia but consisting of fourteen other republics and an even larger number of nationalities, and an external empire, largely controlled by the Soviet Union and including half a dozen countries in Eastern Europe. What followed the Cold War's end was a series of protests and conflicts that might be called the wars of Soviet succession. The division and weakness in Moscow removed much of the glue that had kept nationalist forces in check inside the Soviet Union's internal and external empires alike.

By the end of 1991, the Soviet Union no longer existed. Instead, there were fifteen independent countries, including Russia. In addition, by then the countries of Eastern Europe had become independent in fact as well as in name, with many of them eventually joining NATO and the EU. Most of these changes occurred without bloodshed, although the wars that accompanied the breakup of what was Yugoslavia constituted an important and violent exception. Amid successive rounds of ethnic conflict, it took NATO military intervention in both Bosnia (1995) and Kosovo (1999) to accomplish what peacekeepers, diplomacy, and economic and political sanctions could not. The war in Bosnia was brought to a close by the Dayton Accords late in 1995 and Kosovo declared independence from Serbia in 2008. An uneasy peace in the region has prevailed since, with UN peacekeepers still deployed to Kosovo to this day.

Alongside dealing with ethnic conflict, European governments have been grappling with what degree of integration is desirable and politically feasible among their citizens. In some ways the debate can be summarized as one between two contrasting visions for Europe, best captured by the difference between the phrases "the United States of Europe" and "a United Europe of States."

What the former suggests is a Europe in which authority is increasingly transferred from national capitals to the supranational authority of the EU headquartered in Brussels. Several steps were taken in this direction. The most significant development was the signing of the Maastricht Treaty in early 1992 by the leaders of the twelve countries of the EC, which created the EU. One difference between the EC and the EU was that the latter included the "pillar" of a common foreign and security policy in which the EU would in some cases act, instead of the foreign ministries of the member states.

On the economic side, Maastricht introduced a common currency, the euro, which was launched in 1999, with banknotes and coins entering circulation in 2002. By 1993, a single EU market came into being, one that ensured the free movement of goods, services, and people across national lines. Years earlier, the so-called Schengen Area (named for the city in Luxembourg where it was negotiated) had been established, essentially erasing national borders within the EU when it came to the movement of people. During this period of political integration, the EU expanded its membership from twelve countries to fifteen in 1995, to twenty-five in 2004, and reached twenty-eight members when Croatia joined in 2013.

But the project of building "a United States of Europe" was never to the liking of many, who feared the loss of national identity and sovereign authority, as well as the consequences of the free movement of people across borders. The alternative to this "ever closer union" is best captured by the phrase "a United Europe of States." In this conception, the balance between national capitals and Brussels is much more weighted toward member countries. This is perhaps best exemplified in the case of the United Kingdom, which has long been at the forefront of efforts to check the power of Brussels. The U.K. joined the EC in

MEMBERS OF THE EUROPEAN UNION, 2019

Finland

North Sea · Sweden · Estonia · Russia · Latvia · Lithuania · Belarus

Ireland · Denmark · United Kingdom* · Netherlands

Atlantic Ocean

Belgium · Germany · Poland · Luxembourg · Czech Republic · Ukraine · France · Slovakia · Austria · Hungary · Slovenia · Romania · Croatia · Portugal · Spain · Italy · Bulgaria · Greece · Turkey

■ Use euro as currency

*In 2016, the United Kingdom voted to leave the European Union, but as of January 2020 the UK government had not finalized its exit.

←Malta (uses euro) · *Mediterranean Sea* · Cyprus

1973 but opted to stay out of the monetary union and keep its national currency. In 2005, voters in France and the Netherlands rejected a new European constitution, one that would have further shifted the balance of authority away from governments to what was widely considered an impersonal and unaccountable bureaucracy in Brussels. And in 2016, a slim majority of British voters supported a referendum calling for the country's exit from the EU, popularly known as Brexit.

ECONOMIC AND POLITICAL CHALLENGES

The reality of post–Cold War Europe has not matched the hopes of the EU's strongest backers. As average citizens and elites alike have debated the appropriate distribution of power between national capitals and

Brussels, the EU has been hamstrung by a succession of weak leaders (chosen in part by the leaders of national governments who wanted weak leaders in Brussels) and an unwillingness on the part of governments to devote significant resources to defense or to efficiently use the funds they had. National governments have jealously guarded control of foreign and defense policy; there has also been a lack of coordination between countries on intelligence sharing and law enforcement. When it has come to cooperation on security, Europe has fallen short of what it is capable of.

Economic problems within Europe have been even more significant. As a result, the Continent has had low rates of growth. A number of problems have emerged that stem from the fact that the nineteen countries in the eurozone share a common monetary policy, set by the European Central Bank, but fiscal (tax and spending) policy was and is determined by national governments. Germany, which boasts by far the EU's largest economy, insists (for historical reasons that created a strong aversion to any course of action that could trigger inflation) on maintaining a large budget surplus, a practice that has denied Europe the economic stimulus that would result from a Germany willing to run reasonable deficits. In addition, there is no European banking mechanism in which deposits up to a specified level are guaranteed, as is the case for individuals in the United States; instead, each country is effectively on its own. Adding to its burdens, Europe has an aging population and a worsening ratio of those of working age to those too young or too old to work.

Populist movements have strengthened as a result of stagnating economies, high inequality, and concerns over the influx of migrants from the Middle East. One consequence is that many Europeans now favor an even less integrated, more nationalized version of the Continent than the decentralized vision of "a United Europe of States" would suggest.

GEOPOLITICS

A Russian threat to Europe has reemerged. This might have been inevitable given that the Soviet Union lost the Cold War, saw its external empire in Eastern Europe break free, and then experienced its own internal breakup. Russia accounts for roughly half the population and three-fourths of the land area of the former Soviet Union. It has retained a permanent seat on the UN Security Council and a vast nuclear arsenal and has developed impressive conventional military and cyber assets. But it is a great power more in name than in reality. Russia has an economy roughly the size of Canada's and is heavily dependent on energy, a situation typically associated with a developing country. Its population has declined for two decades; male life expectancy is only around sixty-seven, a result of alcoholism, drugs, crime, and a poor public health system. Power is highly concentrated in the person of Vladimir Putin, who has stripped institutions of nearly all of their independent authority.

A significant source of tension between Russia and both the United States and much of Europe was the decision to enlarge NATO, which started in the late 1990s under the Clinton administration and was continued by its successors. It is rare in history for an alliance born in one strategic context (in NATO's case, the Cold War, where it was formed to deter and defend against a Soviet/Warsaw Pact invasion of Europe) to remain in place once the context has changed and the mission has become obsolete. The question was whether NATO could and should endure—or whether its success would prove to be its undoing.

NATO did survive in a new strategic context, mostly by taking on new missions. These missions were outside the formal treaty area that encompassed much of continental Europe and were instead in locations "out of area" but where the interests of members were nonetheless at stake. NATO morphed into something of an interventionary force for problems in places such as the Balkans, Afghanistan, and parts of the Middle East and Africa. By extending its reach, NATO became less of a traditional alliance built around a shared core security concern and more of a collection of relatively like-minded countries that would henceforth make decisions about joint action on a case-by-case basis. Participation in such actions tends to be voluntary on the part of the countries involved.

NATO also became a body that would consolidate and anchor newly liberated (and, in the case of Germany, newly unified) countries. The Czech Republic, Hungary, and Poland all joined in 1999, motivated in large part by a hope that NATO would provide an insurance policy against the possibility that Russia might reassert itself and resume its tradition of pressuring its neighbors.

Meanwhile, Russia was getting increasingly uneasy with this process. Russia and NATO were on opposite sides of the crisis in what had been Yugoslavia; NATO provided political backing and military support for air assaults on Serbia during the Kosovo war, something Russia (which was sympathetic to Serbia for political, historical, religious, and cultural reasons) opposed. Second, many of Russia's neighbors were joining an alliance that Moscow had long viewed with suspicion. Vladimir Putin, who already felt humiliated over how the Cold War ended and the unraveling of the Soviet Union, viewed NATO's enlargement as an insult and a threat, as did many of his fellow Russians. There is no way of knowing whether the trajectory of relations with Russia would have been better had there been no expansion of NATO and no way to know whether the trajectory of European security and stability would have been worse without it. My own view (a view that is a minority perspective in the U.S. foreign policy world) is that NATO enlargement was an error and that the security concerns of Eastern European states could have been addressed by other means than bringing them into

NATO. This is sure to remain a matter of debate for decades to come; we are where we are, however, and there is no going back. What we do know is that Russia under Putin gradually but steadily lost interest in joining the liberal world order that had been championed by the United States. Instead, Putin's Russia increasingly sought to undermine it.

The rift in the relationship between Russia and much of Europe and the United States widened in 2008 over Russia's decision to intervene in Georgia, a former Soviet republic that had become an independent country, by supplying money and arms and ultimately by sending in troops to fight on behalf of separatist groups. Ukraine, however, was the subject of the greatest differences between Putin's Russia and its Western critics. Ukraine was a republic in the old Soviet Union and became independent in 1991. Russia was uneasy about the possibility of close EU-Ukraine ties, especially if they diminished Russia's influence over Ukraine and might pave the way for Ukraine's entering NATO. Matters reached a full boil in late 2013, when hundreds of thousands of Ukrainian protesters took to the streets in the capital, Kiev, and ousted its pro-Russian president after he tilted away from forging closer ties to the EU. The spectacle of an autocratic president being ousted by protesters who favored moving their country into the EU, NATO, or both was for obvious reasons too much for Putin.

Clashes soon broke out in Crimea, a region of Ukraine with an ethnic Russian majority that had been part of the Russian Republic in the former Soviet Union; Crimea became part of the Republic of Ukraine only in 1954. The fighting quickly escalated as locals of Russian ethnicity gained control of the region, armed with Russian-supplied equipment and backed by Russian soldiers. Within weeks Russia had annexed Crimea, following a referendum passed by an overwhelming majority of Crimea's population. The reaction of the United States and much of Europe was to dismiss the referendum as a sham, conducted as it was in an area mostly controlled by Russian-backed rebels.

Understandably, a military response was ruled out; not only was Ukraine not a member of NATO, but it would have been difficult and risky to defend the territory of a weak country on Russia's border. Instead, as is often the case, economic sanctions became the favored foreign policy instrument, one representing a step more serious than a continuation of unpromising diplomacy, but also one far less costly than military force. The problem is that here and elsewhere history suggests that sanctions can rarely alter what a government decides to do on issues of major importance.

Instability in Ukraine was by no means confined to Crimea. Russian equipment and soldiers (not wearing formal uniforms so as to mask their nationality) also made their way into eastern Ukraine, a region that borders Russia and where a significant minority of the population is ethnically Russian. Low-level fighting between Ukraine's military and local militias supported by Russia continues there, and to date has taken 13,000 lives. A cease-fire and political agreement, termed the Minsk Agreement, was signed by Russia, Ukraine, France, and Germany in early 2015, but it has never been fully implemented, with each side blaming the other for not observing one or more of its parts.

All this is relevant for reasons that transcend the importance of Ukraine, a country of some forty-five million people. What happened broadly affected perceptions of and relations with Russia, which is still the preponderant military power in its neighborhood. It also reintroduced a military dimension to Europe that many observers thought had vanished with the end of the Cold War. Russia paid a political and economic price for its actions. It was expelled from the Group of Eight (G8) gathering of major powers, and the United States imposed heavy sanctions on its economy. But these punishments, along with the decision by the United States in 2018 to provide Ukraine with defensive arms, were not enough to lead Russia to reverse a policy that enjoyed popular support at home. Russia also intervened militarily in Syria starting in 2015; unlike Ukraine, this was done at the government's request, albeit in an often brutal manner. Russia worked to influence both the U.S. presidential election of 2016 and many elections in Europe, including the vote on Brexit, and claimed waters off Ukraine as its own in 2018. The result is that U.S. relations with Russia (and relations between much of Europe and Russia) sharply deteriorated.

LOOKING AHEAD

Europe, as noted earlier, has in a short span of time gone from being the most predictable and stable region—one where history seemed to have truly ended (as suggested in an influential essay published in 1989 by the American political scientist Francis Fukuyama)—to something dramatically different. Democracy, prosperity, and peace all seemed firmly entrenched. Not anymore. Much of what had been widely assumed to be settled is not.

There is no single explanation for these developments. What we are seeing is both populism on the left, the result of stagnating wages, rising income inequality, and a resentment of elites, and populism on the right, fueled by nationalism amid local and global changes, above all an opposition to immigration. The EU, for its part, has gradually lost its hold on the public imagination and will be further weakened by Brexit.

Why this matters should be obvious. Europe still represents a quarter of the world's economy. It contains the largest constellation of democratic countries, a number of which are willing to work to make the world a better place. The last century demonstrated the cost of a breakdown of order on this continent. Europe's trajectory in the twenty-first century, which once seemed pointed toward peace and prosperity, is now less clear.

East Asia and the Pacific

East Asia and the Pacific (mostly referred to here and elsewhere as "Asia") is a study in contrasts. Its thirty-one countries range from China, the world's most populous country (until it is overtaken by India) with nearly 1.4 billion inhabitants, to Nauru, an island country of some 13,000 citizens. Similarly, China has the world's second-largest economy, with an annual output of over $13 trillion (more than eleven times as large as it was in 2000), while Nauru stands at just over $100 million. The region, the venue of intense combat during World War II as well as the Korean and Vietnam wars, has been relatively peaceful and stable over the past four decades and remains so. At the same time, it is also home to many countries with growing militaries, along with multiple territorial disputes and deeply held historical animosities.

The political systems are diverse: Japan, the Republic of Korea (South Korea), Taiwan, Australia, and New Zealand are all robust democracies, while China is decidedly authoritarian and North Korea (more formally the Democratic People's Republic of Korea) is governed by arguably the most closed, repressive regime in the world. There are also a handful of countries in between: the Philippines is a democracy but is backsliding into authoritarianism, Thailand was once a

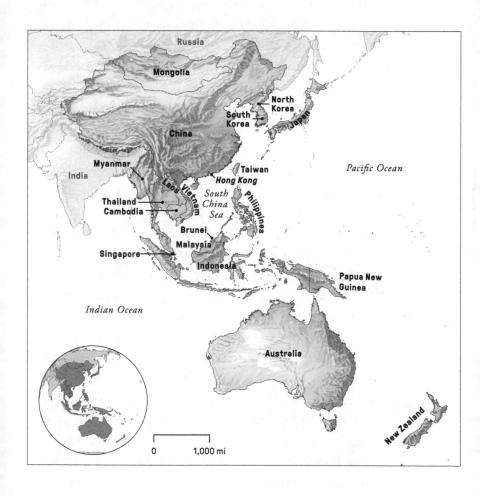

democracy but is now governed by its military, and Myanmar (Burma) recently made progress toward democracy but seems to have stalled.

Wars between Asian countries have been rare—the 1962 Sino-Indian War and the 1979 limited conflict between China and Vietnam being exceptions—as in much of the rest of the world. What makes this remarkable is that the region is home to more territorial disputes than any other. Instability within countries is also rare, in large part because of strong national identities. Many countries are close to being ethnically homogeneous.

The region's economic performance has steadily improved, and it has become a manufacturing powerhouse that accounts for just under one-third of global output. There are several strong regional political and economic institutions, principally the Association of Southeast Asian Nations (ASEAN) and the Asia-Pacific Economic Cooperation (APEC) group that provides a forum for its twenty-one members to discuss ways to promote trade.

The region consists principally of East Asia (China, Japan, the Koreas, and Taiwan); Southeast Asia (eleven countries including Indonesia, Malaysia, the Philippines, Singapore, Thailand, and Vietnam that have a combined population nearly twice that of the United States and a combined GDP on par with France, the United Kingdom, and India); and Australia, New Zealand, and the small Pacific Island nations. Its politics, economics, and security, though, are all heavily influenced by other countries that border Asia, the Pacific, or both, including the United States, Russia, and India. Indeed, more than any other region, Asia is where this era's major powers come into regular, direct contact with one another.

HISTORY

After the tumult of the twentieth century, Asia's present-day success was by no means inevitable. Much of the region suffered a great deal under brutal Japanese occupation before and during World War II. As for Japan, by mid-August 1945 it was a defeated and occupied country. After World War II, China was in the throes of civil war between Nationalists—who were essentially anti-Communist and politically authoritarian and favored economic policies that benefited a wealthy elite—led by Chiang Kai-shek, and Communists—who were politically repressive and opposed to private ownership—led by Mao Zedong. The conflict would continue for four more years, by which time the Communists prevailed and asserted control over mainland China. The Nationalists retreated to the island of Formosa, known today as Taiwan.

The region was also one of the first venues where the Cold War was waged. Following the end of World War II, the Korean Peninsula was divided, somewhat arbitrarily, along the 38th parallel. North Korea, backed by both the Soviet Union and China, invaded South Korea in June 1950 and quickly overran much of the country. The United States, acting with the backing of the newly created United Nations (the resolution was able to pass in the Security Council because the Soviet Union was boycotting the UN to protest the Republic of China (Taiwan) occupying China's seat) and joined by a number of other countries, undertook an audacious amphibious landing at Inchon, regained the strategic momentum, and within months liberated all the territory south of the 38th parallel.

President Harry Truman and the general in charge, Douglas MacArthur, then made the fateful decision to try to unify the peninsula by force. Marching north toward the border between North Korea and

China, they were met by Chinese "volunteers," who in actuality were soldiers, and were forced to retreat. After three years of intense fighting, matters settled to where they had stood before the war, with the peninsula divided into two countries along the 38th parallel. The economic costs of the war were enormous, running in the hundreds of billions of dollars. The human costs were even higher: some 37,000 American troops were killed, and 3.5 million Koreans were either killed or wounded. A formal peace treaty was never signed—an armistice took its place that remains in effect—and the two countries have been in an uneasy and heavily armed standoff ever since. American soldiers have been stationed in South Korea since the war, and nearly thirty thousand remain in the country to this day, with the goal of deterring North Korea from trying to unify the peninsula by force.

Asia went on to experience a number of other conflicts, none more costly and prolonged than the war in Vietnam. Vietnam had been a French colony before World War II but became occupied by Japan during the war. After the Japanese defeat, France moved to reassert control. What ensued was a war for independence, ultimately won by the Viet Minh (the Vietnamese nationalist movement) led by Ho Chi Minh. At the Geneva Peace Conference that followed the defeat of the French garrison at Dien Bien Phu in 1954, Cold War considerations took precedence over local ones, and the country was divided into a Communist north and a non-Communist south. The United States came to see the survival of South Vietnam as critical, fearing that if the country were to be unified under Communist-led North Vietnam it would lead to other countries in the region suffering the same fate, like a row of dominoes.

What ensued beginning in the early 1960s was more than a decade of war, one that simultaneously had the characteristics of a civil war in the South (between U.S.-backed South Vietnam government forces and Communist guerrillas known as the Viet Cong backed by North

Vietnam, the Soviet Union, and China) and a more traditional war involving North Vietnamese troops (again backed by the Soviet Union and China) and U.S. forces. American involvement came to entail the provision of massive amounts of economic and military aid to the South, military advisers, and ultimately American combat forces, at the peak numbering some 550,000. The United States also carried out direct attacks from the air on North Vietnamese targets and on routes in neighboring countries used to supply the Viet Cong fighting in the South.

The high human and economic costs of the war, a military draft, the corrupt and often authoritarian nature of the South Vietnamese regime, and poor prospects for success made the war increasingly unpopular in the United States, triggering widespread opposition to the war throughout the country. For many in my generation, it was a defining issue. My first involvement in politics involved traveling in May 1970 from Oberlin, Ohio (where I was in college), to march on Washington to protest the war, along with hundreds of thousands of others, after four students were killed at Kent State University following demonstrations opposed to the U.S. bombing of Cambodia and the expansion of the war effort.

Against this backdrop, the United States, under the leadership of President Richard Nixon and his national security adviser, Henry Kissinger, turned to diplomacy, and American and North Vietnamese diplomats met to negotiate an end to the conflict. The resulting Paris Peace Accords were signed in January 1973. The agreement did not end the conflict so much as provide a face-saving way for the United States to extricate itself from the conflict. By 1975, following a congressional cutoff of all aid to South Vietnam, its government crumbled and the country was unified quickly and brutally under the Communist government in the North.

As in Korea, the costs of war were horrific by any and every measure. Fifty-eight thousand American soldiers lost their lives; more than one million Vietnamese combatants and civilians lost theirs. The economic cost is impossible to calculate but nearly reaches $1 trillion (if the current value of the dollar is used). One irony is hard to resist: decades later, the United States and a united Vietnam, which is still ruled by the Communist Party, have an increasingly close relationship, a reflection of Vietnam's embrace of a more market-oriented economy and shared concerns over China's intentions.

THE ASIAN ECONOMIC MIRACLE

Yet even with these two conflicts and a number of lesser ones, what took place in Asia since World War II surely qualifies as a miracle. Life expectancy across the region rose from forty-eight years in 1960 to seventy-five half a century later. Robust democracies took root over time in Japan, South Korea, and Taiwan. Arguably the greatest miracle, though, was economic. Many of the region's countries experienced high levels of economic growth over extended periods. The four "Asian Tigers"—Hong Kong, Singapore, South Korea, and Taiwan—experienced average annual economic growth of more than 6 percent from the early 1960s through the 1990s, considerably higher than the world average. For the region as a whole, real gross domestic product (GDP) per capita (in constant 2010 dollars) has risen from roughly $1,300 in 1960 to over $10,000 in 2018.

There are many reasons for this economic success, and there are of course differences that account for what happened in each country. That said, what tended to be common was significant political stability, a culture of hard work, and investment in education. This was complemented by an external order that promoted free trade and for the last half a century mostly avoided conflict.

ECONOMIC GROWTH: ASIAN TIGERS
Real GDP per capita, in 2011 U.S. dollars

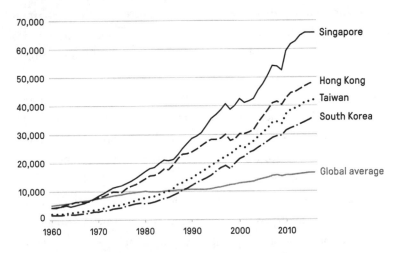

Source: Maddison Project Database, version 2018. Bolt, Jutta, Robert Inklaar, Herman de Jong, and Jan Luiten van Zanden (2018), "Rebasing 'Maddison': New Income Comparisons and the Shape of Long-Run Economic Development," Maddison Project Working paper 10.

The contribution of the United States to this economic boom is worth pointing out. The Asian miracle is in no small part due to American involvement and commitment. U.S. aid to its allies following World War II was significant and helped set the conditions for their future economic success. The U.S. alliance system, which includes Australia, Japan, the Philippines, South Korea, and Thailand, deterred another war on the Korean Peninsula as well as Chinese use of force against Taiwan, discouraged the proliferation of nuclear weapons, and helped bring about professional militaries prepared to accept civilian primacy. U.S. support for free trade and its openness to foreign products provided a mechanism for export-led development and growth for many countries, allowing them to substantially increase the standard of living for their people. U.S. support for democracy and human rights—and pressure on its allies to implement political reform and open their societies—contributed to an evolution of many societies.

Several countries deserve special mention here. The first is Japan, if only because it was the first of the region's success stories. In just two generations, Japan evolved from a defeated imperial militarist country to a functioning democracy, ultimately moving beyond prolonged one-party domination. It became a manufacturing powerhouse, for a long time the world's second-largest economy and now its third largest. Japan also embraced a constitution that limited its military's role in society. Similarly, South Korea evolved from an authoritarian system into a true democracy. Its economy is now the tenth largest in the world.

China followed a fundamentally different path but with no less extraordinary results. It has been some seventy years since China's Communists gained control, and in that time the country's annual economic output has grown from under $100 million to more than $13 trillion. Under Mao Zedong, China was an economic basket case, having experienced the worst human-made famine in modern history, the so-called Great Leap Forward of 1958–1962. This was a coerced, flawed, and overwhelmingly failed effort to ban private farms and collectivize Chinese agriculture that triggered widespread famine and caused an estimated thirty to fifty-five million deaths. The Cultural Revolution (1966–1976), an effort to purge Chinese society of many of its traditional values, followed the Great Leap Forward and had the effect of ruining countless lives and disrupting broad elements of the economy and society by forcing tens of millions of people to leave their homes and jobs in cities, suffer a complete loss of economic and political freedom, and experience a harsh rural existence. It was only after Deng Xiaoping took the helm in the late 1970s, following Mao's death, and began implementing limited market reforms that China was able to right its course. As a result of these changes, hundreds of millions of Chinese citizens have been lifted out of poverty.

GEOPOLITICS

None of this is meant to suggest Asia is without its challenges. The most obvious are geopolitical, with the most pronounced ones relating to the rise of China. China is so large, wealthy (on an aggregate basis), and powerful that it is, in many ways, too much for any other regional country to handle on its own. China is a principal trading partner for many of its neighbors, including Japan, South Korea, and Australia, which also happen to be allies of the United States. The question for them is how to balance these two relationships, and when it comes to security, the question is to what extent they should rely on the United States, become more self-sufficient, or move closer to China.

Meanwhile, it is unclear how China will use its power and how other countries will react. It is acting unilaterally and assertively to increase its military strength in the South China Sea on behalf of territorial claims that many of its neighbors dispute and that some countries (such as the United States) view as a threat to their ability to move their own military forces into and out of the region. China is also using its economic strength, through its "Belt and Road" development initiative that provides loans to countries throughout the region to finance large infrastructure projects, to increase its leverage and access.

There are other disputes in the region worth highlighting. Russia and Japan have yet to sign a formal end to World War II because of competing claims to islands that form the northern part of the Japanese island chain. More seriously, Japan and China cannot agree on who has title to islands in the East China Sea. They cannot even agree on what the islands are called: Japan knows them as the Senkaku Islands, China as the Diaoyu Islands. What makes this particularly perilous is that the competing claims are both a reflection and a cause of larger tensions between the region's two most powerful countries. Should Japan become engaged in a conflict over these islands, the United States would likely become involved; if Japan came to doubt American support, it would increase its military might and possibly develop nuclear weapons.

There is also an uneasy relationship between China and India. Their twenty-five-hundred-mile border is unresolved, and it was a major cause of their 1962 war. But the friction transcends the border dispute and reflects their strategic competition. An important motive for India's acquiring nuclear weapons was the fact that China already had them. China is close to Pakistan, India's archrival, in part because China sees an interest in tying India down so it can focus its energies on its south and east. If it all sounds like classic power politics, that's because it is.

Taiwan is a separate matter. Ever since the Chinese Communists gained control of the mainland in 1949 and the Nationalists fled to Taiwan both sides and most outsiders have maintained that there is but one China, while differing on how to define what China is. Fewer than two dozen countries maintain diplomatic relations with Taiwan (still formally known as the Republic of China), with the rest of the world either recognizing China's claim to Taiwan or asserting that the question remains to be settled. While the United States broke formal diplomatic ties with Taiwan in 1979, it has assumed unique responsibilities to the island, in particular to provide it with defensive weapons and to maintain the ability to come to its defense (without being actually obligated to do so). At the same time, Taiwan is an autonomous political and economic entity and has most of the characteristics of an independent country. The mainland is committed to unification with Taiwan and has stated on multiple occasions that force is an option to bring this about. Other countries are neutral on whether Taiwan becomes definitively a part of China but care about the process by which it comes about. They want whatever happens to be peacefully resolved and entered into voluntarily and therefore on terms acceptable to Taiwan. The question is whether a peaceful settlement on terms both sides can live with is feasible or whether events—for example, Taiwan declaring independence, an economic crisis on the mainland that leads its government to force the pace of unification or steps taken by the United States to upgrade Taiwan's status—will trigger a crisis that could involve the use of force.

A final potential source of geopolitical instability in the region is the Korean Peninsula. As already noted, the Korean Peninsula has been divided along the 38th parallel since after World War II. Aside from small incidents, deterrence has held. Both sides are heavily armed, and there is always the chance North Korea will be tempted to attack given the proximity and vulnerability of Seoul, South Korea's capital. Adding to the stakes in recent years is North Korea's steady development of nuclear weapons and long-range missiles, making it a threat not just to South Korea and Japan but to the world, including the United States. It is an open question whether some mixture of diplomacy and deterrence can continue to prevent war between the two Koreas as well as between North Korea and the United States. It is just as much a question as to whether the United States is prepared to live with a North Korea that can threaten it directly and accept a negotiated outcome under which North Korea agrees to limit but not eliminate its nuclear and missile capabilities. There is also the question of how stable North Korea really is; it has been ruled dynastically for its entire existence and is one of the poorest and most closed countries on earth. And finally there is the question of whether China would be willing to allow the two Koreas to reunify on terms that favored the United States and would result in a U.S. ally on its border.

The deteriorating U.S.-China relationship will influence each of these regional issues and in some instances make them more fraught.

The modern Sino-American relationship can be said to be in its fourth phase. The first phase, which lasted from the establishment of the People's Republic of China in 1949 until rapprochement under President Richard Nixon, was one of open hostility. The United States much preferred that the Communists not win the internal struggle for power that resumed following World War II, and after they did, the two countries fought on opposite sides during the Korean War. The second phase was animated by a shared antipathy toward the Soviet Union, and saw the United States and China work together to counter the Soviet threat. It was a relationship built on realism: when China's government killed hundreds and perhaps thousands of pro-democracy demonstrators in Tiananmen Square in 1989, the George H. W. Bush administration chose to preserve the bulk of the relationship in order to keep the pressure on the Soviet Union. Once the Soviet Union collapsed in 1991, the relationship entered its third phase, typified by increasing investment, trade, and China's integration into the global economy. While Americans benefitted from cheaper Chinese goods and access to China's market, and China received much-needed capital and technological know-how, Americans eventually soured on this relationship as it failed to create a more open, market-oriented, and cooperative China at the same time it helped to bring about an economic competitor. It can be said the U.S.-China relationship is now entering its fourth phase, and is currently looking for a rationale. Without a strategic or economic underpinning, the relationship is becoming increasingly adversarial.

One critical factor in determining the region's future will be the role that the United States chooses to play going forward. As already noted, one reason for the region's phenomenal success over the past seventy years is the presence of the United States. Yes, the United States badly overreached by trying to unite all of the Korean Peninsula by force and then again in making a commitment to Vietnam that was not justified by its direct interests. But the U.S. military presence, its political and diplomatic involvement, its support for trade and investment, and its reputation for reliability also contributed mightily to the region's success. The obvious question is whether the United States will be willing to play such a role moving forward. If not, one can imagine a future of increased Chinese influence, Japanese rearmament, and conflict on the Korean Peninsula, over Taiwan, or owing to one or more of the other outstanding territorial disputes.

LOOKING AHEAD

The direction of the U.S.-China relationship will be critical for the region's future. What will determine its trajectory more than anything else will be whether the two countries can reach a modus vivendi in the economic sphere, particularly regarding advanced technologies and the role of the Chinese state in its economy. Geopolitical issues such as the South China Sea and Taiwan, and differences over how China treats its minority groups, are unlikely to be resolved. The foreign policy challenge, therefore, will be to manage these differences so that they do not get out of hand or preclude cooperation where the interests of the two countries overlap.

Not all of the challenges facing the region are geopolitical. One is demographic. The region is aging more rapidly than any region in history. The principal causes are increased life expectancy, low immigration levels, and declining fertility, something often associated with economic success. Many of these countries (in particular Japan and China) will face a future in which a declining percentage of the population will be of working age and will nonetheless be forced to support a large number of old people who are retired.

There are also internal political and economic challenges facing several countries. Chinese leaders face not just an aging population and an abundance of men over women (both related to years of imposing a one-child limit on families, something that led many to opt for boys) but also widespread corruption, environmental degradation, and an economy overly dependent on access to the markets of others. There is a potential tension between the Communist Party's desire to build an innovative modern economy and its desire to impose strict limits on individual freedom. It is not clear China can enjoy the benefits of an open economy while maintaining a closed political system. The overriding question is whether the Chinese government can maintain political stability amid lower levels of economic growth, and, if it cannot, whether it resorts to a more nationalist foreign policy in order to distract attention from domestic frustrations.

The question naturally arises: Can Asia continue to be a modern miracle? Can it sustain its economic growth, political stability, and peace? It is possible, but it is by no means assured given shifting power balances, continued military modernization, the emergence of a more capable and assertive China, unresolved territorial disputes, expected changes within societies, and questions over what the United States is willing to do in order to maintain the region's stability.

South Asia

South Asia consists of eight countries that constitute roughly 25 percent of the world's population, under 4 percent of its landmass, and approximately 4 percent of its economy. The region includes India, the world's most populous democracy, which will soon overtake China as the world's most populous country. South Asia's overall population and its share of the global population are both predicted to rise for the next few decades. The region also includes three of the four countries with the world's largest Muslim populations: India, Pakistan, and Bangladesh. In fact, by 2050 India is projected to have the world's largest Muslim population, overtaking Indonesia. (It should be pointed out, though, that roughly 80 percent of Indians are Hindu.)

Most of South Asia's countries were once British colonies. They now live in the shadow of India and Indo-Pakistani tensions, which are pervasive. Regional ties are weak. The local regional organization, the South Asian Association for Regional Cooperation, has had negligible impact, failing to hold regular summits due to disputes between India and Pakistan. This is the world's least economically integrated region; trade between and among the region's states is small and represents only a fraction of their foreign trade.

If there is a thread that captures the essence of South Asia, it is one

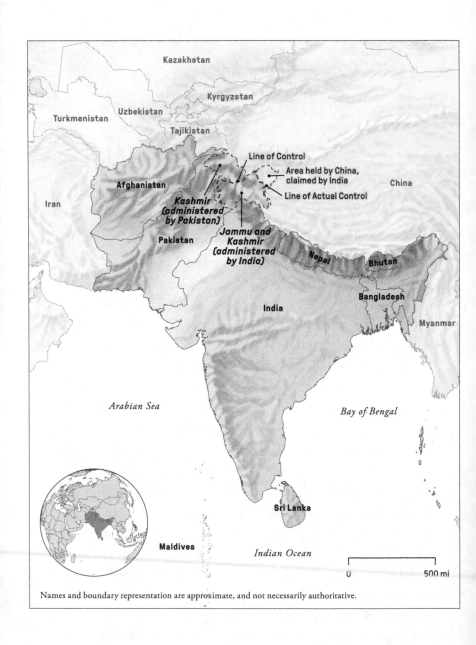

Names and boundary representation are approximate, and not necessarily authoritative.

of struggle. The modern history of the region began with conflict, and war has been a regular feature ever since. The region is far behind most of the rest of Asia economically. Alas, there is little reason to predict the future will be fundamentally different or better, because South Asia will have to contend with the reality or possibility of war, climate change, and larger populations that are likely to absorb gains in economic output.

Some lump in the five countries of Central Asia (Kazakhstan, Kyrgyzstan, Tajikistan, Turkmenistan, and Uzbekistan) with South Asia to form a region known as South and Central Asia, but these countries are best understood as distinct. Their modern history goes back to the Soviet Union, when they were component republics, gaining their independence in 1991, when the Soviet Union unraveled. There are important differences, in particular between the energy-rich nations (Kazakhstan, Turkmenistan) and the countries that are poorer, less stable, and less connected to the world (Kyrgyzstan and Tajikistan). What these countries (with the partial exception of Uzbekistan, which is introducing a number of economic and political reforms) have in common is authoritarian political systems, a large state role in their economies, considerable corruption, and close ties to Russia and China.

INDIA AND PAKISTAN

Any discussion of South Asia begins and ends with India. In addition to its rising population, India's economy is large and growing, in recent years at the robust rate of around 7 percent annually. India's economy is the world's seventh largest and will soon be in the top five, trailing only the United States, China, Japan, and Germany (overtaking France and the United Kingdom in the process). It was not always thus; Indian economic growth averaged only 3 to 5 percent annually (quite low for a

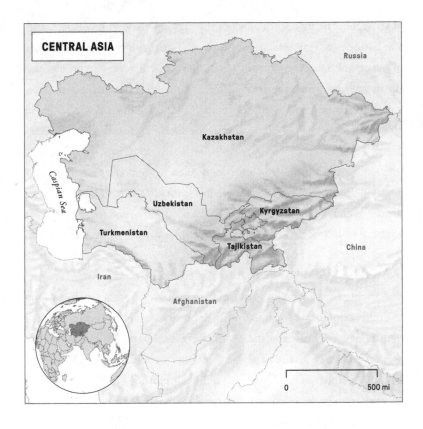

developing country) for its first four decades following independence. India's economy is only about one-fifth the size of China's, even though they have comparable populations and started from a similar base half a century ago. It was not until 1991 and the adoption of market-oriented reforms that India's economy began to accelerate, thirteen years after China adopted its own set of market-oriented reforms and began its economic ascent. But even with these reforms, India's economy continues to be held back by corruption, poor infrastructure, and complex political and legal bureaucracies. These realities have discouraged foreign investment. Also reducing the impact of economic improvement is the large and fast-growing population; gains in output are largely offset by increases in population. India's GDP per capita is only around $2,000, which does not even merit a ranking in the world's top hundred by that metric.

India has seen social as well as economic progress. Life expectancy has more than doubled since independence in 1947. Literacy has more than quadrupled over that same period. In the past fifteen years, India has made remarkable strides in lifting its people out of extreme poverty. But even so, poverty remains widespread, several hundred million Indians are illiterate, and inequality is stark. Billionaires live alongside slums. India has made a huge push to extend electricity into its remote villages, but roughly 200 million Indians still do not have regular access to electricity. Half the people on the planet who lack access to basic sanitation or toilets live in India. Caste, or the stratification of Hindus into tiered social groups according to birth, has reduced social and economic mobility and continues to weigh down India, especially in rural regions. In many ways, it is helpful to speak of "two India's," one relatively modern, urbanized, and middle class, another more traditional, rural, and poorer.

With the exception of a short period in the mid-1970s, India has maintained a robust democracy since it gained its independence. For much of its modern history, India was led by the secular, center-left Indian National Congress, or Congress Party, whose leaders were associated with resistance to British rule and governed the country in the decades following independence. In this century, however, it is the Bharatiya Janata Party, a party with a nationalist Hindu identity, that has emerged as a major political force at the national and state levels. Such an exchange of power is in principle welcome because it is essential for the institutionalization of democracy; in this, India resembles

Japan and Mexico, two other countries headed for decades by one party that have similarly evolved into more pluralistic polities.

Pakistan, whose name is an acronym derived from the country's component parts, has not fared as well as India either economically or politically. Its economy is barely more than one-tenth that of India's, and at just over $1,500 its GDP per capita places it near the bottom 25 percent of all countries. Politically, Pakistan has been and remains a democracy in name only. Real power is held by the army and the intelligence services. Elected politicians, other than those who are retired military officers, tend to exercise little authority.

Bangladesh is often overlooked but should not be. It is a more important country than Pakistan in terms of global trade. Bangladesh is second only to China when it comes to exports of ready-made garments; U.S. trade with Bangladesh is greater than its trade with Pakistan. It is deeply embedded within European companies' supply chains and with many American brands and retailers.

Bangladesh has also quietly delivered significant improvements in human development to its citizens. It is doing better than both Pakistan and India on many development measures. Bangladesh has solved its border dispute with India, has taken a strong stance against terrorism, and is the host for nearly a million Rohingya refugees fleeing Myanmar (Burma). Less positively, Bangladesh has suffered from dysfunctional and, at times, authoritarian leadership, but its democracy seems to be strengthening. Its high population density is also a problem, with the equivalent of half the population of the United States packed into an area smaller than Wisconsin. The country is also ground zero for a likely climate refugee crisis given that its densest areas of population are at sea level on the coast.

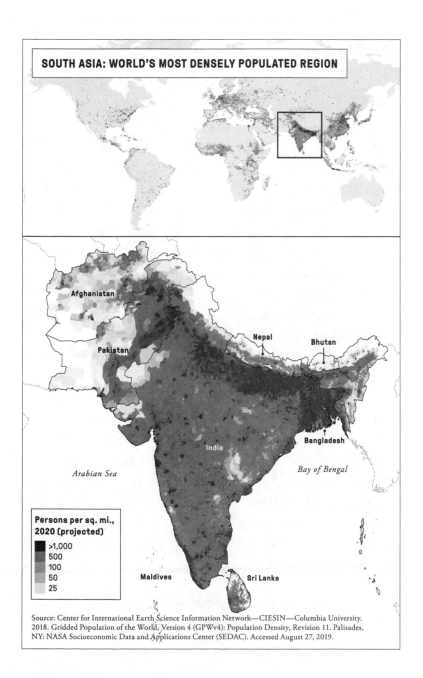

SOUTH ASIA: WORLD'S MOST DENSELY POPULATED REGION

Afghanistan

Pakistan

Nepal

Bhutan

India

Bangladesh

Arabian Sea

Bay of Bengal

Persons per sq. mi., 2020 (projected)
>1,000
500
100
50
25

Maldives

Sri Lanka

Source: Center for International Earth Science Information Network—CIESIN—Columbia University. 2018. Gridded Population of the World, Version 4 (GPWv4): Population Density, Revision 11. Palisades, NY: NASA Socioeconomic Data and Applications Center (SEDAC). Accessed August 27, 2019.

HISTORY

The modern history of the region has its roots in the British Empire. India, which included what we now call Pakistan and Bangladesh, was its jewel. But World War II left the British exhausted, and that, coupled with the rise of nationalism in India, a strong desire for self-rule, and an effective, nonviolent resistance movement led by Mahatma Gandhi, spelled the end of the colonial period. As was often the case elsewhere when the colonial period came to an end, violence ensued. Many of India's Muslims, led by Mohammed Ali Jinnah, sought independence not just from Great Britain but from India. Gandhi and the Indian National Congress saw India not as a Hindu country but as a democratic, secular society and initially resisted partition. But after much fighting and communal violence between Hindus and Muslims that cost as many as one million lives and created as many as twenty million refugees, Pakistan got its wish and became an independent country.

But the birth and separation of the two former colonies did not bring stability. Many Indians, viewing themselves as a secular and tolerant democracy, never accepted the need for a separate country based on religion; many Pakistanis never came to trust their larger neighbor. In addition, India and Pakistan disagreed over boundaries, in particular over Jammu and Kashmir, a Muslim-majority region (often referred to simply as Kashmir) on the Indo-Pakistani border. Pakistan faced additional challenges because it originally consisted of two separate parts—East Pakistan and West Pakistan—that were separated by India's territory.

As is the case with the Middle East and the Israel-Arab and Israel-Palestinian disputes, it is possible to speak of the region's modern history in a shorthand of wars—1947, 1965, 1971, and 1999—and periodic near wars. Kashmir was at the center of many of these, although the 1971 conflict was triggered by widespread repression in East Pakistan that in turn led to a massive influx of refugees into India. This demographic pressure in turn led to an Indian military intervention designed to end the flow of refugees and permanently separate western from eastern Pakistan, with the latter becoming the separate country of Bangladesh. The most recent crises have involved differences over Kashmir or Indian reactions to Pakistani support for acts of terrorism within India.

South Asia was also a venue of Cold War competition. The United States hoped that India would become a model of non-Communist development and an alternative to China. India was one of the largest recipients of U.S. foreign aid. India, however, was not interested in being a poster child for American development strategies, and embraced a position of nonalignment, spurning a formal alliance with both the West and the Soviet bloc, although it often was close to the Soviet Union in practice. India's leaning in the direction of the Soviet Union also reflected the large Indian government role in the country's development and its mistrust of Pakistan and America's close relationship with Pakistan. Ironically, the U.S. relationship with Pakistan, while at times too much for India, was rarely if ever enough for Pakistan, which viewed the United States with suspicion given U.S. unwillingness to stand by it unconditionally.

GEOPOLITICS

What has made the Indian-Pakistani pattern of conflict more significant than it already was is the fact that both developed nuclear weapons. India and Pakistan now represent two of the world's nine nuclear weapon states. India first tested a nuclear device in 1974, in part as a response to China's development of nuclear weapons. India and China fought a short war in 1962 that China won easily, and the two continue to view each other warily. The border between them remains in dispute, despite dozens of rounds of negotiations. But whatever the reason for India's nuclear program, Pakistan followed suit, both to deter any Indian threat and to compensate for its inability to match India's conventional forces.

The existence of nuclear weapons adds a whole new layer of concern to Indo-Pakistani friction in that one of the two (most likely Pakistan given its position of conventional military inferiority, its development of low-yield or tactical nuclear weapons, and its refusal to rule out being the first side to use nuclear weapons) might be tempted to actually use them. Pakistan is thought to have the world's fastest-growing nuclear arsenal. There have been several crises that led to wars, and the possibility exists for nuclear weapons to be introduced in a war growing out of historical resentments, the dispute over Kashmir (which intensified in 2019 following India's decision to revoke much of its autonomy), or Pakistan's harboring (and, at times, outright support) of terrorists who target India. There is also the fear that Pakistan could lose control over one or more of its nuclear weapons or nuclear material due to political instability and the divided loyalties of some of its soldiers, some of whom are suspected of sympathizing with radical Islamic groups and terrorists. Pakistan is also a proven proliferation risk, because the principal architect of its nuclear program, A. Q. Khan, sold information on nuclear weapons to North Korea, Libya, and Iran.

AFGHANISTAN

Afghanistan has had its own overlay of geopolitics. While not a British colony in the formal sense, it was a venue of British influence and, during the nineteenth century, an arena of competition between Great Britain and Russia. Several wars were fought between British (and Indian) soldiers and Afghan troops loyal to the ruling emir in the nineteenth century as Great Britain sought to shape local politics. Afghanistan declared its independence in 1919.

Two of the formative episodes in Afghanistan's modern era are the overthrow of its monarch in 1973 and the Soviet Union's military campaign in 1979, when it intervened on behalf of a left-wing, relatively secular government that had come to power in a coup d'état a year earlier. The Soviet decision to deploy troops against a radical Islamic guerrilla movement turned out to be an expensive one; Soviet military and financial sacrifices along with the unpopularity of the war effort back home contributed to the demise of the Communist government and the breakup of the Soviet Union in 1991.

The United States played its own role in the Soviet-Afghan War, one that also would prove to be an expensive policy over the long run, in this case for Americans. Together with Pakistan, the United States funneled arms and money to the Afghan resistance, the so-called mujahideen, which fought the Soviets. It was a textbook example of covert action, where the United States provided arms and intelligence in a manner designed to cloak its involvement and limit its direct role. Many of these "freedom fighters" supported by the United States came to embrace a radical vision of Islam. The defeat of the Soviets led not to their disbanding but rather to an effort to take over and remake Afghanistan in their radical image.

The last Soviet troops departed Afghanistan in February 1989. The Soviet-supported regime managed to hang on to power for several years but ultimately gave way to an alliance of Afghan tribes affiliated with the United States. These tribes proved unable to work together and in 1996, after some four years of civil war, were defeated by the Taliban, the word for "students" in Pashto (the dominant language of southern

Afghanistan). The Taliban were and are Sunni fundamentalists who adhere to an extreme orthodox version of Islam and believe that society should be organized according to a literal interpretation of Sharia, the Islamic legal code. Such views are incompatible with human rights, gender equality, or democracy. In addition, the Taliban provided safe haven to terrorists, putting them at odds with much of the world.

Years later, on September 11, 2001, terrorists affiliated with the terrorist group al-Qaeda (literally "the base," a network of Sunni fundamentalists animated by an antimodernist, anti-Western creed who received sanctuary in Afghanistan) hijacked four airplanes, flying two of them into both towers of the World Trade Center and a third into the Pentagon. The fourth plane was reportedly bound for the White House but crashed into a field in Pennsylvania after passengers resisted the hijackers. Three thousand innocent people lost their lives. I was working at the State Department at the time, as head of the Policy Planning Staff under Secretary of State Colin Powell. But I was also the U.S. envoy to the Northern Ireland peace process and as a result found myself in Dublin at the time of the attacks. With flights back to the United States temporarily halted, I continued with my mission, which seemed odd because it was Northern Ireland and not the United States that for so long was associated with terrorism. I took time out from my diplomatic efforts to write a lengthy message to the secretary of state, arguing among other things that the time had come to put Pakistan on notice that the United States would no longer tolerate it providing a sanctuary to the Taliban. This was done, but over time the United States shifted its focus, and Pakistan went back to its ways. What was lasting, though, was American vulnerability, the power of modern-day terrorists, and the radicalization of a significant number of young Arabs who embraced a view of Islam that made them enemies of much of the West and modernity itself.

The Taliban government that controlled Afghanistan provided a home to the terrorist group al-Qaeda that carried out the 9/11 attacks. The U.S. administration at the time, that of George W. Bush, demanded the Taliban hand over al-Qaeda members who were operating out of Afghanistan, and when it refused to do so, the United States joined forces with many of the same tribes that had run Afghanistan following the fall of the former king. This coalition succeeded in removing the Taliban from power in 2002. President Bush asked me to coordinate U.S. policy toward the future of Afghanistan from my perch at the State Department. We managed to help the Afghans form a new unity government, but it proved unable to govern the entire country or to end the fighting.

In the ensuing decade, civil war raged, because the government, supported by forces from the United States and other NATO countries, could not secure the country against Taliban fighters who continued to enjoy great support in the south of Afghanistan (where they had ethnic and tribal ties) and sanctuary in neighboring Pakistan, which opposed the establishment of a government in Kabul with close ties to the United States and India. In subsequent years, the civil war continued, with the Taliban gradually coming to control a larger percentage of this country of thirty-five million people, the poorest nation in this part of the world. It is too soon to know what if any impact peace talks might have on the country, even if there were to be an agreement.

LOOKING AHEAD

South Asia is also increasingly an important region in the context of China. The United States, Japan, Australia, and France are building stronger relationships with India partly to balance China. India is modernizing its military and has the world's fourth-largest military budget, strengthening itself so that it can project power into the Indian Ocean, where China is also deploying its forces. China, for its part, is growing closer to Pakistan and is making inroads by investing in Pakistan, Sri Lanka, and the Maldives as part of its Belt and Road Initiative that promotes infrastructure and development projects to increase Chinese influence abroad and support high levels of economic activity at home.

For all these reasons, South Asia has been and remains an uneasy and uncertain part of the world. The region's two most powerful countries are locked in a cold and sometimes hot conflict against the backdrop of their respective nuclear arsenals, a contested border, and Pakistani support for terrorism against India. India is a democracy with a relatively healthy economy but is held back more than anything by its large and still growing population, one that includes a vast number of poor people. Also casting a cloud over its future is India's increasingly discriminatory treatment of its large Muslim minority, something that poses questions for India's secular democracy and social cohesion. For its part, Pakistan has a large and growing population but also a weak civilian leadership under the sway of the military. The country's long-term stability cannot be assumed, and if it were to come undone it could easily trigger regional or even broader conflict.

Meanwhile, the struggle for Afghanistan's future continues. Bangladesh has its own unique struggles as it faces the realities of climate change because flooded coastal areas may turn millions into refugees. South Asia is likely to be a part of the world that continues to struggle to maintain peace and provide its large and still growing population with a decent standard of living.

The Middle East

The Middle East has been, is, and quite likely will remain the most tumultuous of the world's regions. Its history since World War II (when most of its countries gained their independence) is more often described in terms of various wars than anything else. Even a partial list would include the 1948 war between the Arab countries and the newly created state of Israel, the 1956 war in which Israel, the United Kingdom, and France joined forces against Egypt following its nationalization of the Suez Canal, the 1967 (Six-Day) and October 1973 wars between Israel and its Arab neighbors, the war between Israel and Lebanon that began in 1982, the Iran-Iraq War of the 1980s, the 1990–1991 Gulf War between an international coalition led by the United States against Iraq following its invasion and subsequent absorption of Kuwait, and the 2003 Iraq War initiated by the United States. Today there are numerous conflicts within and between countries, some of which have been raging for the better part of a decade at terrible human cost. There is as well the all-too-real potential for additional conflict.

Even the region's name is not universally agreed on; for some it remains the Near East (given its proximity to Europe as compared with

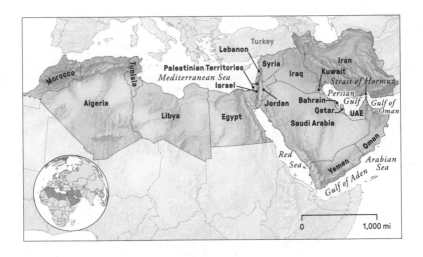

the Far East or Asia), and for others it is Southwest Asia, which again is not all that surprising if one looks at a map. In reality, the region is made of three geographic elements. There is Egypt and the four countries of North Africa (Algeria, Libya, Morocco, and Tunisia, sometimes referred to as the Maghreb), the four countries of the Levant (Israel, Jordan, Lebanon, and Syria, as well as the Palestinian territories), and the nine countries of the Persian Gulf or, if you prefer, the Arabian Peninsula or Arabian Gulf (Bahrain, Iran, Iraq, Kuwait, Oman, Qatar, Saudi Arabia, the United Arab Emirates, and Yemen). Some refer to it as the Greater Middle East to underscore the inclusion of all three subregions. It is, however, most often called the Middle East, which we shall call it here.

The total population of the region today is around 450 million, approximately one third the population of either China or India. The distribution of people is uneven; Egypt has a population on the order of 100 million, while Bahrain numbers under 2 million. Most are Arab, an ethnic designation for those people descended from the region's tribal peoples. Almost all are Muslim, although it should be noted that more than three-fourths of the 1.8 billion Muslims in the world are not Arab. The Middle East's Muslims are predominantly Sunnis, defined in terms of what they understand to be the rightful succession to the Prophet Muhammad and increasingly differentiated by separate traditions and identity from Shia Muslims, who are mostly in Iran, which is neither Arab nor Arabic-speaking. There are also Kurds, as well as many other Muslim minorities, including the Alawites who have ruled Syria for decades, and small communities of Christians. Israel is notably distinct, because it is predominantly Jewish and Hebrew-speaking.

The region's GDP is modest, at around $3.5 trillion approximately 4 percent of the world's total. Germany, with less than one-fifth of the people, has a larger economy than the entire Middle East. Manufacturing of goods desired beyond the region is negligible. Innovation outside Israel is rare or nonexistent. Many of the governments, especially those in the Persian Gulf, are overwhelmingly dependent on revenues from the sale of oil and gas. For the region as a whole, oil exports account for more than half of total merchandise exports. Governments dominate the economies. Corruption is widespread. Most of the farming, with Israel again the exception, is neither modern nor large scale.

The human statistics are little better. The vast majority of the region's young people has access to education until the age of sixteen, but the education they receive is poor and does little to prepare them to compete in the modern world. Not surprisingly, youth unemployment is far above the global average, as is participation by girls and women in the economy.

The overwhelming majority of the governments are to one degree or another autocratic. Several are ruled by hereditary monarchies. Most others are ruled by individuals with close ties to the military or the dominant political party. National identities and loyalty to country in many cases compete with other loyalties, be they to a tribe or a sect or a religion.

Just why so much of the region's modern history is characterized by a lack of democracy and a prevalence of violence within and between countries is a matter of more than a little conjecture and controversy. Some blame it on the legacy of colonial powers, who often drew borders that ignored local identities and did not do enough to develop what functioning democracies and markets require. This is true, but as an explanation for what accounts for the region's ills, it is wearing thin now that half a century or more has passed since the colonial powers departed the scene. Countries in Asia that were also colonies at the same time are thriving. It is also the case that the United States, fearing the instability that could ensue, has not made the promotion of democracy a priority of its foreign policy in the region. Others, however, attribute the region's trajectory more to its people and culture, particularly the absence of a line between the political and the religious in Islam, as well as Arab reactions to the challenges posed by modernity and globalization. But whatever the cause or causes, what cannot be disputed is that the Middle East has largely failed to produce conditions of freedom, stability, and prosperity.

So why does a region that accounts for only a small percentage of the world's people, land, and economy figure so prominently in the news? Why does the Middle East matter as much as it appears to? One reason is energy. Middle Eastern oil and gas literally fuel a good part of the global economy. The Middle East is home to just over half the world's proven oil reserves; Saudi Arabia has the second-largest oil reserves (after Venezuela), is second to the United States in oil production, and is the world's largest oil exporter. The region is also the source of just under half of the world's known natural gas reserves, with three countries (Saudi Arabia, Qatar, and Iran) that rank among the world's top four. Many of the most powerful members of the Organization of Petroleum Exporting Countries, or OPEC, the cartel that has so influenced world oil supply and prices for nearly sixty years, are to be found in the Middle East.

A second explanation of the region's importance is religion. Jerusalem is central to three of the world's faiths: Christianity, Islam, and Judaism. Billions of people of these faiths live all over the world and care passionately about what happens here. International relations is not just about statecraft and national interests; it is also about ideas and ideals and what motivates people, and religion surely qualifies.

A third set of reasons is decidedly negative. The Middle East is riven by violence. Terrorists are in abundance. In recent years, the region has accounted for almost half of all terrorist attacks worldwide. In 2014 alone, these attacks claimed the lives of more than twenty thousand people. Additionally, there are a number of large paramilitary organizations and militias that governments cannot control. There is as well the proliferation danger, in that Iran under certain scenarios might acquire a nuclear capability, which could trigger a conflict, cause other countries to follow suit and develop nuclear weapons of their own, or both.

Last but not least is Israel and the Israel-Palestinian conflict. Israel was created in 1948, the culmination of the Zionist movement that gained traction in the first half of the twentieth century and came to fruition in the aftermath of the Holocaust, which saw six million Jews murdered at the hands of Nazi Germany. Jews came to believe that the only way to ensure such a tragedy did not happen again would be to have a country of their own. Many governments in the world agreed, and a vote at the UN established the state of Israel. At the same time, most in the Arab world resent or reject Israel as a Western creation imposed on them and paid for by the Palestinians, who remain without a country of their own. It is a conflict that has been waged for seventy years and has captured the world's attention to a degree that at times seems to transcend the immediate stakes.

MIDDLE EAST & NORTH AFRICA AND GLOBAL ENERGY RESERVES

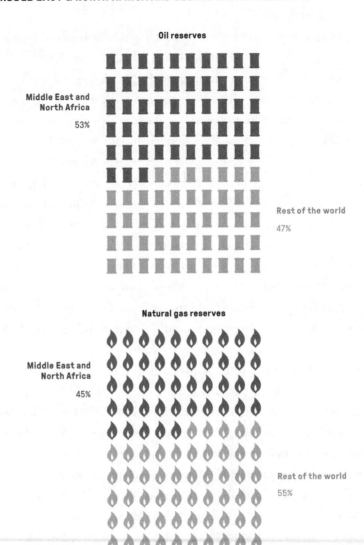

Oil reserves

Middle East and
North Africa

53%

Rest of the world

47%

Natural gas reserves

Middle East and
North Africa

45%

Rest of the world

55%

Note: Data as of 2017 or most recent available for each country.

Source: *CIA World Factbook.*

HISTORY

As is almost always the case, it is useful to review the history to better understand the present. The modern Middle East dates back to the late eighteenth century. There was the long, slow decline of the Ottoman Empire, with its base for much of its existence in present-day Istanbul and which over some five centuries stretched over a good deal of what today constitutes the Middle East, North Africa, southeast Europe, and parts of Asia. The second trend was the emergence of a more assertive Europe that sought colonies. These two trends intersected during World War I, which heralded the demise of the Ottoman Empire (replaced in part by the rise of the modern, secular Turkish republic with its capital in Ankara) and the division of a large part of the former Ottoman Empire into European colonies.

The transition from Ottoman to European colonial rule was embodied in the Sykes-Picot Agreement, reached secretly in 1916 while World War I was still being fought, in which a British and a French diplomat essentially divided what had been the Ottoman-controlled Middle East into British and French spheres of influence. This European era lasted barely four decades, ending with the exhaustion of the European powers following two world wars. Arab nationalism was on the rise and with it a desire for countries of their own.

The emergence of the Cold War and the Suez Crisis of 1956 were pivotal in ushering in a new era for the Middle East. Egypt's nationalist leader, Gamal Abdel Nasser, seized control of the Suez Canal, an economically and strategically vital waterway. In response, the United Kingdom, France, and Israel conspired politically and collaborated militarily to weaken Nasser, whom the Europeans saw as a threat to their interests in the region and Israel saw as a dangerous rallying point for the Arab world. The U.S. president, Dwight Eisenhower, however, saw the U.K.,

French, and Israeli seizure of the Canal as misguided, believing it could push the Arab world closer to the Soviet Union and turn international attention away from the Soviet Union's brutal use of force to crush dissent in Hungary. It was American economic and diplomatic pressure that forced the three countries to return control of the Canal to Egypt. It was a classic use of economic tools to advance political ends, sometimes referred to as geoeconomics. From this moment forward, the Europeans would play at most a supporting role in a region dominated by locals and their superpower backers.

The next few decades were punctuated by conflicts that shaped the region's trajectory in lasting ways. The 1967 war between Israel and its Arab neighbors (triggered by Egypt's blockading of the Straits of Tiran used by Israeli vessels going to and from the Red Sea but begun by Israeli air strikes on Egyptian military airfields) was one such conflict. After six days of fighting, Israel seized the Sinai Peninsula and the Gaza Strip (both controlled by Egypt), the Golan Heights (controlled by Syria), and the West Bank and East Jerusalem (then under Jordanian authority). More than any other conflict with the possible exception of the 1948 war between the Arab countries and Israel that followed Israel's creation, the 1967 war defined the parameters of Middle Eastern diplomacy for the next half a century, with the focus of the dispute shifting away from Israel's existence to its territorial reach.

Six years later, in October 1973, there was another war between Israel and its immediate neighbors, known by many as the Yom Kippur War, because it began on that holiday, the Jewish Day of Atonement. Initiated by Israel's Arab neighbors, the war was an attempt on their part to undo the post-1967 status quo or at least demonstrate to the superpowers that it was too dangerous to be allowed to persist. Israel prevailed, but only after some initial setbacks. The war was also an occasion for U.S. and Soviet involvement, both diplomatic and through the provision of military assistance to their respective friends and allies.

More positively, the conflict set the stage for diplomacy initiated by the Egyptian president, Anwar Sadat, who in 1977 broke precedent and visited Israel, addressing the Israeli parliament and calling for peace. Sadat's visit set in motion negotiations that ultimately brought about formal peace between Israel and Egypt as well as the return to Egypt of

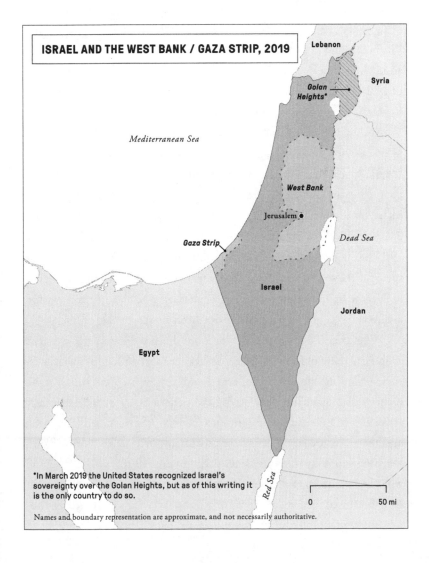

ISRAEL AND THE WEST BANK / GAZA STRIP, 2019

Lebanon

*Golan Heights**

Syria

Mediterranean Sea

West Bank

Jerusalem ●

Dead Sea

Gaza Strip

Israel

Jordan

Egypt

Red Sea

*In March 2019 the United States recognized Israel's sovereignty over the Golan Heights, but as of this writing it is the only country to do so.

0   50 mi

Names and boundary representation are approximate, and not necessarily authoritative.

land taken by Israel in the 1967 war. Subsequent talks established peace between Israel and Jordan along with a degree of stability (although not formal peace) between Israel and Syria.

What the 1973 war did not do, however, was alter the Palestinian predicament. The Palestinians remained stateless and divided, with some living on land Israel gained from Jordan in the 1967 war (variously called the West Bank, the occupied territories, or, by many Israelis, Judea and Samaria), others living in Gaza (which Egypt had administered before 1967), and still others who were forced out or voluntarily left during the 1948 war and decades later remained as refugees in neighboring countries, especially Lebanon and Jordan.

Multiple diplomatic efforts, mostly led by the United States, as well as one notable undertaking in Oslo in the early 1990s that was spearheaded by Israelis and Palestinians themselves, have failed to produce a comprehensive outcome acceptable to both Palestinians and Israelis. All such efforts have been premised on UN Security Council Resolution 242, which called for Israel to withdraw from territories it gained in the 1967 war, a just settlement of the Palestinian refugee problem, and respect for the sovereignty, territorial integrity, and political independence of every state in the area along with their right to live in peace within secure and recognized boundaries free from threats or acts of force.

What this and subsequent resolutions did not do was offer specifics as to how these objectives should be realized. So-called final status issues, including the borders of Israel and any future Palestinian state, security arrangements, the fate of Palestinian refugees living outside Israel as well as Israelis living in settlements in the occupied territories, and the status of Jerusalem, were left for negotiators to hammer out. Deep divisions emerged in Israel over how much to compromise and what to require in exchange. Prospects for diplomacy have receded as Israelis created settlements in significant parts of the occupied territories, making it more difficult to give them back—because hundreds of thousands of Israelis had come to live on them—and more difficult to create the territorial basis of a viable Palestinian state. The fact that Palestinians were and are divided not just geographically but politically has also made it difficult to reach any agreement because Palestinian leaders have shown themselves to be unwilling to accept American and Israeli proposals that offered the Palestinians much even if not all that many wanted. Violent resistance in the form of terrorism or broad-based intifadas (literally, "casting off" in Arabic, but essentially sustained protests that involved both civil disobedience and violence) have likewise failed to alter the fundamentals.

Some observers believe the time for a two-state solution has passed and that the Palestinians should have embraced previous Israeli offers that are no longer on the table. Others believe the prospects are poorer than they were for a two-state outcome but still exist. Still others are looking at additional alternatives, including a plan under which Jordan would gain control over certain Palestinian areas. Other ideas include separate Palestinian states in the West Bank and Gaza alongside Israel (a three-state approach) or a one-state solution in which Palestinians would become permanent residents or even citizens of Israel, an outcome that some fear would threaten either Israel's Jewish identity or its democracy. All alternatives have drawbacks; the most likely reality for the foreseeable future is a continuation of the occupation that now exists, or a version of it where Israel annexes certain territories where settlements are concentrated while Palestinians have a degree of self-rule in remaining parts of the West Bank and Gaza.

IRAN AND IRAQ

It is impossible to tell the story of the modern Middle East without noting the significance of Iran and Iraq. Unlike most of the other countries in the region, Iran is neither Arab nor of the Sunni branch of Islam. Instead, it is Persian and predominantly Shia, a branch of Islam that stemmed from a dispute over the proper succession to the Prophet Muhammad but over time came to reflect different practices and traditions.

For more than three decades following the end of World War II, Iran was a stable, relatively secular, and pro-Western, pro-American country, in part because many Iranians feared (with good reason) Soviet ambitions. Like most other countries in the region, it was led by an authoritarian figure, Shah Reza Pahlavi, who ruled for nearly forty years. The Shah, as he was commonly known, was supported by the U.S. and U.K. governments, which covertly came to his aid and helped to overthrow a nationalist prime minister who was voted into power in the early 1950s and moved to weaken the Shah's role and distance Iran from the West.

Iran's political stability and orientation proved to be temporary, however, and in 1979 a revolution overthrew the Shah. Ayatollah Ruhollah Khomeini, a senior religious figure, led this revolution and instituted a unique theocratic system that fused religious and political authority and insisted on building a society that conformed to a strict interpretation of the Koran. There are some democratic elements to the Iranian system such as parliamentary and presidential elections, but it is not a democracy given the outsized role of religious and military authorities in the political realm and their willingness to use force to crush dissent.

Iraq for its part is, at least on paper, the Arab country that has it all: oil, water, arable land, and a large and educated population. Emerging from decades of Ottoman and British rule, it should have evolved into a Middle Eastern "tiger," one resembling similar medium-sized countries in Asia that boomed economically and transitioned, at least in part, from authoritarianism to democracy.

Things did not work out that way. The leadership shares a good deal of the blame, above all Saddam Hussein, who for a quarter century (from 1979 until 2003) ruled violently on behalf of a Sunni minority to the detriment of the Shia majority, the large Kurdish population, and Iraq's neighbors. Iraq's political culture and traditions could also explain its plight, because even before Saddam Iraq was characterized by repressive governments and frequent conflicts between and among its many factions.

The histories of both Iran and Iraq are inextricably tied to each other and to another conflict that took place during the Cold War but had little to do with it. The Iran-Iraq War began in 1980 with an Iraqi invasion of Iran; even in retrospect, it is difficult to be sure of Iraq's motive, although it might well have been to reduce the appeal and reach of the new radical Islamic regime in Iran that had come to power just months before and was calling for revolution throughout the region. Saddam Hussein viewed such a call as inflammatory, fearing his own sizable Shia population might rise up against him and his fellow Sunnis. Whatever Iraq's motives, the war lasted for eight years, claimed nearly one million lives, and took a terrible toll on both countries, in part due to Iraq's use of chemical weapons. The war ended in stalemate but helped sow the seeds of Saddam Hussein's 1990 invasion of Kuwait because he felt the Arab countries never did enough to compensate Iraq for taking on Iran. The war also left many Iranians embittered over the lack of international outcry over Iraqi aggression and more supportive of their leadership that had defended the country.

The end of the Cold War brought about another era in the region, one dominated initially by the sole remaining superpower, the United States. The era opened with Saddam Hussein's invasion and occupation of Kuwait in August 1990. Led by President George H. W. Bush, the United States and almost the entire world resisted the Iraqi action so as to deny Iraq Kuwait's energy resources and avoid establishing the precedent that armed force could be used to change borders. After diplomacy backed by economic sanctions failed to persuade Saddam Hussein to withdraw his troops, a U.S.-led international coalition of several dozen countries and as many as 750,000 soldiers turned to military action and liberated Kuwait after just seven weeks of war. Saddam, however, managed to maintain power, setting the stage for additional showdowns in years to come.

There are many analyses as to what led the U.S. administration of George W. Bush to initiate the 2003 war with Iraq, including concern that Iraq had a secret nuclear weapons program and a belief that if it were to become democratic it would set an example the rest of the region would be compelled to follow. I was serving as a senior official in the State Department during the lead-up to the Iraq War, and argued against going to war with Iraq. I tried to make the case that the United States had better options to protect its core interests and that transforming Iraq into a democracy would be both extraordinarily difficult and costly.

Those advocating for war won out, and the result was a conflict that proved expensive by every measure. Hundreds of thousands of Iraqis lost their lives, and more than four thousand Americans perished in what I described in a previous book as a "war of choice that was ill-advised." Ousting a government was one thing; putting something better in its place that could endure is something altogether different and more difficult. In this instance, regime change proved possible but nation-building, defined as an effort to build functioning political, economic, security, and social institutions in another country, proved elusive. The high human and financial cost of the war, along with the simultaneous war in Afghanistan—where the results in no way justified the costs—soured many Americans not just on military intervention but on an active U.S. role in the world more generally. Ironically, Iran emerged as a major beneficiary of the war because its archrival Iraq was left too weak and divided to continue to counter it. Iraq, meanwhile, was consumed by civil strife among its Kurdish, Sunni, and Shia populations that emerged in the absence of a strong central government and due to a lack of consensus regarding how power in a post-Saddam Iraq ought to be shared.

THE ARAB SPRING

When citizens rose up in protest against their authoritarian leaders in much of the Arab world beginning in the final days of 2010, hopes were high in many quarters that the region would improve markedly. Dubbed the Arab Spring, what these protests had in common was popular frustration with governments that were often corrupt, autocratic, and unable to deliver a decent standard of living to most of their people. A good many commentators as well as activists in the region hoped this wave of popular protests that began in Tunisia and spread to Egypt, Libya, Syria, Bahrain, Yemen, and elsewhere would at long last usher in political reform to societies that had known little in the way of freedom or democratic participation. Many thought new technologies, in particular cell phones, the internet, and social media, would tip the balance of power away from authoritarian governments and toward individuals by facilitating communication and the flow of information.

Things did not work out that way. In Egypt and Libya, rulers were forced from office, but in Egypt authoritarianism was restored after a one-year interval in which the Muslim Brotherhood, a movement that sought to dramatically increase the role of religion in the political sphere and decrease individual freedom, was first voted into office and then removed by the military amid great popular unrest. Egypt faces a difficult future given a population that is increasing by more than one million per year, an economy that cannot support them, and a political system that relies as much on repression as on support for its survival. In Libya, the removal of the longtime ruler Muammar al-Qaddafi led to prolonged chaos and the effective division of the country into three regions. In both countries, no viable alternative to either repression or chaos emerged. Meanwhile, in non-Arab Iran, the government used force to quickly crush demonstrations.

Protests in Syria against the government of Bashar al-Assad turned violent, and the government cracked down against the opposition. Tens of thousands of radical Sunnis came from around the region and beyond to fight the government, which was and is dominated by an Alawite minority associated with the Shia branch of Islam. Full-fledged civil war ensued, with the government gradually prevailing owing to the support of Iran and Russia and the reluctance of the United States and others to intervene meaningfully on behalf of the opposition. Some 500,000 Syrians have lost their lives, and more than half the population has been forced from their homes. The costs of rebuilding the country are immense, but international help is unlikely to be forthcoming absent meaningful political compromise, which shows little sign of happening.

The United States did intervene militarily in Syria, not to overthrow the regime, but to attack the Islamic State (or ISIS), a terrorist organization that had moved into Syria in force. American policy is open to criticism, however, for what it failed to do. In 2012, President Barack Obama publicly warned Bashar al-Assad that using chemical weapons would cross an American "red line." A year later, it was clear Assad had used chemical weapons on his own people, but President Obama was unwilling to act militarily. This had implications not just for Syria, where Russia soon intervened militarily, all but guaranteeing the Assad regime's survival, but for the entire region and the world. Doubts had been raised among America's friends and allies about U.S. reliability and its willingness to act. These doubts would lead allies as well as adversaries to pay less heed to U.S. interests. If there is a date to choose to pinpoint the end of American primacy in the Middle East, 2013 is as good as any. The token military strikes used by Obama's successor, Donald Trump, in the wake of additional chemical weapons attacks by the Syrian government, did nothing to change this impression. The perception of a United States in retreat was then reinforced by the decisions of the Trump administration not to respond with military force to Iranian attacks on Saudi

Arabian oil facilities in September 2019 and to withdraw its support of Kurdish forces who had done so much to weaken ISIS in northern Syria. President Trump's subsequent decision to authorize the targeted killing of Qassim Suleimani, the leader of Iran's Islamic Revolutionary Guard Corps overseas forces, temporarily reversed this impression, but the scope of the U.S. commitment to the region remains in question.

One issue that has recently reasserted itself, in the wake of the U.S. invasion of Iraq in 2003 and the implosion of Syria more recently, is the fate of the Kurds. The Kurds, a group of mostly Sunni Muslims with roots in Persia (Iran) who have their own traditions and language, never received their hoped-for country in the aftermath of World War I. It was something of a diplomatic game of musical chairs, and when the music stopped, there were not enough chairs to go around and the Kurds were left standing. The Kurds, now numbering more than thirty million overall, find themselves mostly in Turkey, Iran, Iraq, and Syria. All four governments are determined to frustrate Kurdish independence because it would pose a threat to the cohesion of their countries.

One alternative to self-determination and a separate country is greater autonomy for a particular people living within one or more existing countries. Increased autonomy, including elements of self-rule, provisions for the use of the Kurdish language, and respect for Kurdish culture, could and should be achievable without redrawing existing borders. Even this, however, might be too much for some or all of the countries where Kurds live in large numbers to accept.

The monarchies, including Jordan, Kuwait, Morocco, Saudi Arabia, and the United Arab Emirates, have fared better than most other regimes in the region, in part because their leaders tend to be viewed as more legitimate by a majority of their people. The question is whether this will continue to be the case, especially in Saudi Arabia, which matters a great deal given its significant energy resources, responsibility for Islam's holiest sites, wealth, and relatively large population. Its leaders are now looking for a way to maintain stability at home while at the same time introducing a limited degree of needed political and social reform resented by the most conservative elements of the population. Saudi Arabia's leaders are also seeking to diversify the country's economy away from its near-complete dependence on oil and gas, manage a political transition to a new generation representing mostly one faction of the royal family, and wind down what many see as an ill-advised and unwinnable war in Yemen. The Saudi government has further complicated its task by repressing and in some cases killing its critics, a practice that has stained its reputation. It is highly unlikely the emerging generation of Saudi leadership can accomplish all that it seeks; the question is what will happen when it does not.

Iran, no longer balanced by a hostile and strong Iraq, has emerged as a regional power. It is an ambitious country that seeks to spread its influence throughout the region, using not just its own armed forces but also militias and paramilitary groups such as Hezbollah (a Shia-based militia and political party that dominates Lebanon) and support for local Shia populations, as it does in Yemen and Iraq. It has intervened directly and indirectly in Syria. In the process, it has turned itself into the largest regional concern for Saudi Arabia and the other Arab Sunni states, Israel, and the United States. How this competition—one that in many ways has superseded the Israeli-Arab dynamic that for decades dominated the Middle East—plays out will have an enormous impact on the future of the Middle East.

Regional organizations have made little contribution to stability or prosperity in this part of the world. The Arab League, founded in 1945 and now numbering twenty-two Arab countries, has largely ignored internal issues that have held back most of its members and focused instead on maintaining a confrontational, united front against Israel or, more recently, Iran. The Gulf Cooperation Council, essentially comprising the Sunni Arab countries of the Persian Gulf, has become little more than a Saudi-dominated front against Iran. There is no regional organization that includes Israel, Turkey, and Iran in addition to the Arab states—which is to say there is no regional organization in a position to tackle regional issues.

LOOKING AHEAD

One additional factor merits discussion. The Middle East includes one country with nuclear weapons, and that is Israel. Israel developed nuclear weapons in the 1960s, largely through its own efforts but also with French assistance, presumably as the ultimate instrument of self-defense given the hostility of many of its neighbors to its existence. The details of the Israeli program are uncertain, though, because it has purposely decided on a public policy of ambiguity to avoid sanctions and so as not to increase the desire of its neighbors to develop their own nuclear arsenals. At least twice Israel has attacked neighbors to prevent them from going down such a path, launching air strikes on facilities in Iraq in 1981 and Syria in 2007. Several years later, the United States and Israel are widely believed to have inserted malware into the Iranian nuclear program in an effort to slow its development.

The question is whether the Middle East can continue to avoid a dangerous nuclear competition. Iran came close to developing nuclear weapons but backed off in the face of economic sanctions and the risk of being attacked. What followed were negotiations among Iran, the United States, China, France, Russia, the United Kingdom, and Germany that culminated in 2015 in the Joint Comprehensive Plan of Action, or JCPOA. The agreement temporarily reduced Iran's ability to amass the fuel required to build a nuclear weapons arsenal; in exchange, Iran received considerable sanctions relief. Under President Trump, though, the United States in 2018 exited the agreement on the grounds that its terms (negotiated under the Obama administration) were not demanding enough given that important elements of the pact would expire in a decade or so and also because the agreement did not restrain either Iran's missile program or its malign regional activities. At the same time, new economic sanctions on Iran were introduced. In response, Iran decided to breach the limits on uranium enrichment specified under the JCPOA, use its proxy forces to disrupt shipping in the Strait of Hormuz, attack Saudi Arabia, and target U.S. personnel in Iraq. There are several questions: Will U.S. sanctions persuade Iran to agree to new constraints on its nuclear program and missile development in order to achieve much-needed sanctions relief? Or, will Iran seek to enrich enough uranium to put itself in a position to make a number of nuclear weapons with little warning? Will it achieve a nuclear capability that in turn leads others (particularly Saudi Arabia, but possibly Turkey and Egypt as well) to follow suit? Or, will the United States and Israel use military force to attempt to destroy critical elements of Iran's nuclear program before it becomes operational?

Whatever happens involving Iran, what is certain is that the Middle East lacks many of the prerequisites of stability. The map of the region conceals the reality that many of the borders are contested and several of the governments are not in control of what goes on within their borders. There is no balance of power and no shared sense of what the region should look like or how change should come about. Increasingly, the region is a venue of often violent competition among the most powerful local countries—Iran, Saudi Arabia, Turkey, Israel, and Egypt—that is further complicated by the regional interests of several of the major powers—mostly the United States, Russia, and to a lesser extent China—and the actions of a troubling range of non-state actors such as al-Qaeda, ISIS, Hezbollah, and various Kurdish militias. All of this suggests a future for the Middle East that is like its past, defined by violence within and across borders, little freedom or democracy, and standards of living that lag behind much of the rest of the world.

Africa

Africa is difficult to characterize because it is a continent of contra-dictions, of successes and failures, of economic progress and extreme poverty, of emerging democracies and old-fashioned tyr-annies, of countries that are stable and others racked by conflict. Its sheer size makes it even more challenging to encapsulate. It is made up of forty-nine countries occupying territory larger than the combined area of the United States, Western Europe, and India.

For the purposes of our discussion, Africa refers specifically to Africa south of the Sahara or sub-Saharan Africa. This is an ad-mittedly imprecise geographic designation used to distinguish the countries and peoples constituting the bulk of the continent from those of northern Africa that are normally treated as part of the Middle East given their use of Arabic, their religion (Islam), and their identity. The countries of northern Africa view themselves as part of the Arab world, even though they retain their membership in Africa's regional body (the African Union). Making matters even more confusing is that a number of other countries, including Sudan, Somalia, and Djibouti, are sometimes grouped on linguistic and religious grounds with the Maghreb countries of northern Africa.

HISTORY

Arbitrary groupings aside, the history of sub-Saharan Africa, or simply Africa as it will be called here, goes back centuries before the Europeans arrived and exploited its resources and people. The Europeans enslaved more than ten million Africans and transported them to the Western Hemisphere, beginning in the sixteenth century and lasting until slavery was outlawed in the nineteenth. There was a parallel, trans-Sahara slave trade in which Arabs enslaved millions more Africans and transported them to North Africa and the Middle East. That traffic lasted longer than the transatlantic trade, starting in the Middle Ages and continuing until the twentieth century.

Once the slave trade began, it was not long until Europeans established colonies in Africa. France, Portugal, and Great Britain, to be followed by Germany, Belgium, Italy, and Spain, all built outposts on the continent. By the early twentieth century, Europeans had laid claim to most of the continent.

The details of the division of the continent into colonies reflected European interests more than African realities. Colonial lines were drawn with little or no attention given to local tribal, religious, or clan-related identities or commercial patterns. Seeds were thus sown for instability both within and between the countries that emerged from colonialism.

The colonial era in Africa proved to be relatively short-lived, lasting less than a century. Following World War II and the advent of the Cold War, neither the United States nor the Soviet Union was much interested in African colonies; the United States in particular opposed any extension of the European colonial era lest it provide opportunities for the Soviet Union to make inroads by backing nationalist forces. In addition, the Europeans themselves mostly grew weary of African colonies, given the mounting cost of maintaining them at a time when their citizens questioned the benefits of such sacrifices. France, which tended to see its colonies less as colonies than as extensions of France itself, tried to stay the course in Algeria but in 1962 gave up after a ruinous eight-year war that cost upwards of fifteen thousand French lives and hundreds of thousands of Algerian lives and threatened political stability back home.

As was the case in the Middle East and South Asia, the rapid end of the colonial period after World War II was often occasioned by conflict. Wars dominated the postcolonial years of what had been the Belgian Congo, Nigeria, and a number of other newly independent countries. It is also true that few of the former colonies were prepared to meet the demands of self-rule. Ever since, for most African countries, their biggest challenge has been establishing good governance. Those that have succeeded are more the exception than the rule. More common have been autocratic and corrupt governments and countries characterized by a lack of stability and economic opportunity for the majority of their people.

One of the most compelling and important episodes in Africa's modern history is that of South Africa. The area was colonized successively by the Dutch and the British. There were at times extended armed conflicts between them and the African tribes who were living there when they arrived. The last of these wars, the Second Boer War fought between the British and the Boers, who were the descendants of Dutch settlers, ended in 1902. The British won the war, but it was a Pyrrhic victory in many ways, and over the course of the century the modern-day Boers, or Afrikaners, gradually gained the upper hand.

What we now call South Africa became a self-governing nation within the British Empire in 1910. Nearly four decades later, in 1948, the National Party was elected to power and formalized existing policies of racial discrimination, which became known as apartheid, or separateness. Under this system, citizens were classified as White, Coloured, or Black. A white minority ruled over a black majority that was disadvantaged by every economic, social, and political measure.

This cruel reality provoked two reactions. One was the rise of political and military movements dedicated to overthrowing the system. The best known is the African National Congress, later led by Nelson Mandela. The other was the eventual response of the international community that included economic and political sanctions to isolate and weaken the minority regime. In 1961, following a referendum, South Africa terminated its status as a dominion with the queen of England as ceremonial head of state and became a republic. That same year, South Africa withdrew from the Commonwealth of Nations because of its members' hostility to apartheid. Matters came to a head in the early 1990s with black riots and a declining economy, the latter in part a result of sanctions.

Change when it arrived did so quickly and, for the most part, peacefully. Historical precedents would have predicted a violent transition. It was avoided in this instance, however, due to the leadership of two remarkable individuals. One, Nelson Mandela, an anti-apartheid activist, had been a political prisoner for twenty-seven years, eighteen of which were spent on Robben Island, a rock quarry near Cape Town. Nevertheless, after his release his message was one of reconciliation, not revenge. The other was F. W. de Klerk, who turned out to be the last president of the Afrikaner-dominated system. It was de Klerk's understanding that change in the form of majority rule was inevitable. His concerns were when it would happen, how it would come about, and whether it would be violent or peaceful. Neither Mandela nor de Klerk acting alone could have succeeded. Decades ago I wrote about ripeness, and the bottom line is that diplomatic success requires leaders on both sides of a struggle who are willing and able to compromise. To have had such leaders was South Africa's good fortune. In the end, change came without prolonged or large-scale violence, and Mandela in 1994 became the first president of postapartheid South Africa. But as will be discussed below, that development, as significant as it was both for what it meant and for what it avoided, did not guarantee a successful future for the country.

GEOPOLITICS

There is relatively little in the way of geopolitical competition for influence—be it between local countries or outside powers—in contemporary Africa, especially when it is compared with the Middle East, South and East Asia, and Europe. If colonialism constituted the first phase of contemporary African history, and the era of decolonization and the Cold War the second, modern Africa is now in its third phase. There has been some European, American, and, increasingly, Chinese investment in infrastructure and minerals. And there is periodic terrorism. But again, the continent is more distinguished by a relative lack of geopolitics. Wars within countries are more common than between them, and when conflicts are instigated by external factors, it tends to be less for reasons of coercion or conquest than because of refugee flows or ethnically based violence.

ECONOMICS

As is the case with everything else in Africa, the economic reality is mixed. Africa's collective GDP has grown sharply over time but is still small, constituting only a few percent of the world total. In recent years, overall growth has averaged between 3 and 4 percent, lower than it needs to be for most Africans to enter the middle class given the low starting point and the fact that the region's population continues to grow rapidly. Still, the percentage of Africans living in what is judged to be poverty

GEOGRAPHIC DISTRIBUTION OF THOSE LIVING IN EXTREME POVERTY

Number of people living on less than $1.90 per day

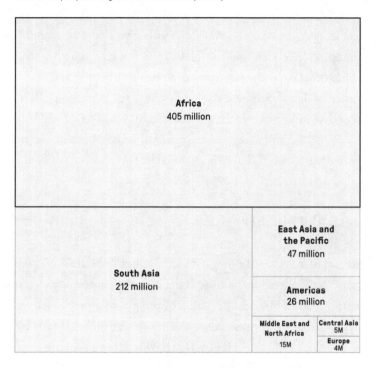

Africa
405 million

East Asia and
the Pacific
47 million

South Asia
212 million

Americas
26 million

Middle East and
North Africa
15M

Central Asia
5M

Europe
4M

Note: Data is for 2015 or the most recent year available for each country.

Source: World Bank.

has gone down, but the absolute number of Africans living in poverty has gone up. More than half of the world's poor live in sub-Saharan Africa, with 400 million people living on less than $2 per day. Half of the people in the world lacking regular access to electricity live in this region. Tax collection tends to be minimal; corruption tends to be extensive. Literacy has improved to the point where as many as 60 percent of Africans are literate, but the number of illiterate people has actually increased.

Intra-African trade is negligible. Imports from outside the region constitute a large share of what is consumed. Exports are largely primary commodities, such as oil and minerals. Infrastructure is inadequate; in sub-Saharan Africa, only Nigeria and South Africa rank among the top one hundred connected countries globally. Given visa requirements, it is often easier for Americans to travel around Africa than it is for Africans themselves. Manufacturing is also modest and is growing slowly. It is too soon to determine whether the African Continental Free Trade Area established in 2018 will make a meaningful difference, but there is reason to doubt that it will given the many obstacles to its implementation.

PEOPLE AND SOCIETY

There has been important progress in the realm of health. Over recent decades, life expectancy has increased across the continent and is now over sixty years, although this still lags the global average of seventy-two years. Infant and maternal mortality rates are down. Many infectious diseases, including HIV/AIDS and malaria, have largely been brought under control.

Africa still remains highly vulnerable, though, to infectious diseases, as evidenced by periodic outbreaks of Ebola. Less dramatic but arguably no less important, Africa is increasingly bearing the burden of noninfectious, noncommunicable diseases (NCDs) such as diabetes, heart disease, and cancer, often associated with a sedentary lifestyle, poor diet, and the use of tobacco products. Health-care systems are inadequate.

Africa's population, now more than one billion, is the world's fastest growing. It is also the youngest. The region's population has quadrupled in the last fifty years and is predicted to double again, to two billion, by mid-century. It is steadily becoming more urbanized. Also likely, though, is that this population increase will prove to be more of a burden than an asset because it is unlikely that there will be sufficient jobs for those entering the workforce. The real danger is that population increases will mean that many Africans will continue to lack many of the essentials of life even if a higher number of Africans come to have them. Adding to the troubling forecast for the people of Africa, this population increase will take place against the backdrop of technological innovation that in many instances will threaten existing jobs or create new ones that will require training that few will be able to acquire.

AFRICA'S POPULATION IS PROJECTED TO GROW FROM 1.1 BILLION TO 3.9 BILLION

Projected population, in billions

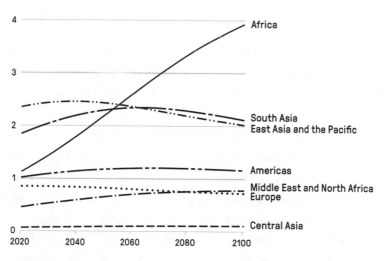

Source: United Nations Population Division.

POLITICS

There are meaningful examples of political progress in Africa, and these will likely continue. Democracy is gaining ground in many countries. More than half of all Africans live in countries that are free or partly free and can be accurately described as functioning (if not full-fledged) democracies. Increasingly, incumbents are being voted out of power; also increasing is the number of constitutions that impose term limits on heads of state. Still, it is premature to conclude that the tide of history is running in democracy's favor in Africa or that it can be concluded that democracy in any particular country is there to stay. Too many African countries have experienced internal conflict. The Rwandan civil war in the early 1990s claimed as many as 800,000 lives, many of whom perished in a genocide that targeted the country's Tutsi minority. More recently, there have been violent internal conflicts in Sudan, the Central African Republic, and the Democratic Republic of the Congo. There is no sign that such conflicts are becoming either less frequent or less intense.

The two most important countries in Africa are arguably South Africa and Nigeria. They represent more than one-fifth of Africa's population and more than 45 percent of its economic output. They are the continent's two anchors.

As noted above, 1994 marked the arrival of a postapartheid South Africa ruled by its black majority. As is often the case, one-party rule (in this instance, under the African National Congress) has proved disappointing. Inequality remains high; for many blacks, political change has not brought economic change. Corruption has been extensive. The world's largest population with HIV/AIDS lives in South Africa. The bottom line is that the promise of postapartheid South Africa has not been realized.

For its part, Nigeria was a British colony for a century before gaining its independence in 1960. The country's subsequent history can only be described as deeply troubled; its initial decades were marked by civil war, secessionist challenges, and military rule. Its politics seem to have stabilized, in that civilian leaders have sidelined the military from politics. But the challenges confronting the country are significant, in no small part because of its religious, tribal, geographic, and linguistic divisions and also because of the country's poor infrastructure. The burden of disease, above all HIV/AIDS, is great.

Nigeria's population of close to 200 million is the continent's largest. Its economy is also Africa's largest, although a good deal of its annual economic output reflects oil production rather than employment-intensive manufacturing, services, or agriculture. Corruption has been and remains extensive. Terrorism is a large and growing problem, as Boko Haram, a violent Islamist organization, seeks to overthrow the current democratic, secular system and replace it with strict Islamic (Sharia) law, something supported by a portion—but far from a plurality—of its Muslim population and opposed intensely by its sizable Christian population. An even bigger problem might be the lack of allegiance many Nigerians feel toward the government in Abuja and the federal state.

REGIONAL INSTITUTIONS

Regional institutions have played only a modest role in Africa. The most famous, the Organization of African Unity, was created in 1963 in the immediate aftermath of decolonization but accomplished little. It was succeeded four decades later by the African Union, or AU. On paper the AU appears to be an improvement, in that among other things it sets terms (for example, in the instance of genocide) under which its members can intervene in the affairs of another member. It is far from clear, however, whether in practice the AU will prove to be significantly better than its mostly ineffectual predecessor because it often lacks the necessary resources and capabilities to take on demanding missions, particularly peacekeeping.

LOOKING AHEAD

The bottom line is that Africa's future, like its recent past, is likely to be uneven. There will be countries characterized by good governance and broadly shared economic growth, and those plagued by illegitimate autocrats, corruption, and violence. The biggest common challenge will come from an expanding population that will place extraordinary pressures on economies to provide adequate schooling, health care, housing, and food along with jobs for millions of young people every year. How well this challenge is met will determine, as much as anything, the continent's trajectory in the twenty-first century.

The Americas

The Americas—more specifically, North, South, and Central America and the Caribbean—constitute the Western Hemisphere. The region includes thirty-eight countries (along with several territories mostly associated with the United Kingdom and France) in which just over one billion people live. It is home to Canada and the United States, which are the second- and third-largest countries in the world as measured by landmass. Both are slightly larger than China but each is roughly half the size of Russia, which spans eleven time zones and is by far the world's largest country.

The United States, with a GDP just over $20 trillion—accounting for one-fourth of global output—has the world's largest economy and is the dominant country in the Americas. It represents nearly a third of the region's population and approximately three-quarters of its economic output and possesses power and influence on a different scale from the other countries in the region. The United States enjoys many advantages, such as a rich variety of natural resources combined with soil and weather conducive to agriculture, a degree of protection provided by two oceans, and friendly neighbors to its north and south. Other U.S. advantages are man-made, including its political stability, its rule of law, its ability to adapt, its great universities, and a tradition

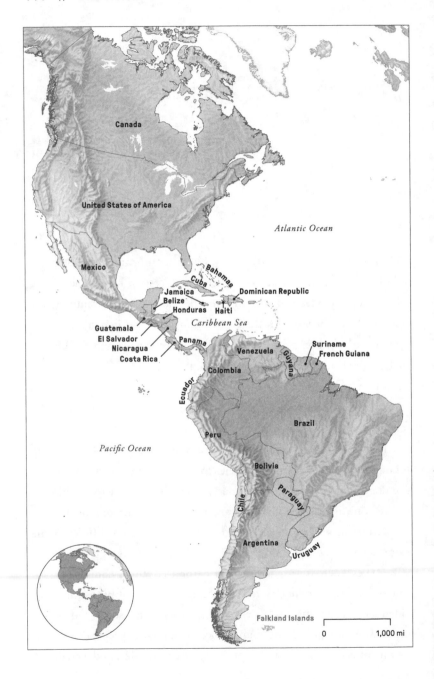

Canada

United States of America

Atlantic Ocean

Mexico

Bahamas

Cuba

Jamaica
Belize
Honduras

Guatemala
El Salvador
Nicaragua
Costa Rica

Dominican Republic

Haiti

Caribbean Sea

Panama

Venezuela

Guyana

Suriname
French Guiana

Colombia

Ecuador

Brazil

Peru

Pacific Ocean

Bolivia

Paraguay

Chile

Argentina

Uruguay

Falkland Islands

0   1,000 mi

(at times violated) of being open to immigrants, which has provided great talent and allowed the country to avoid demographic imbalances (too many elderly compared with those of working age) that would be difficult to sustain.

But the story of the Americas is much more than just the story of the United States. Brazil has more than 200 million people and Mexico more than 100 million, and both have significant, growing economies. The region is home to vast energy resources. Venezuela possesses the world's largest proven oil reserves; three of the top ten countries in terms of oil reserves (Venezuela, the United States, and Canada) are in the Americas. Even when the United States is removed from the picture, the region is deeply meaningful to the world economy given its size as an export market and its abundance of commodities.

The Americas is critical strategically to the United States, in that the region's relative stability and the overall positive relationship between the United States and other regional countries enhance its ability to be a great power. The United States has the rare luxury of being able to focus its attention and energies beyond its hemisphere. For instance, the United States is the region's only nuclear power, while China must contend with four nuclear powers on its borders. The United States also does not need to deploy the bulk of its military forces to deterring or dealing with threats in the Americas and can instead send its military to Europe, the Middle East, and Asia, if it so chooses.

One attribute worth highlighting about the region at the outset is its relative lack of geopolitics, or politically motivated interactions between countries. Territorial disputes are few, wars between countries rare, armies small. Prospects for nuclear proliferation appear remote. Unlike Europe or Asia, the Americas is, for the most part, not a region with a tradition of great-power rivalry and conflict, although there were such moments during the Cold War and China appears intent on developing its economic presence in the Americas now. Unlike the

Middle East, the Americas is not a source of terrorism that threatens the world.

But stability between countries is not the same as stability within them. A good many countries of the region are racked by violence, from gangs and criminal cartels to homicide and domestic abuse. Military and police forces are often unable to contend successfully with these domestic challenges. Legal and prison systems are likewise inadequate. Mexico, as well as many of the countries of Central America, suffer from the problem of state weakness, which in this part of the world is more of a challenge to security and stability than countries with disproportionate strength.

THE AMERICAS LEADS THE WORLD IN HOMICIDES

Homicide rate per 100,000, 2017

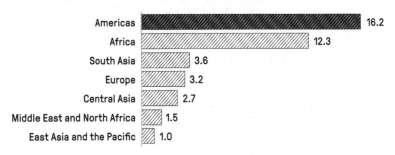

Note: A homicide is defined as an "unlawful death inflicted upon a person with the intent to cause death or serious injury." War-related deaths are not included.

Source: United Nations Office on Drugs and Crime.

There has been a recurring tension in the Americas between democratic and authoritarian systems. Right now the balance favors democracy, because countries such as Chile, Brazil, and Argentina have all successfully put into place some of the features of strong democracies, including an independent judiciary, a free press, and fair elections. But this was not always the case and cannot be assumed going forward.

Indeed, until the late twentieth century, the balance was overwhelmingly in favor of top-heavy, authoritarian governments, whether civilian or military led. Mexico was characterized by one-party rule for decades. And even now, democracies face a daunting array of challenges, including corruption, drug- and gang-related violence, high inequality, poor education, inadequate checks and balances against ruling parties, and in many instances prolonged low economic growth and public expectations for government support that cannot be met or sustained. Backsliding into populist (where personal power and considerations take precedence over rules and institutions) or illiberal (near-authoritarian) governments is a real danger.

HISTORY

To understand the Americas, it helps to go back to the fifteenth and early sixteenth centuries, known as the age of exploration. Spain and Portugal divided much of the New World between themselves. But if this colonial period began earlier than was the case in much of the Middle East and Africa, it also ended earlier, because both Spain and Portugal were too weak and distracted to maintain colonies owing to the Napoleonic Wars that ravaged Europe in the early nineteenth century. The result was that many of the countries that make up the Americas today trace their modern origins to this period some two hundred years ago.

The United States gradually became more involved in the region around this time, mostly in an effort to limit European involvement in ways that might threaten U.S. interests. The principal expression of this U.S. approach was the Monroe Doctrine, articulated by President James Monroe in 1823, which made clear American opposition to any new effort by Europeans (no longer constrained by having to deal with

Napoleon) to colonize the Americas. In 1898, as one part of its own experiment with colonialism, the United States fought a war with Spain, a short conflict that ended with Cuba gaining its independence from Spain and the United States taking control of Puerto Rico as well as the Philippines and Guam. A few years later, President Theodore Roosevelt initiated the construction of the Panama Canal. Completed in 1914, the Canal dramatically reduced the time and cost for shipping goods crossing the Atlantic and Pacific oceans.

President Theodore Roosevelt's impact on the Americas and U.S. foreign policy went beyond the Canal. In 1904, he effectively amended the Monroe Doctrine with what became known as the Roosevelt Corollary, which stated a U.S. right to intervene in the Americas if it deemed it necessary. President Franklin Delano Roosevelt, Theodore Roosevelt's cousin, walked back this "right" thirty years later, although the United States intervened in the region both before and after these declarations.

The region was an important venue of the Cold War and the host to several of the period's signature crises. Fidel Castro led a Communist guerrilla movement that succeeded in 1959 in overthrowing a corrupt, authoritarian government in Cuba. Castro then proceeded to install an anti-democratic, Communist government with close ties to the Soviet Union. A covert U.S. effort, led by the CIA, to overthrow Castro's pro-Soviet and anti-American government two years later failed dismally. A modest invading force of Cuban exiles was trapped at the Bay of Pigs, and a hoped-for public uprising in support of the "liberators" never materialized. President John F. Kennedy, who had just taken office, held back promised U.S. military assistance that even if authorized would not have altered the fate of the misconceived and poorly executed undertaking.

A year later, in the fall of 1962, U.S. intelligence (in this case, using aerial reconnaissance) discovered preparations by the Soviet Union to place ballistic missiles capable of carrying nuclear warheads in Cuba. Less clear to intelligence analysts was what motivated the Soviets. It could have been a bargaining chip: the Soviets might have hoped that they could make an agreement not to place nuclear warheads in Cuba in exchange for the Americans giving up their commitment to West Berlin, their missiles in Turkey, or any new plan to invade Cuba. The Soviet move might also have been an attempt to shift the nuclear balance or a bid to get the best of President Kennedy, who was still relatively new and untested and was widely judged to have mishandled the Bay of Pigs fiasco.

But whatever the motive or motives, the Soviets miscalculated. Although the United States was already in range of and vulnerable to Soviet missiles based in the Soviet Union, President Kennedy and his advisers judged that having Soviet missiles so close to American territory posed an unacceptable political and military challenge, in part because of the reduced warning time that would be associated with any missile attack and in part because U.S. acceptance of the Soviet deployment might have been seen as a sign of weakness.

The United States held off any armed attack, fearing it could escalate into a nuclear exchange in which both societies would be decimated. Instead, the United States put into place a selective naval quarantine (effectively a blockade) that was intended to prevent any Soviet missiles from reaching Cuba. In the end, the Soviets backed down rather than risk a direct confrontation. In return, the United States pledged publicly not to invade Cuba and privately promised that it would remove medium-range nuclear missiles of its own that were based in Turkey and that could reach the Soviet Union. More than half a century later, decades after the Cold War came to an end, Cuba remains a nondemocratic, Communist country with an active foreign policy that often places it at odds with the United States and many of its neighbors.

Central America also became a major venue of Cold War competition in the late 1970s and early 1980s, one that absorbed a good deal of my energies when I worked in the State Department at the time. It was a typical proxy struggle, with the Soviet Union backing leftist guerrilla movements and governments, and the United States doing what it could to strengthen anti-Communist (although not necessarily democratic) governments or backing groups that sought to weaken Communist governments. El Salvador, Nicaragua, and Honduras were the principal battlegrounds. By the mid-1980s, peace had largely come to a region dominated by non-Communist governments.

One additional episode worth highlighting, one that turned into a full-fledged conflict that lasted several months, involved a group of small islands off the coast of Argentina. To Great Britain, which had controlled them for well over one hundred years, the islands were known as the Falklands; for Argentina, which claimed them as its own, they were the Malvinas. In 1982, Argentina's military-led government, most likely in a bid to rally public opinion, invaded and quickly occupied the defenseless islands. The British prime minister, Margaret Thatcher, however, judged this unacceptable and mounted a military expedition that quickly reasserted British control. This conflict contributed to the fall of the military government in Argentina, which made the outcome of the Falklands War a gain for both the rule of law and democracy.

CONTEMPORARY ISSUES

The relative lack of geopolitical jockeying for advantage between regional states or the major powers does not mean the Americas is without its share of challenges. Already discussed is the widespread lack of state capacity and the fragility of democracy. Venezuela is the most acute problem, a failing country and a near dictatorship. Oil production is down significantly. Food supplies are inadequate, as is the health-care system. Hyperinflation rages. Tens of thousands of people are leaving every month, in the process emptying the country of significant human talent and placing a great strain on its neighbors, especially Colombia. And even if political change comes to the country and a legitimate government replaces the current one, the task of rebuilding the country will be immense, requiring massive resources and decades of effort by Venezuelans and outsiders.

Brazil is dealing with endemic corruption (although its courts thus far appear, for the most part, to be stepping up to the challenge) and a large public sector and benefits for citizens that the economy cannot sustain. Argentina has struggled to find leaders who could simultaneously be democratic, effective, and popular. Mexico faces an epidemic of drug- and organized-crime-related violence, as do the countries of the Northern Triangle (Guatemala, Honduras, and El Salvador). Murder rates in these countries are among the world's highest. Such violence undermines the local economy and causes people to flee, thereby increasing immigration pressures on the United States and other neighbors. These pressures cannot be dealt with effectively at the U.S. border; instead, what is needed is a policy that "goes to the source" and creates local conditions in which people are less motivated to leave for reasons of physical and economic security.

Canada is also part of the Americas, although like the United States much of its focus lies elsewhere. Canada boasts the world's eleventh-largest economy and is in the top fifteen when it comes to GDP per capita. It is a robust democracy of nearly forty million people. Along with China and Mexico, it is one of the three largest trading partners of the United States; it is also a member of NATO, the Group of Seven (G7), and the Group of Twenty (G20). It is thus a frequent partner of the United States in the world and in dealing with threats to North America. Again, having such a friend as a neighbor is one reason the United States has been able to focus its energies elsewhere, an advantage unknown to most great powers throughout history.

Regional institutions have a mixed record. The Organization of American States lacks the ability to get much done given its requirement for consensus and the lack of military and economic resources at its disposal. The Lima Group, formed by a dozen countries in the region to promote a peaceful outcome in Venezuela, has yet to demonstrate it has much heft. More significant are the various trade groups, above all NAFTA, the U.S.-Mexico-Canada free trade pact that entered into force in 1994 and did so much to increase trade volume among the three countries and in particular spur Mexico's development and growth, in the process reducing the desire of many Mexicans to emigrate. Some argued

NAFTA SIGNIFICANTLY INCREASED TRADE WITHIN NORTH AMERICA

68% of Canadian exports go to the U.S. and Mexico

28% of U.S. exports go to Canada and Mexico

64% of Mexican exports go to the U.S. and Canada

Trade among the three countries rose from $352B in 1994 to $1.3T in 2018

$1.2T
$0.9T
$0.6T
$0.3T
$0

Global Financial Crisis

1994   2018

Exports as of 2018.

Source: International Monetary Fund.

that NAFTA disadvantaged American workers and led to job loss in the United States. This was true in certain specific circumstances but not overall. In any event, the Trump administration renegotiated NAFTA with Canada and Mexico, resulting in the United States-Mexico-Canada Agreement, which was passed by the U.S. Congress in January 2020 and subsequently signed into law. Rhetoric and politics aside, the new agreement resembled the old one in many ways.

More broadly, the challenges facing the region include the need by governments to build the capacity to deal with internal security challenges, to improve the quality of public education so the workforce has the skills needed to compete globally, to promote civil society and thereby make their democracies more robust, to reduce public debt, corruption, and the role of the state in economies to a sustainable level, to do more to increase trade between countries of the region, and to see that geopolitics does not enter the region in a meaningful way. There is as well the question of whether Brazil will act responsibly in protecting the Amazon rainforest, the preservation of which is critical to global efforts to combat climate change. Finally, there is the enormous challenge posed by forced migration, where every day thousands of people are fleeing Venezuela and to a lesser extent the Northern Triangle countries, in the process all but overwhelming their neighbors. It is a demanding agenda.

Part III

$\circ\!\!-\!\!\!-\!\!\!-\!\!\circ$

THE
GLOBAL
ERA

Each era of history is defined by its principal forces, powers, and challenges and how people and governments fare in the face of these issues. Usually this puts great powers, be it their rivalry or rule, at the center of the narrative. This has been true for the preceding eras of history, and may yet be true of the current or next one, especially if either was to become defined by the growing competition between the United States and China. But it is by no means certain that the United States and China will find themselves in a new or second cold war. And even if they do, it is not certain that their relationship will come to define the era.

Another possibility is that globalization will define this era. Globalization is about the flows, often vast in scale and fast in speed, of just about anything you can think of, from people and emails to viruses and carbon dioxide, across the world and across borders. In some cases, governments are not aware of all that is entering and leaving their territory; in other cases, they are but they either choose not to regulate it or cannot do so even if they want to.

Borders have always been crossed. What is different about contemporary globalization is the scale and variety of the phenomenon and its importance and potential impact. Globalization has the potential to dramatically change human life as we know it.

It is important to underscore what globalization is not. It is not—with few exceptions—a policy preference. Globalization is a reality. It is both good and bad, benign and malign. In some realms, globalization is something countries will want to embrace or steer. In others, they can choose to resist or even opt out in whole or in part. In other realms, there is little or no choice.

The initial chapter in this section is devoted to globalization itself. Subsequent chapters are devoted to various manifestations of globalization, namely terrorism, nuclear proliferation, climate change, migration, cyberspace, health, international trade, monetary and currency issues, and development.

Each chapter describes the specifics of one particular form of globalization, looks at its causes and consequences, and discusses the options available to countries and the world as a whole for contending with it. Success or the lack thereof in dealing with any of these manifestations of globalization could matter as much as anything else when it comes to giving this era of history its character.

Globalization

lobalization—the emergence of an increasingly interconnected world marked by greater flows across borders of workers, tourists, ideas, emails, oil and gas, television and radio signals, data, prescription and illicit drugs, terrorists, migrants and refugees, weapons, viruses (computer and biological), carbon dioxide and other gases that contribute to climate change, manufactured goods, food, dollars and other currencies, tweets, and a good deal else—is one of the defining realities of modern existence.

To be clear, globalization is not entirely new. People and goods have always moved around the world, be it over the ancient Silk Road in Asia or on the high seas. But what is new is the scale, velocity, and range of what crosses borders today. There are more than 1.5 billion departures per year for international tourists, up from 600 million just twenty-five years ago. There are also between twenty-five and thirty million refugees. Foreign direct investment flows top $1 trillion a year. Trade in goods is valued at some $20 trillion: seven times what it was thirty years ago and nearly one hundred times what it was fifty years ago.

The flows are not just vast but often fast. Some things move at or near the speed of light, which allows someone in New York to video chat with someone in Japan, or someone in London to transfer money

THE SPEED OF COMMUNICATION

How globalization has changed how fast we can communicate

1 Month 3,546 miles	10 Hours 3,669 miles	0.2 Seconds 3,787 miles	Instantaneously All across the world
1776 News of the Declaration of Independence reaches London via mail.	**1858** President James Buchanan responds to Queen Victoria in the first transatlantic telegram exchange.	**1928** President Calvin Coolidge places the first telephone call to a European leader—King Alfonso XIII of Spain.	**2015** President Barack Obama praises Pope Francis in the first U.S. presidential tweet to a foreign leader.

Sources: *The London Gazette*; *The New York Times*; Smithsonian.com.

to an account in Hong Kong, almost instantaneously. Other flows, such as long-distance travel, may take hours or days. Either way, the speed combined with the scale is such that it is often impossible for governments to monitor, much less control, everyone and everything that crosses their borders.

What has led to this phenomenon? In no small part it is technology. The internet, jet planes, mobile phones, shipping containers, and satellites have all played a significant role. But so, too, have policies that have facilitated trade and access to markets. Such policies are the reason why an American company can manufacture its products in China or open stores of its own in China.

Geopolitics, the competition among countries for power and influence, also has played a role, but in contradictory ways. Stability and the absence of large-scale war on the scale of the world wars of the twentieth century have made it possible to trade, invest, and move around with considerable ease. On the other hand, local instability and problems have created pressures for individuals to move, something that accounts for the significant number of refugees.

Globalization is also reinforced by business decisions. The United States, for example, is home to less than 5 percent of the world's people. Trade is essential for American firms to gain access to the other 95 percent of the world's population. Other sorts of businesses, from illegal drugs to guns to human trafficking, have also sought markets outside their own borders. This, too, is globalization.

At the core of globalization is the notion of interconnectedness, which refers to webs and networks of ties of every sort. A similar concept is that of interdependence, the reality that every country and person is affected to some extent by what takes place everywhere else and by what others do. There is increasingly one global market for many manufactured and agricultural goods, for oil, for investment, and even for some services such as technical support for computers and cell phones. Such interconnectedness means that what happens in one place can affect conditions in another place. What begins at the local level can quickly become global. This is true of infectious disease (the 2014–2016 Ebola crisis), financial contagion (the effects of the U.S. financial crisis of 2008 and the resulting Great Recession that rippled around the globe), or a video that goes viral. Interdependence of any kind can be mutually beneficial, or it can bring vulnerability.

Some of the consequences of globalization are simultaneously good and bad. Trade is an example. The ability to export can provide jobs for the workers involved, and the ability to import can be a source of goods not made domestically or not otherwise available to domestic consumers at a lower price but of comparable (or even better) quality. But imports can also eliminate jobs, be it because of differences in the cost of labor or production or because of government subsidies and currency manipulation.

Similarly, there will be those who view the broad flow of information and ideas as a wonderful thing. But others will take offense at some of the content, and some governments can and do oppose the spread of information that they believe threatens domestic political stability and their continued rule.

Oceans, deserts, and walls cannot isolate a country from the consequences of globalization. But governments do have a range of options when it comes to how to respond to various dimensions of globalization. If governments are inclined to try to slow down globalization or reduce their country's involvement, they can choose to take a number of steps.

Governments can and often do erect tariffs—which cause price increases that must be paid by their own citizens on imported goods—and other barriers to make it more difficult for others to export to them. This is classic protectionism. They can also install provisions that make it more difficult for outsiders to invest in their country and to make it more difficult for those funds that do come in to exit. Walls can be built and guards stationed to keep people out. Coastlines can similarly be guarded by ships and airspace by planes and missiles. Those entering legally through airports can be limited in number or in how long they can stay. People can be screened for high fevers and denied entry on the possibility they are carrying an infectious disease. Packages and shipping containers and luggage and trucks can be searched, although in reality this can be done only a tiny percentage of the time lest business and tourism grind to a halt. Broadcast signals can be jammed; the internet can be closed off.

But to say that governments and peoples have options vis-à-vis globalization is not to suggest any country is able to opt out of globalization entirely. Climate change, for example, respects no borders. The same can be said of the spread of radiological material from a nuclear incident. An economic slowdown or financial crisis that begins in one country can quickly spread to another; the term "contagion" is used for good reason. Connection to the internet confers vulnerabilities as well as advantages. Ideas often have a way of entering even closed societies. Any visitor could carry disease. No economy possesses or produces everything it needs or can sell everything it makes at home.

Moreover, being closed to the outside is not without its costs. North Korea is by most measures one of the most closed countries in the world. It is also one of the poorest. Cutting off imports denies residents access to consumer goods and can generate retaliation in kind, making it more difficult to export, in the process sacrificing jobs and growth. Cutting off flows of people translates into an absence of tourism and little business or investment.

The result is that nearly all governments choose to both go along with and resist elements of globalization. Another way to say this is that governments try to promote what they judge to be positive and resist what they see as negative or threatening. Managing globalization is a challenge for every government, because they are often held accountable for the effects of globalization, be it immigration or climate change or disease outbreaks, even if they are not able to control them.

Another way governments contend with globalization is through collective rather than national responses. This is the essence of multilateralism. No country on its own can shield itself from all the downsides of globalization or harvest solely the positive aspects; what has emerged as a result is a set of global arrangements—legal, political, and commercial— for dealing with everything from health, trade, the internet, and climate change to trafficking in nuclear materials, persons, and drugs. There is no global *government*, but there is a degree of global *governance* to help deal with virtually every domain of globalization. The political reality, though, is that there is little consensus over how various manifestations of globalization should be seen and, as a result, little consensus over whether and how globalization should be governed or regulated.

Globalization is controversial. One reason has already been noted, which is job loss. Foreign competition (and imports) are often blamed for the disappearance of jobs. Sometimes this is the case, but more often than not the real cause is technological innovation that has made it possible to produce a given product or service more cheaply, of higher quality, or both. Still, globalization is often viewed with suspicion. One reason is that the benefits are widely spread but more incremental in nature, while the downsides can be highly concentrated and more deeply felt. Americans on the whole benefit from cheaper cars and can save money or get more value for their money by buying imported vehicles. For those Americans who lost their jobs when factories closed because of cheaper or better imports, however, their entire lives have been turned upside down. While economists agree that the country as a whole is better off, a small portion is worse off.

Globalization can also be seen as a threat to local identity and culture. It can be difficult for small businesses to compete with large global firms that enjoy economies of scale and famous brands. McDonald's and Starbucks stores span the globe. It can also be difficult for traditional lifestyles to resist the appeal of exciting new images and ideas from elsewhere that are presented via television and movies or are available on the internet. The competition is uneven, in that it is often easier for globalization to affect individuals and societies than it is for individuals and societies to affect globalization.

All of which brings us back to the notion that globalization is a powerful force in the modern world, one that generates benefits and challenges alike. The task for individual governments and for the world collectively is to promote those aspects of globalization that do the most good, to push back against those doing the most harm, and to assist those individuals and countries that are having the most difficulty.

Terrorism and Counterterrorism

Terrorism is best defined as the intentional use of violence by non-state actors against civilians in pursuit of political objectives. Several words are critical to this definition. To qualify as terrorism, an action must involve violence or the threat of violence in some form, be intentional, be taken in pursuit of a political objective, be carried out by a non-state actor, and target civilians. As such, terrorism is something very different from crime, which is normally motivated by objectives that are not political. It also differs from traditional warfare, which is conducted by sovereign states and for the most part by uniformed soldiers. Finally, when civilians are not targeted but become victims all the same, that is not an act of terrorism.

Some will ask why terrorism is only a tool of individuals and groups other than states. If a state carries out purposeful violent actions against the citizens of another country, we already have a name for it: war. Countries, however, can choose to support terrorists if they see them as a useful tool, in which case the government risks being judged a state sponsor of terrorism and attacked or sanctioned as a result. This was exactly what happened to Afghanistan's Taliban government following the attacks of September 11, 2001, when the United States and its allies

COUNTRIES MOST AFFECTED BY TERRORISM
Number of terrorist attacks, 2017

Iraq
2,466

Afghanistan
1,414

India
966

Pakistan
719

Philippines
692

Nepal
247

Libya
190

Turkey
181

Thailand
179

Democratic Republic of the Congo
143

Mali
141

United Kingdom
122

Colombia
117

Somalia
614

Syria
243

Cameroon
94

Palestinian Territories 83

United States 65

Myanmar
115

Yemen
226

Sudan
106

Nigeria
484

Egypt
224

Kenya
97

All others
972

Note: A terrorist attack is defined as "the threatened or actual use of illegal force and violence by a non-state actor to attain a political, economic, religious, or social goal through fear, coercion, or intimidation."

Source: National Consortium for the Study of Terrorism and Responses to Terrorism (START), University of Maryland (2019). The Global Terrorism Database retrieved from www.start.umd.edu/gtd August 22, 2019.

judged that the Taliban had provided safe haven to the al-Qaeda terrorists behind the attacks and had to be removed.

While the definition of terrorism above is the one most commonly used, no universally accepted definition exists. It is impossible to remove all subjectivity from the issue, because individuals and governments are often reluctant to label as terrorism actions done in pursuit of goals they support. The old adage was that one person's terrorist was another person's freedom fighter. In recent years, however, there seems to be greater, although far from total, agreement among governments that no cause or goal justifies terrorism.

Terrorism itself is not new. One can find examples that stretch back centuries or even millennia. A century ago, a terrorist assassinated Archduke Franz Ferdinand, heir to the Hapsburg throne, which set in motion a train of diplomatic and military events that led to World War I. Terrorism was a central means used to bring an end to colonialism, an era of European control of many territories and peoples around the world. In the 1960s and 1970s, the Provisional Irish Republican Army employed terrorism in an attempt to force British troops out of Northern Ireland and bring about Irish unity, and the Palestine Liberation Organization used terrorism to target Israel in an attempt to bring about the state of Palestine. The most recent wave of international terrorism is associated mostly with individuals and groups such as al-Qaeda, ISIS (sometimes called ISIL, the Islamic State, or Daesh), Boko Haram, Lashkar-e-Taiba, and others acting in the name of their vision of Islam.

Terrorists can be individuals or groups and can be directed by some authority or simply inspired by one. Countries can be involved in terrorism in two ways. The first is by choosing to provide resources, be they financial, intelligence, military, or territory, to a terrorist group. As already noted, such states (Iran for one) are commonly known as state sponsors of terrorism. Second, a state can allow a terrorist group to use its territory or gain access to some of its resources not out of choice but out of weakness. This was the case with ISIS in Iraq and Syria. Increasingly, terrorist groups have found ways of accessing needed resources directly, relying less on state supporters.

Terrorists' motives vary. Groups in Spain (the Basque separatist organization ETA comes to mind) have fought against the central government, seeking to establish an independent state for the population they claim to represent. Others (such as ISIS) have acted to bring down the existing authority and replace it with their own. An armed guerrilla group in Colombia that used the acronym FARC sought to bring about a different central government with very different policies. Still others (such as al-Qaeda) seem to be motivated mostly by a desire to cause suffering and damage. The evidence suggests that most modern terrorists are motivated much more by political agendas than by a desire to alleviate poverty or economic inequality.

Terrorists' methods also vary. The perpetrators of 9/11 used box cutters to immobilize flight crews and take control of aircraft that they either flew into occupied buildings or failed while trying. Other terrorists have used car and truck bombs and guns, driven trucks into crowds, or strapped explosives to their chests. An average of nearly twenty thousand people a year lost their lives to terrorism from 2005 to 2017, including more than twenty-six thousand in 2017 alone. Most terrorists are to be found in the Middle East, South Asia (especially Pakistan), and Africa (especially Nigeria).

There is concern that future terrorists will not limit themselves to such "conventional" methods and instead turn to what is described as grand terrorism. One possibility is a radiological or "dirty" bomb, which would combine conventional explosives with radioactive material, in the process leaving a defined area uninhabitable for years. Far worse in its effects would be detonating an actual nuclear weapon. Fabricating such a device is almost certainly beyond the capacity of any non-state group, but stealing, buying, or otherwise coming into possession of one is a possibility. Terrorists could also build and use chemical and biological weapons as well as use cyber weapons to disrupt or disable critical infrastructure such as dams, power plants, or water treatment facilities that people in the targeted society depend on.

Efforts to frustrate terrorists and terrorism are known as counterterrorism. Counterterrorism includes a range of actions that can diminish recruitment of new terrorists or reduce the commitment of existing terrorists. This can be done in many ways, including influencing what is said and taught in classrooms and religious institutions and expressed in social and traditional media. Governments individually or together can also make it more difficult for terrorists and terrorist organizations to acquire the necessary human, financial, and physical resources they require. Other elements of a comprehensive counterterrorism policy include deploying law enforcement and intelligence agencies to collect information on terrorist planning; applying economic sanctions and other pressures against governments to discourage or penalize support for terrorists; and offering negotiations that provide an alternative path for those terrorists who harbor limited aims.

There is one additional option: to attack terrorists directly. Such attacks can be carried out by law enforcement, military, or intelligence units. They can be preemptive, against terrorists about to launch some specific, imminent action, or they can be preventive, against known terrorists but absent information relating to a specific imminent action on their part. The aim can be to arrest individuals (which has the added advantage of obtaining information and intelligence) or to kill them, as U.S. Special Forces did when they entered Pakistan with the mission of killing Osama bin Laden. Countries can launch weapons from afar, using drones, cruise missiles, or fighter aircraft, or they can insert special operations forces on the ground. Efforts can be small scale and short duration or large scale and long term, much along the lines of what U.S. intelligence and military personnel did in collaboration with local partners against the Islamic State in Iraq and Syria. Cyber-related technologies can also be used to disrupt terrorist planning and operations.

Much can be done to reduce the potential effectiveness and impact of what terrorists do even if prevention fails. Governments can build their counterterrorism capacity so they can better contend with threats from terrorists, something the United States did in the aftermath of the September 11, 2001, attacks. Governments at all levels can also take steps to make a society less vulnerable to terrorist attacks. This falls under the rubric of defense and embraces law enforcement, the physical and cyber hardening of would-be targets, and the introduction of pro-cedures to make it more difficult for terrorists to succeed. Such steps could include screening and searches at airports, government buildings, and places of work. And beyond increasing protective measures, socie-ties can work to enhance their resilience in order to reduce the effects of successful terrorist attacks. Resilience can include training personnel who would respond to attacks in order to decrease casualties. It can also include stockpiling medical supplies and warehousing spare items that are costly and hard to produce quickly, such as critical electricity grid components, so that they can quickly be replaced following an attack.

Ending or eliminating terrorism is often articulated by governments as an objective but is impossible to do. It is not only that identifying and arresting or killing known terrorists can be difficult but also that pre-venting the emergence of new terrorists is impossible. There will always be individuals who are dissatisfied with the status quo and are prepared to employ violence on behalf of their goals. Particular terrorists and acts of terrorism can be stopped, but terrorism will on occasion succeed. It can also be difficult to deter terrorism given the zeal of many individu-als and groups, something that can lead them to sacrifice their lives for their cause. The challenge for governments and societies is to reduce the threat posed by terrorism to a level that is not unduly disruptive to a country's way of life, the safety of its citizens, and its economic well-being. Adding to the challenge is the reality that many counterterrorist actions come at a price, one that can reduce economic growth, efficiency, privacy, and freedom and, in some circumstances, breed more terrorism if what is done (for example, a military attack that kills innocents) persuades some individuals to support the terrorists.

Nuclear Proliferation

Proliferation can refer to just about anything, from cells to ideas, that is increasing in number. But when it comes to foreign policy and international relations, the term is most often used in the context of spreading military technology or systems. In particular, it refers to weapons of mass destruction, or WMD, which is a category that includes nuclear, chemical, and/or biological weapons and the means to deliver them, above all ballistic missiles. Nonproliferation refers to policies and tools used to halt the spread of these weapons.

In principle, countries can proliferate weapons of mass destruction in two ways. They can pursue vertical proliferation, which means adding to their inventory or improving their capabilities. This was the case during the Cold War, when the United States and the Soviet Union regularly modernized and increased their stockpiles of nuclear weapons. Vertical proliferation also applies now to the nine countries that currently possess nuclear weapons and missiles and to varying extents appear to be modernizing and/or increasing their arsenals.

Proliferation is mostly used, however, in the horizontal sense, meaning a country or some other actor adding a new class or category of weapons (such as nuclear or chemical weapons or ballistic missiles) to its arsenal. It is horizontal proliferation that most people have in

THE NUMBER OF NUCLEAR WEAPONS IN THE WORLD HAS DECLINED

Number of stockpiled warheads

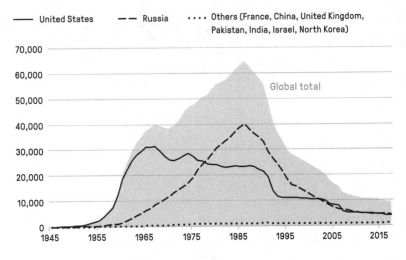

Sources: *Bulletin of the Atomic Scientists*; Federation of American Scientists.

mind when they speak of nuclear proliferation and when they speak of nonproliferation policy—the tools used to halt the spread of these weapons.

There is a view that nuclear proliferation is not to be feared and under certain circumstances could or even should be embraced. Behind this thinking is the belief that nuclear weapons helped keep the Cold War from going hot; expressed differently, the fear of a conflict escalating to a nuclear war that would be ruinous beyond belief introduced a degree of caution and restraint that would have otherwise been absent. What helped to keep the peace between the United States and the Soviet Union, it is sometimes argued, could help keep the peace between other rivals such as India and Pakistan, China and Japan, or Israel and Iran. Some prominent scholars have even taken this argument to its logical (if extreme) conclusion, asserting that if more countries had nuclear weapons it would be a more peaceful and stable world, because no nuclear country would attack another one and risk nuclear retaliation. This is a distinctly minority view for good reason. The emergence of additional countries with nuclear weapons is far more likely to be dangerous than stabilizing and could lead to conflict, including one where a weapon of mass destruction might be used with horrendous consequences. Creating conditions of deterrence such as existed during the Cold War so that there is no incentive to strike first is difficult because it requires robust arsenals that can survive an initial attack and still be able to deliver a devastating retaliatory response. Absent such qualities, a balance between two nuclear-armed entities would be precarious because there would be great incentive to attack first in a crisis. There would also be an incentive to strike to interrupt the emergence of a capability—something termed a preventive strike—or to attack the site of a weapon of mass destruction just before intelligence suggests it is to be used. This would constitute a preemptive strike. There is as well the danger that nuclear weapons could be used by accident or "fall into the wrong hands," especially those of terrorists, if custody or control over weapons and materials were to be somehow lost or compromised. Finally, some make the argument that certain regimes cannot be deterred, because they have an apocalyptic or messianic vision of the world and are willing to use nuclear weapons and "sacrifice" themselves in order to realize their vision.

It was concerns such as these that helped bring about the Treaty on the Non-Proliferation of Nuclear Weapons, commonly known as the Non-Proliferation Treaty, or NPT, an international agreement that went into effect in 1970. The NPT requires the five countries that possessed nuclear weapons at the time of its signing and that it recognizes as legitimate "Nuclear Weapons States" (the United States, the Soviet Union, China, Great Britain, and France) not to transfer nuclear weapons or assist, encourage, or induce any state without them to acquire them. (The Soviet Union's obligations passed to Russia in 1991.) It also sets forth the principle that these states will avoid a nuclear arms race and move toward ridding themselves of all their nuclear weapons. It asks those states without nuclear weapons not to produce or acquire them. It guarantees access to nuclear energy for peaceful purposes. And it asks the non-nuclear-weapon states to accept "safeguards," which are essentially inspections the International Atomic Energy Agency (IAEA) carries out to verify they are complying with the treaty.

The NPT is limited in what it can do, however. No country can be compelled to sign it; in fact, three countries with nuclear weapons— India, Israel, and Pakistan—have never joined the treaty. There is also no penalty for withdrawal, as was made clear when North Korea exited the treaty. Those without nuclear weapons often complain that those in possession of such weapons are not making sufficient progress toward disarmament even though U.S. and Russian nuclear stockpiles are but a fraction of what they were at the height of the Cold War. The NPT states that all signatories have the right to technology for generating peaceful nuclear energy, which comes close to contradicting its aim of preventing proliferation. Many of the materials that would be needed to develop nuclear weapons are also needed to generate nuclear power for peaceful purposes. Making things even more problematic is that the inspections regime that was established is cooperative, in that the IAEA gets to inspect only those facilities admitted to by the country in question. It is an honor code system in a world where people are not always honorable.

In addition to the NPT, there are any number of policies and tools employed to discourage proliferation. Some are positive, such as security guarantees. The United States, for example, covers its allies Japan and South Korea under its "nuclear umbrella," in part so that they do not see a need to develop their own nuclear weapons.

Most of the policies used to prevent or slow proliferation, however, have been negative in the sense that they are designed to make it difficult for governments to acquire many of the components that go into nuclear weapons. Various so-called supplier groups have been created to prohibit the export of certain technologies and systems or to interdict illegal shipments that are taking place. States have used cyberattacks to infect and thereby disrupt computers running the centrifuges carrying out uranium enrichment. There has also been work toward developing proliferation-resistant reactors that are meant to allow countries to attain nuclear energy without the ability to divert materials toward making nuclear weapons. Also related to nuclear energy are arrangements whereby a country with nuclear power ships out its spent nuclear fuel for reprocessing to ensure that it is not able to covertly enrich it to weapons-grade material.

Sanctions have also been threatened or introduced to discourage would-be suppliers from providing technology or materials and would-be recipients from accepting them. Arms control has also been a tool to slow or reverse vertical proliferation (for example, involving both the United States and the Soviet Union or Russia) or to prevent horizontal proliferation, most significantly in the case of Iran.

Iran's recent history is worth highlighting. The United States, China, France, Great Britain, Russia, and Germany applied pressure on Iran, mainly in the form of economic sanctions, to persuade it to accept limits on its nuclear activities. The limits were detailed in a 2015 agreement (formally known as the Joint Comprehensive Plan of Action or JCPOA) by which Iran accepted temporary constraints on its ability to produce and store the fuel needed for a nuclear bomb. In exchange, most of the sanctions that had been put into place against Iran were removed. Iran complied with the agreement, but the United States exited it in 2018 on the grounds that the limits on Iranian activity were of too short a duration and that the agreement did not address

Iran's ballistic missile program or what were seen as its malign activities throughout the Middle East. To be sure, Iran made an open-ended commitment not to produce or acquire nuclear weapons, but critical limits on activities associated with producing and storing enriched nuclear fuel were due to expire by 2025 or 2030, after which Iran could amass much of what it would require if it decided to make a sudden, secret dash to produce nuclear weapons and present the world with a fait accompli (known as breakout). It is still unclear if Iran will try to become a country with nuclear weapons and how other countries would respond to its efforts should it proceed. Diplomacy could in principle succeed in establishing new ceilings on Iranian capabilities, denying it a nuclear weapon for a prolonged period or even permanently, although it is far from certain such arrangements could actually be negotiated.

There are now nine countries in the world known to possess nuclear weapons: the original five countries permitted to do so under the NPT along with India, Israel, North Korea, and Pakistan. States pursue nuclear weapons for a number of reasons, including security and prestige. They are seen as the ultimate security guarantee, because no nuclear state has ever gone to war with another nuclear-armed state. Nuclear weapons also act as a sort of status symbol; it is no coincidence that the five permanent members of the UN Security Council all possess nuclear weapons. It is very difficult to stop a country that is determined to develop nuclear weapons from doing so, especially if it possesses the necessary scientific and industrial capacity and is prepared to pay a price in the form of economic sanctions and a degree of international isolation.

Once a state develops or otherwise acquires nuclear weapons, there are a number of options for dealing with it. One is to sanction the country to pressure it to give up its nuclear weapons. This is precisely what happened with South Africa, which in the face of sanctions gave up its nuclear weapons program in the late 1980s. Ukraine voluntarily

STOCKPILED NUCLEAR WARHEADS, 2019

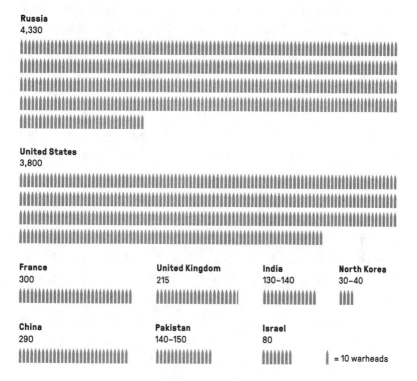

Russia
4,330

United States
3,800

France	United Kingdom	India	North Korea
300	215	130–140	30–40

China	Pakistan	Israel	
290	140–150	80	▌ = 10 warheads

Sources: Federation of American Scientists; Institute for Science and International Security.

relinquished the many nuclear weapons it inherited with the breakup of the Soviet Union. Libya and Iraq, which had nascent nuclear weapons programs, also gave up their nuclear ambitions in the face of sanctions and the threat of attack. As already noted, though, a number of governments so value nuclear weapons that sanctions are unlikely to persuade them to give these weapons up. In addition, sanctions can be hard to sustain, because there are almost always competing economic or strategic interests that argue against keeping them in place.

In the case of North Korea, sanctions, threats, and inducements are likely not enough to force it to give up its nuclear weapons. The United States, working closely with China, Japan, Russia, and South Korea, has sought to persuade North Korea's government to give up its nuclear weapons and related systems (denuclearize) through a mix of sanctions, threats of military attacks, and economic incentives. Many observers (including this one) are skeptical that North Korea would ever take such far-reaching steps given the prestige and security that nuclear weapons confer. The fact that Ukraine was invaded by Russia and lost Crimea to it despite promises enshrined in the 1994 Budapest Memorandum signed by Russia, Ukraine, the United Kingdom, and the United States that its security would be respected once it gave up the hundreds of nuclear weapons it had inherited from the Soviet Union obviously decreases the likelihood that North Korea would follow in Ukraine's footsteps. This reluctance is further reinforced by the fact that the governments in both Iraq and Libya were removed through foreign intervention in the wake of their having given up their nuclear weapons programs. What remains to be seen is whether diplomacy can limit the scale and quality of the North Korean nuclear and missile programs and, depending on what can be negotiated and verified, how others will choose to react either vis-à-vis North Korea or in terms of their own capabilities.

There is as well the option of trying to forestall the use of nuclear weapons if efforts to prevent or dissuade a country from developing them ultimately fail. This would entail trying to establish deterrence, making it clear that any use of nuclear weapons would be met with a devastating response. The problem is that deterrence cannot be guaranteed to work if an individual or government is prepared to act in ways most would view as irrational. There are as well the dangers of misperception, miscalculation, and miscommunication. Nuclear weapons can give a government confidence that it can act with impunity. And as noted earlier, there is the danger that a government in possession of nuclear weapons could decide to transfer them to another country or terrorist group or simply lose physical control of its weapons to such a group.

Defense, which entails deploying systems that make it difficult for aircraft or missiles carrying nuclear warheads to reach their targets, is another option for countering proliferation. Still, there is the probability—given the technical difficulty in developing systems that are effective against missiles—that one or more warheads might still reach their target, causing great destruction and loss of life. There is no such thing as invulnerability. There is also the risk that improved defense will cause other countries to upgrade their nuclear arsenals so that their leaders can be assured that they can pierce the opposing defenses, which may trigger an arms race.

There are options that would use conventional (non-nuclear) military force or other means, including cyberattacks, to interfere with or destroy nuclear-related facilities and materials, weapons, and/or their delivery systems before they could be used. A preventive strike would seek to destroy them while such capabilities were being developed or stored. Israel, for example, carried out preventive strikes against nuclear-related facilities in Iraq in 1981 and Syria in 2007. A preemptive strike, by contrast, would seek to destroy nuclear-capable systems while they were being readied for actual use. Either of these actions involves costs and risks, including the chance that the attack will not destroy the system in question and then surviving systems would be used or that the preventive or preemptive attack could trigger retaliation and escalate a situation into a broader conflict.

Discouraging or frustrating the spread of nuclear weapons can be difficult or even impossible. But it is also important not to lose sight of the fact that more than seventy years after the United States introduced nuclear weapons for the first time in the final days of World War II against Japan—and close to sixty years since a young candidate for president named John F. Kennedy predicted that as many as twenty countries could achieve a nuclear weapons capability by the end of 1964—there are only nine countries known to have nuclear weapons. And since the attacks on Hiroshima and Nagasaki, nuclear weapons have not been used. Several countries (including Ukraine and South Africa) voluntarily gave them up, while many others with the capacity to build them have opted not to (for instance, Japan, South Korea, and Taiwan). The challenge remains to ensure that those with nuclear weapons limit or reduce their stockpiles and those that do not possess nuclear weapons do not come to possess them. It is a challenge that shows no signs of abating.

Climate Change

Global climate change—sometimes called global warming—is the observable shift in climate patterns around the world due to a warming of the atmosphere's temperature. This is principally caused by human activity—mostly the burning of fossil fuels, primarily coal, oil, and natural gas—that releases carbon dioxide and other so-called greenhouse gases in high concentrations into the atmosphere where they trap the sun's rays and cause an increase in temperature.

Climate change is thus very different from pollution. Pollution tends to be mostly (although not exclusively) local in its causes and effects. It has an impact on air or water quality, health, marine life, and structures such as bridges that can face accelerated rusting and weakening. Climate change by contrast is global; the effects are felt everywhere even if there is no local contribution. Borders count for naught.

Climate change is also something fundamentally different from weather. Weather is the day-to-day temperature, precipitation, wind, and the like. On any given day, the weather can be cold or hot, wet or dry. Climate reflects underlying trends and shifts in temperature, precipitation, wind, and more, and although there will be days that do not fit the overall trend, over time the weather will largely reflect the evolution of the climate.

Evidence of climate change includes measures of average air temperature that show a distinct increase, an increase in the average temperature of the world's oceans, clear signs that polar ice is melting away, and rising sea levels. While there are natural phenomena, such as volcanoes, that add carbon dioxide to the earth's atmosphere, scientists are able to measure the source of the unusually high levels of carbon dioxide that have accumulated in the atmosphere since the Industrial Revolution. Careful analysis of atmospheric carbon dioxide allows scientists to conclude that human activity is the source for today's buildup of carbon dioxide in the atmosphere. Data also show a marked increase in the concentrations of certain gases, such as carbon dioxide and methane. For instance, the second decade of this century was the hottest ever recorded. 2019 was the second-warmest year ever, trailing only 2016. The years 2015 to 2019 were the five hottest years ever. In addition, the rate at which the world's sea level is rising has been accelerating.

As a result of climate change, we are seeing higher sea levels in coastal areas, more severe storms, higher average temperatures everywhere, and expanding desertification. This process is reducing the amount of land that can support human life. The effects of climate change will only increase over time given the lag between energy use and the effects of carbon already released as well as the reality that vast amounts of carbon dioxide and other gases causing climate change continue to be released.

Rising sea levels and flooding put low-lying coastal areas and entire island countries at risk. Climate change (in its effects on temperature as well as the spread of salt water) also poses potentially irreversible threats to various forms of animal, marine, plant, and insect life. As a result, it will affect crop yields, disease prevalence, and much else.

It is a question of when—not if—large and growing areas of countries become uninhabitable owing to prolonged freshwater shortages,

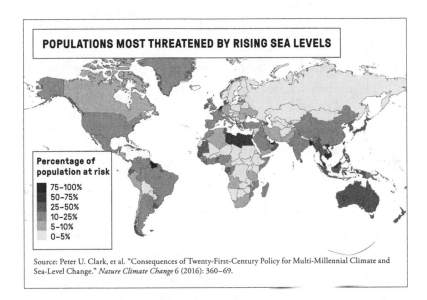

POPULATIONS MOST THREATENED BY RISING SEA LEVELS

Percentage of
population at risk

75–100%
50–75%
25–50%
10–25%
5–10%
0–5%

Source: Peter U. Clark, et al. "Consequences of Twenty-First-Century Policy for Multi-Millennial Climate and
Sea-Level Change." *Nature Climate Change* 6 (2016): 360–69.

extreme heat, widespread flooding, and frequent, costly storms. Bangladesh may well be the first country with a substantial population to face this problem on a large scale. The amount of land able to support human existence is shrinking and will continue to shrink, while the world's population will continue to grow, which may lead to food and water shortages and even political instability. One statistic sure to increase is the number of people forced to move within their countries (becoming internally displaced) when coastal areas become uninhabitable owing to higher sea levels; the number of refugees will also rise when their home countries can no longer support them. Climate change is not just a major humanitarian, economic, and health problem but a national security issue as well.

Climate change has come about because of the sharp increase in the consumption of fossil fuels. Over the past fifty years, consumption has nearly tripled. What accounts for the greater use are population increases and economic growth, initially in the United States and the rest of the developed world but increasingly in the developing world and in China and India in particular. Much of the use is associated with transportation, buildings, and industrial production.

Oil generates roughly one-third of the energy consumed, while nearly 30 percent comes from burning coal. Natural gas is third, at just over 20 percent, which means that fossil fuels combine to account for close to 85 percent of all energy use. Hydropower accounts for 7 percent of primary energy consumption, renewable forms of energy such as solar, wind, and tidal account for 4 percent, and nuclear power for another 4 percent. The difference between these last two categories is that use of renewables is growing in absolute and relative terms and nuclear power is shrinking as a result of costs and politics.

Deforestation is a significant cause of global warming, responsible for a good deal of global carbon emissions. Healthy tropical forests absorb carbon dioxide, but when they are cut down to make room for agriculture or to produce timber, not only are they no longer able to absorb carbon as effectively, but their stored carbon is also released into the air. Brazil and Indonesia, in particular, are two countries whose forests are shrinking, and unless their governments take steps to protect these forests responding to climate change will be more difficult.

That global warming is a reality caused by human activity is widely accepted by scientists, although a small minority questions whether what is taking place is in fact an enduring trend caused by the use of fossil fuels or is instead part of a cycle of warming and cooling that the planet has seen before (although at a much slower pace). But there is a near consensus in the scientific community that climate change is real and that human activity is its principal cause. To refuse to act on the basis that the evidence is not 100 percent certain is not justifiable given the overwhelming strength of the evidence and its implications. We all purchase insurance, even though we do not expect to have our homes flooded or destroyed in a fire. Even climate skeptics should be able to support some policy efforts as a hedge against the possibility that climate change is in fact real and costly. The most urgent debate is not whether climate change is real but what we should do about it.

The critical policy question is how to best mitigate, or effectively reduce, overall carbon and other emissions and therefore reduce the pace and scale of climate change. Many mitigation approaches involve developing and deploying technologies that increase the efficiency of those fuels that are used. Increasing the number of miles automobiles can drive on a gallon of gas is one example, while creating more fuel-efficient jet engines for airplanes is another. Technology can also help to filter emissions so that fewer greenhouse gases are released into the atmosphere. Other technologies are designed to "capture" carbon and other gases so they are not released into the atmosphere but are instead (to cite one strategy) injected underground or converted to a useful product. There are costs associated with mitigation, but there are also jobs to be created and profits to be made given the growing market for cleaner energy. The notion that responsible policy and economic growth are at odds is not backed by the evidence.

Mitigation can also involve shifting to alternative fuels that release little or no greenhouse gases. These include wind, hydroelectric, and solar power, the so-called renewables whose use is now the fastest growing among all fuels, as well as nuclear power. The development of electric cars that don't use any gasoline is another example of successful mitigation. (This is true even if the electricity that powers an electric car comes from fuels that release greenhouse gases because overall there is a reduction in the amount of carbon dioxide released.) Another tactic for mitigation is shifting from one fossil fuel (say coal) to another (such as natural gas) that releases lower levels of greenhouse gases while producing an equivalent amount of energy. Increasing energy efficiency (or lowering what is termed energy intensity, the relationship between economic output and energy input) by adopting new technologies also helps. Encouraging forestation or discouraging deforestation is also an effective strategy, because forests absorb carbon and thereby reduce climate change.

All this and more is taking place, but it would be wrong to exaggerate what can be expected as a result. Given expected increases in global population and economic growth, it will be extremely difficult to lower energy use from fossil fuels. Coal emissions alone have been responsible for one-third of the 1.0 degree Celsius increase in average global temperature, according to calculations by the International Energy Agency. To date, the benefits of falling coal use in Western Europe and North America have been offset by rising coal use in Asia. China now accounts for about half of the world's coal use, and it would have to dramatically alter its policies to change the landscape. Under a business-as-usual scenario where no further regulations are made in China and India, coal, which produces the greatest amount of carbon for the amount of energy it generates, is projected to account for some 20 percent of all energy use in 2040, down from 27 percent today. Oil (projected to account for 28 percent of all energy use in 2040) will remain the most widely used form of energy. Renewables (wind, solar, tidal, geothermal, and so on) are expected to reach some 15 percent of all energy consumed in 2040, still trailing coal and natural gas. Nuclear power (owing to high start-up costs and political opposition) is expected to account for only 5 percent of energy consumed. In short, despite greater efficiencies and an improved mix of fuels, increased global energy consumption will continue to add to the climate change challenge for the foreseeable future.

No global body or mechanism is in a position to mandate mitigation-related efforts. Rather, mitigation takes place voluntarily and at the national or local level, although there is a global effort to encourage broad nonbinding international agreements for countries to undertake more ambitious efforts to lower their emissions of the gases causing climate change.

Several approaches for setting global climate policy have been suggested. One idea (often termed cap and trade) is for the world's governments to agree on a total amount of emissions. Each country would receive a quota. In principle, a market could be established in which permits for emissions could be purchased by those governments wishing to exceed their quota and sold by those who would rather receive money than use up their full quota. The goal would be both to place a ceiling on total emissions worldwide and to incentivize reductions at the national level. The same approach could also be introduced by individual countries at the national level even if other countries did not participate.

Another idea that has garnered considerable interest would be to levy a tax on emissions, thereby encouraging lower levels. This is usually described as a carbon tax. The tax would discourage activities that produce large amounts of greenhouse gases and encourage the replacement of some fuels and energy forms with others that are more efficient or release lower levels of greenhouse gases.

Most governments have yet to endorse either cap and trade or a carbon tax. Wealthier countries fear they would be pressured to slow their economic growth in order to meet more stringent emission targets, transfer large sums of money to developing countries, or both. Certain businesses judge that costs would rise and profits would decline. This concern tends to be overblown. The automobile industry, for example, has demonstrated an ability to adapt by increasing the fuel efficiency of its vehicles and introducing electric vehicles. Climate concerns can stimulate opportunity and growth—for example, in solar and wind and other so-called green technologies.

Developing countries are wary of and unable to pay for any

consequential constraints on carbon. They also need funds to cope with climate change and have yet to receive the full access to capital that has been promised from the industrialized nations. Countries such as China and India have been slow to make substantial cutbacks in coal use and ask why they should not be allowed to develop to a level where their average citizen can enjoy the same quality of life as an average American or European. Around the world, political opposition to pricing carbon has been intense. Disagreements such as these mean that international efforts, begun in earnest in 1995, are far from achieving necessary action.

Instead, the world seems to have agreed for the time being on a path in which individual governments set their own goals ("nationally determined contributions") for emissions ceilings. Meeting in Paris in 2015, nearly all of the world's governments did just this. In addition, they set a collective goal of limiting the total increase in average global temperature to 2 degrees Celsius or some 3.5 degrees Fahrenheit over preindustrial levels. One problem is that the national goals articulated at the gathering represented intentions rather than firm commitments and that even if each country met its emission targets, the increase in temperature would still be higher than the overall ceiling the governments set. The sad truth, though, is that even these modest and admittedly inadequate targets will not be reached. Governments agreed to review their climate goals every five years, something that holds open the possibility of their adopting more ambitious objectives. One complicating factor is the U.S. decision under President Donald Trump to exit the Paris Agreement, which leaves open the question of what the world's second-largest emitter of carbon dioxide will do to address climate change.

Climate change will thus likely become more severe and outpace international efforts meant to limit or counteract it. Thus, a second area of national and international activity has grown up in which local

THE WORLD IS WARMING

Global temperature change over pre-industrial average (Celsius)

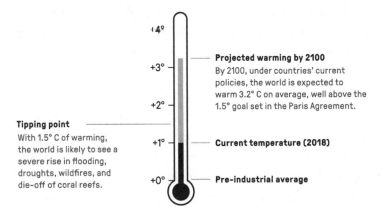

+4°

Projected warming by 2100
By 2100, under countries' current policies, the world is expected to warm 3.2° C on average, well above the 1.5° goal set in the Paris Agreement.

+3°

+2°

Tipping point
With 1.5° C of warming, the world is likely to see a severe rise in flooding, droughts, wildfires, and die-off of coral reefs.

+1°

Current temperature (2018)

+0°

Pre-industrial average

Source: Climate Action Tracker; *The New York Times*.

and national governments take steps to decrease their vulnerability to existing or projected effects of climate change. Such steps, termed adaptation, can involve such things as discouraging or prohibiting people from living in coastal areas that are vulnerable to flooding or in regions susceptible to wildfires. Barriers can be set against higher seas and flooding. Funds can be made available at the local, national, or international level to assist victims of climate change or to reduce vulnerability to its manifestations. Regulations can affect where and how homes are built. None of this resolves the climate change challenge, but such efforts can help stave off its worst effects. The financial cost of adaptation, however, is certain to be significant.

A third, nascent policy area would attempt to reverse climate change—for example, by putting particles in the atmosphere that would block out some of the sun's rays. Such actions (termed geoengineering) are controversial because their effects cannot be confidently predicted. The science is still in its early days. There is no process for approving what could have far-reaching or irreversible impacts. (A 1978 international convention that prohibits actions that would modify the environment with the intention of harming another country would not apply here.) But if there are technology advances, geo-engineering could emerge as a viable potential policy alternative or complement to both mitigation and adaptation if, as seems likely, global climate change advances with the projected disastrous effects.

Short of some technological revolution that would transform global energy use, we should be concerned, even alarmed, about the future impact of climate change on the world. It is the quintessential global challenge in that no single country can solve this problem on its own and there is no way for any single country to shield itself from its effects. Generating the required collective response, however, seems highly unlikely. As a result, climate change could conceivably be *the* defining issue of this century.

Migration

Migration, the movement of people within and across borders, has long been a feature of international relations. Such movement can be voluntary, for example, to pursue economic opportunity, or it can be forced, for instance, to escape armed conflict or persecution. The term "migrant" is not defined under international law, nor is there a commonly accepted definition. The UN, however, defines a migrant broadly as a "person who moves away from his or her place of usual residence, whether within a country or across an international border, temporarily or permanently, and for a variety of reasons." Elsewhere, migrants are defined as those "who live temporarily or permanently in a country of which they are not nationals" and where the decision to do so "has been taken freely by the individual concerned." This narrower definition is more useful, because it distinguishes migrants from those forced to leave their homes, who are termed internally displaced persons (IDPs) if they remain within their country or refugees (or at times "asylum seekers" or "forced migrants") if they cross an international border.

Current statistics suggest there are some 250 million international migrants in the world. The vast majority of these leave voluntarily for economic reasons. They tend to settle in countries with relatively high average incomes, in particular the United States, which is home to just under 50 million immigrants. Statistics such as this underscore the economic dimension of international migration and the reality that most of it is voluntary.

But as of 2019, 71 million people, or close to one out of every one hundred in the world, are involuntarily or forcibly displaced. Of these, 41 million are IDPs and have moved elsewhere within their home country, while 26 million are refugees who have been forced to leave their home country to escape persecution or violence and 3.5 million are asylum seekers.

ONE PERCENT OF THE WORLD'S POPULATION HAS BEEN FORCIBLY DISPLACED

71 million	**41 million**	**37,000**
people are forcibly displaced worldwide by conflict, the most since World War II	of them are internally displaced, while the rest are refugees or are seeking asylum	people were forced to flee their homes each day, on average, during 2018

Source: UNHCR, June 2019.

Migrants are subject to the decisions and immigration laws of the country they wish to enter and reside in. Each country has the prerogative to decide whether to admit a migrant and the terms of admission. Some countries, such as Canada, Australia, and New Zealand—and to a lesser extent the United States—select immigrants based on educational attainment, skills, and/or wealth. This helps to explain why many immigrants contribute to the economy of their adopted country as well as to their former country through sending payments (remittances) back home.

The United States has more immigrants than any other country in the world. Approximately one million people obtain permanent resident status in the United States each year. Most of these decisions are based on grounds of family reunification. Once one person legally migrates to the United States, he or she can sponsor family members to also move there. The United States permits no more than 7 percent of immigrants each year to come from any single country, which puts a cap on large "sending" countries like India, China, Mexico, and the Philippines. Some immigrants enter on the basis of skills, education, and wealth. Over time, many immigrants become citizens; in 2017, for example, nearly one million immigrants applied to become naturalized American citizens.

History suggests immigration can help a society by bringing in enough working-age men and women so that the ratio of those working as compared with those either too young or too old does not reach a point difficult to sustain. Many Asian countries are now grappling with the challenges posed by a rapidly aging population, partly the result of their restrictive stance toward immigration. And as the American technology sector demonstrates, immigrants can also be a major source of innovation and talent. Almost 45 percent of companies in the 2019 Fortune 500—a list of America's biggest companies—were founded or co-founded by an immigrant or the child of an immigrant.

This is not to suggest that immigration does not have downsides. There is evidence that immigrants with lower education levels and skills can compete with and replace workers with similar education and skills. Immigrants can also increase the burden on education, health care, and other public services. And there is the anxiety (often cited in Europe) that immigrants can pose what some see as a cultural challenge when they resist integrating into the society.

There is a considerable disparity in the numbers of immigrants (as well as refugees) governments around the world admit, ranging from none to more than a million annually. Immigration policy, including openness to refugees, has become a matter of intense political debate in many countries in Europe, in Japan, and in the United States, the result of real or imagined consequences for the potential host country's security, employment, and identity.

Global efforts to shape migration (and immigration) policy have had a limited impact. A global "compact" on migration adopted by many of the world's governments (but not the United States and some two dozen others) in 2018 set nonbinding guidelines and standards for the treatment of migrants but left it up to individual governments to determine their policies.

International efforts have had greater impact on the status and treatment of those who migrate out of necessity rather than choice. The number of IDPs and refugees is the highest it has been since World War II and quite possibly ever, with much of the increase a result of conflicts within countries. In fact, the population of forcibly displaced persons has nearly doubled over the past decade. Eighty-five percent of the world's refugees are in developing countries, and nearly 60 percent of all current refugees have come from Syria, Afghanistan, and South Sudan.

Why does this issue, or more accurately set of issues, matter so much? Partly the reason is humanitarian; the number of lives affected is staggering. There is also the economic dimension, in terms of both cost (dependents to be housed, clothed, fed, protected, and provided with education and health care) and opportunity, in that immigrants (be they refugees or migrants) have often proved a great source of innovation and valuable labor.

Large numbers of IDPs and refugees can also have significant political and national security effects. Wars have broken out to stem flows of refugees. For example, the 1971 war between India and Pakistan that gave rise to Bangladesh was triggered by large flows of individuals streaming out of East Pakistan and into India in order to escape repression. And even without triggering conflict, large inflows of refugees can cause a political backlash and alter the politics of countries in their path. Contemporary European politics are a case in point: much of the populism that emerged in the second decade of this century was the result of a backlash to immigration from the Middle East and Africa.

A 1951 international convention (subsequently amended and complemented by various regional organizations) gives refugees specific rights and protections. Refugees are defined as persons outside their own country with a "well-founded fear of being persecuted for reasons of race, religion, nationality, membership of a particular social group or political opinion" and who for these reasons are unwilling or unable to return to their country. The United Nations High Commissioner for Refugees leads an agency charged with providing protection to refugees and seeking permanent solutions to their problems, and there are also a large number of private organizations whose mission it is to assist refugees.

This set of arrangements is helpful but inadequate. Persecution, the operative word in the 1951 international convention, is too narrow a basis for determining refugee status, because someone could reasonably deserve to have the status and rights of being a refugee if, for example, he were to flee his home to avoid a war or gang violence rather than persecution per se. In addition, the decision whether to grant refugee status is left to each government to make for itself. There is no international judge or organization that makes this determination, even though governments are often reluctant to make such a determination lest they be required to let people inside their borders and provide them with assistance.

As the above makes clear, refugees must be able to convince the country they are seeking to enter that they qualify for such treatment and protections, because in principle someone could pose as a refugee when in fact he or she is an economic migrant. Refugees are often termed asylum seekers until the government decides whether their justification is legitimate and they can remain. (The Trump administration has sought to make it impossible for such individuals to even enter the United States until such a determination has been made lest they be able to stay for years while their case is being adjudicated.) Countries have varying policies and mechanisms for determining whether someone merits refugee status, how many refugees to accept, where to allow them to stay, and whether to allow them to remain in the country under a different, more permanent status. In addition, refugees cannot be forced to return to their country of origin if conditions there have not improved to the point where they could expect to live free from violence or persecution.

International efforts to assist refugees largely fall into four areas. The first and most basic is to prevent the conditions that create refugees (or to alter the conditions if they do). Conflict is the most common cause of large-scale refugee flows. The problem is that ending wars can require an enormous commitment, one often beyond the capacity or willingness of most countries, the relevant regional organization, or the United Nations to undertake successfully. This has certainly been the experience with respect to Syria in recent years.

Other causes of large refugee flows can be just as difficult to contend with. One is climate change, which can make large swaths of territory uninhabitable. It is only a matter of time before climate change becomes the greatest cause of refugee flows. Also difficult to deal with is internal violence and crime, which just like war make people flee to safety. But as we are seeing in Central America, where endemic violence and crime have generated significant refugee flows, combating these conditions is often beyond the capacity of the state. A mixture of crime, political repression, and economic hardship has led in recent years to millions of men, women, and children fleeing Venezuela.

A second area of international effort involves taking refugees in on a temporary basis, although this often turns out to be an open-ended if not permanent commitment. The countries that have accepted the largest number of refugees in recent years include Turkey, Pakistan, Uganda, and Sudan, all neighbors of those countries where conflict has generated large flows of refugees.

A third area of assistance is to help those countries that absorb a large number of refugees. Such help is typically economic. This financial aid, for the most part, has come from the United States, Canada, individual European countries, and the European Union itself. The countries that absorb refugees, along with private organizations, also provide significant support.

A fourth and final area of international support for refugees involves how they are treated. The 1951 convention and other documents detail the rights of refugees, although the unfortunate reality is that all too often men, women, and children do not receive the services, including health care and education, or the physical protection that they require and deserve.

Internally displaced persons are defined in a 1998 UN document as those "who have been forced or obliged to flee or to leave their homes or places of habitual residence, in particular as a result of or in order to avoid the effects of armed conflict, situations of generalized violence, violations of human rights or natural or human-made disasters, and who have not crossed an internationally recognized State border." The document goes on to identify the rights of such persons, which are much the same as any citizen, but the reality is the document does not have the force of law and is not binding. It is not just that governments have not formally signed on to it. Rather, the reality is that IDPs receive considerably less attention and protection than refugees because, by definition, they remain within their country of residence (and under the sovereign jurisdiction of that government), something that limits the reach of international law.

What appears certain is that whatever answers there are to the global challenge of migration will most likely originate on the national and local levels. A consistent international response is highly unlikely.

Conditions that generate the decision by people and families to migrate (be it out of choice or necessity) will continue to reflect local conditions and prospects. Most of those forced to leave their homes will end up either inside their country or in a neighboring country. And governments will continue to set their own policies for whom to admit and what resources to make available for alleviating the burdens associated with migration. Those requiring a new permanent home will surely outnumber the availability of such homes. Resolving the conditions that lead to migration has the highest payoff. But if the past is prologue, it will be difficult to address either the cause of migration or its consequences.

The Internet, Cyberspace, and Cybersecurity

The internet is central to modern life. Developed over the past few decades, it has evolved at a speed and scope and gained an importance that was truly unimaginable to its creators. Nearly 300 billion email messages are sent every day. The internet allows the flow of enormous amounts of data and information among billions of users at extraordinary speeds—be they individuals, businesses, governments, or organizations. Geography and distance count not at all.

The technology associated with cyberspace has its constructive and destructive uses, although there is no international consensus as to what kind of action would fall into each category. What we know is that the internet functions smoothly for the most part, facilitating a worldwide flow of information and communications. At the same time, we also know that the internet can be used to steal money and intellectual property (for instance, manufacturing secrets and cutting-edge technology); compromise identities; violate individual and corporate privacy; influence political processes; inspire, train, and instruct terrorists; interfere with communications central to managing military operations; and, perhaps in the future, carry out attacks no less consequential than those conducted with military force. The very connectivity and openness of the system also makes it vulnerable, as does the rapid pace of change.

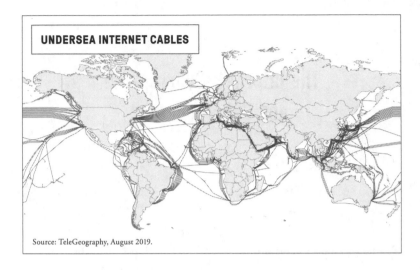

UNDESEA INTERNET CABLES

Source: TeleGeography, August 2019.

Furthermore, we are introducing new weaknesses and complexities as billions of sensors and devices are connected to each other through the Internet of Things, and millions more are coming online.

The relative lack of oversight and policing of a domain and a technology so critical to so many aspects of life and work is surprising. What has "governed" the internet is not a single authority so much as a collection of individuals, civil society groups, corporations, and governments, sometimes working together, at other times in parallel or not at all. It has been more of an informal bottom-up process than something formal and top-down. Much of this evolution took place when the internet was new and before it took on the significance it currently holds.

How the internet should be used and who should have access to the data that users generate are hotly contested topics. Related to this is the question of who has the authority to decide policy when it comes to the internet and whether governments and formal international authorities ought to take over.

To be clear, there is some international governance of the internet. In 1998, the Internet Corporation for Assigned Names and Numbers, or ICANN, was created as a nonprofit organization to bring some order into what would otherwise be chaos. As its name suggests, ICANN established a process to manage the granting of domain names and addresses, that is, what you type into a browser when you want to go to a website. There have also been international conferences and agreements to facilitate commerce, advance human rights, protect privacy, and combat crime and terrorism. For instance, the UN has recognized that people have the same human rights online as off. There have also been bilateral efforts to determine what is permissible in cyberspace. In 2015, for example, the United States and China agreed that they would not "conduct or knowingly support cyber-enabled theft of intellectual property" for commercial gain. But there is no overall global consensus; there are few rules and few ways to enforce what rules there are. For instance, there is a prevailing view in the United States that China has not kept its end of the bargain in living up to the 2015 accord.

The U.S. government in 2011 called for the internet to be open, interoperable, secure, and reliable. Not everyone agrees, and the internet already appears to be fragmenting, resulting in the creation of several distinct internets. (This trend is sometimes described as the "splinternet.") Citing sovereignty, some governments, most prominently China, want to restrict what the internet can bring into their country as well as the ability of people in their country to communicate with one another. Some governments fear the internet will be used by political opponents to bring about what they view as threatening political change, while others believe certain content judged harmful (say, pornography) should be restricted. It is also becoming more common for governments to completely shut down the internet or social media websites in response to terrorism or acts of communal violence, fearing that people will use the internet to spread rumors or fan the flames. In 2019 alone, Sri Lanka, Iran, and India all shut down social media or the entire internet amid crises.

Improving global governance will be extraordinarily difficult. There is probably no realistic way of preventing or even discouraging espionage by one government against another. In this, cyber is little different from other modes of communication, from old-fashioned mail to telephone calls, that are targets of intelligence agencies. But there are other government activities that might be ruled out of bounds, including preparing for or carrying out attacks on one another's physical infrastructure (for instance, shutting down its power grid), interfering with one another's politics (as Russia did during the 2016 U.S. presidential campaign), stealing intellectual property, or sabotaging an entity such as a corporation, as North Korea did to Sony Pictures.

One question sure to emerge is whether there ought to be an exception to any potential ban on using the internet to attack another country. Some would argue that an exception should be made that allows countries to attack terrorists or countries that are seeking to develop weapons of mass destruction or advanced delivery systems. The United States and Israel appear to have carried out such cyberattacks to slow Iran's nuclear program, and the United States reportedly carried out cyberattacks to disrupt North Korea's nuclear and missile programs. Others might embrace such a rule in principle but violate it in practice, seeing cyberattacks as a useful tool of war, be it to deter or retaliate against an adversary that is stronger by more conventional military measures. In this sense, the cyber domain can be a weapon of the weak, because it is low cost and can cause a tremendous amount of damage to a militarily superior enemy. For instance, North Korea, which by all measures is one of the most impoverished countries in the world, also has one of the most sophisticated cyber arsenals. Depending on the targets selected and their effectiveness, cyberattacks have the potential to be as costly and consequential as those conducted with conventional arms or even weapons of mass destruction.

Gaining widespread endorsement of such rules and exceptions

might well be impossible. Calls for a "digital Geneva Convention" have gained little traction. And even if some collective agreement were possible, collective enforcement would not be. What comes to mind as a parallel are the international rules and norms as to when and how armed force should be used. Such rules can serve a purpose in shaping behavior but frequently are ignored if economic or national security interests are judged to be important.

Beyond the lack of agreement, there is the reality that the relevant technologies are quickly evolving and will continue to do so. This makes it hard, if not impossible, for any international rule-making body to keep up. Indeed, any such effort would need to include not just governments but corporations central to the functioning of the internet. What's more, there are a number of tensions and trade-offs when it comes to regulating cyberspace. One is between individual privacy and collective security. The Internet has emerged as a principal and widely shared means for communicating. As a result, governments must determine under what circumstances law enforcement and intelligence agencies could read what is sent by one citizen to another with the presumption that it is between them and no one else. There is as well the issue of what data pertaining to individuals corporations should be allowed to collect and keep. Even between close friends and allies, such as the United States and the countries of the European Union, there is strong disagreement on these issues, with the Europeans arguing for further protections for individuals and more restrictions on technology companies. In fact, in 2018 the EU implemented the General Data Protection Regulation, which provides certain protections to individuals in the EU regarding their data and has fined U.S. companies such as Google for violating this law.

There are alternatives to building an international consensus on how best to govern and regulate cyberspace. Even absent formal agreement, there is the possibility of influencing the behavior of governments.

Deterrence is often discussed as one way to discourage certain unwanted actions, including interference in democratic elections. But it is difficult to make deterrence real, mostly because the vast majority of cyberattacks are below the threshold for responding with an armed attack or use of force. Imposing sanctions might not have the desired effect. It can thus be difficult to find a response that imposes costs but is not disproportionate and unduly risky. In addition, the source of the illegal or hostile action cannot always be determined. This makes retaliation (the threat of which is central to deterrence) often impossible to implement.

If, however, a government can determine who was behind some action in cyberspace that it deems illegal or hostile, there is a range of potential responses. Those violating the law can be treated as criminals and punished. In the case of terrorists, a response could involve a physical attack. If a government is behind the cyberattack, either directly or by supporting some individual or group, economic sanctions, military action, and even some cyber-related response can be options.

There are alternatives—or, better yet, complements—to fostering restraint. Steps can be taken to make systems less vulnerable even if not invulnerable. As is so often the case, there exists a running battle between offense and defense, between those technologies that would attack in one form or another and those that would defend. Many actions for individuals and small companies come under the rubric of cyber hygiene, such as using complicated, random sets of characters for passwords (as opposed to something like "password123"), not writing passwords down next to your keyboard, using a password manager, and enabling two-factor authentication on social media, email, and banking accounts. Encryption may be an option. A user can also make sure he or she is running the most recent software and continue to update that software. There is also a case to be made for resilience, including making critical equipment redundant, creating multiple backups of critical information, and ensuring business continuity under severely degraded conditions. Here and elsewhere, efficiency and security (along with potential risks and costs) will need to be considered and balanced. One thing is sure: governing the internet promises to be one of this century's greatest and most important challenges, and right now those favoring establishing rules are losing out to fast-changing technologies that, unlike nuclear weapons, for example, are increasingly available to the many and not just a few.

Global Health

There is a persuasive case to be made that global health is considerably better now than at any other time in human history. And there is a case to be made that people and governments nevertheless should be concerned given developments in the health sphere and the gap between these challenges and the readiness of the world to meet them. In this latter sense, global health is but another example of the gulf between globalization's challenges and the adequacy of the collective response.

The reason all this matters stems from the obvious—we all want to live long lives in which we are able to perform mentally and physically at a high level, and for humanitarian reasons we would like others to as well—to the less than obvious, including the relationship between a society's overall health and its economic performance, political stability, and national security. Health-related costs and crises can turn a strong, successful society into a weak and dysfunctional one. Preventing, detecting, and responding to outbreaks in other countries can slow or prevent those outbreaks from spreading to your country. Health care is also central to the global economy because close to 10 percent of global economic output is spent on it. In the United States, spending on health is now estimated to be no less than 18 percent of its gross domestic product.

The world's population is approaching eight billion, eight times the population two centuries ago, four times what it was one century ago, and roughly twice as large as it was as recently as fifty years ago. A principal reason for this increase is that life expectancy has dramatically risen. The typical person in the world today can expect to reach his or her seventy-second birthday. In some of the wealthier countries, a person can expect to reach his or her eightieth birthday; Japan is a global leader, with a life expectancy of eighty-four years. Increasing numbers of people live into their nineties and even beyond. This average longevity is more than double what it was a century ago, which reflects a sharp increase in the average life span of those living in poorer or developing countries. The reasons for longer lives include better diet, enormous progress in the fields of medicine and health—in particular, both child and maternal mortality are down—and fewer large-scale wars. The average woman lives several years longer than her male counterpart. Due to the decline in under-five mortality since 2000, fifty million children's lives were saved.

Many factors account for this progress, including improvements in medical care ranging from prevention to diagnosis to treatment, breakthroughs in technology and drugs, education that has changed individual behavior for the better, improvements in diet and nutrition, and aid provided to low-income countries to bolster their health-care systems. The eradication or near eradication of several infectious diseases that previously ravaged populations is a case in point. Smallpox was officially eradicated as of 1980. Polio cases have decreased by more than 99 percent since 1988 and are now extremely rare. New HIV infections are down, and the number of people dying from AIDS-related causes is now around one million a year, half of what it was since the peak in 2004 and a small fraction of what would have been the case without changes in behavior and the development of drugs that allow individuals to manage the disease. Incidence of both malaria and measles has plummeted.

Notwithstanding all these gains, the global health agenda remains full and demanding. Life expectancy in several African countries is barely above fifty years, while the average life expectancy for sub-Saharan Africa as a region is sixty years, a figure that represents a sharp improvement of twenty years over its 1960 level but one that is still relatively low. Infectious disease remains a threat, in part because globalization itself (for instance, the ease of travel) has made it much easier for diseases to spread. Urbanization and warmer temperatures have likewise created an environment conducive to outbreaks and transmission of diseases. Large refugee populations have also become vulnerable to outbreaks of diseases such as cholera and diphtheria.

The overuse of existing antimicrobial drugs and underinvestment in new ones mean drug-resistant organisms are becoming more common and are more difficult to treat. Then there are viruses, for which there is often no means to ensure either prevention or successful treatment of the infected. In recent years, the world has experienced life-threatening outbreaks of diseases including severe acute respiratory syndrome, Middle East respiratory syndrome, Zika, and Ebola.

At the same time, a large-scale global epidemic—a pandemic—cannot be discounted. Vaccines cannot anticipate specific strains of flu, and it is possible that a particularly virulent form could emerge one season and quickly go global. By the time the influenza virus had been identified, it likely would have spread and taken root. During the Spanish flu pandemic a century ago, it is estimated that at least fifty million people died. Literally hundreds of millions (especially the young and the old) would be at severe risk today from the outbreak of a virulent form of flu, and the global economy could suffer a major blow because travel would be interrupted, health systems overloaded, and people discouraged from going to work or anywhere where they could come into contact with people who might be contagious. In the realm of contagious diseases, little stays local for long.

The other large emerging threat to global health stems not from infectious diseases but from noninfectious or what are termed noncommunicable diseases. NCDs include cardiovascular disease, respiratory diseases, cancers, and diabetes. In 1990, three of the top seven causes of death in the world were the result of NCDs; by 2015, the number was six in seven. NCDs are the leading cause of death globally and were responsible for thirty-eight million—or 68 percent—of the world's fifty-six million deaths in 2012. By 2030, NCDs are projected to cause nearly five times as many deaths as communicable diseases worldwide. This shift is the result of progress realized in the fight against infectious diseases (which among other things increased life spans) but even more reflects the result of a much greater prevalence of NCDs.

NCDs can result in part or whole from genetic disposition, for instance, cardiovascular disease. A separate cause is prolonged exposure to or interaction with a polluted environment. NCDs are often a consequence of individual behavior, be it sedentary lifestyles, poor diets, smoking, and drug and alcohol abuse. NCDs also encompass mental illnesses, including dementia and Alzheimer's, which most affect those living lives longer than was common just decades ago.

NCDs tend to be costly to treat. Many drugs are prohibitively expensive. NCDs also affect economies because individuals who have NCDs often must leave the workforce prematurely. The adage "an ounce of prevention is worth a pound of cure" applies here. Education and consumer information about risks associated with certain consumption and behaviors (along with the benefits of others) are one thing. Regulation and taxation can make it more difficult and expensive to smoke or drink alcohol. Workplaces and environments can be inspected and required to meet certain standards with sanctions and penalties introduced if such standards are not met. Increased access to primary health care in developing nations would also make a big difference, because people are often diagnosed too late and treatment becomes more difficult. However,

PREMATURE DEATHS FROM INFECTIOUS DISEASES ARE DECLINING, WHILE DEATHS FROM NONCOMMUNICABLE DISEASES ARE RISING

Total deaths under 70 years old, selected diseases

—— Infectious (communicable)   — — Noncommunicable

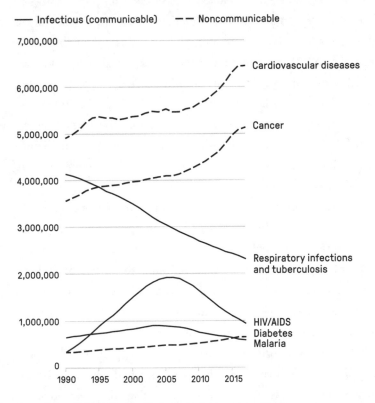

Source: Institute for Health Metrics and Evaluation. Used with permission. All rights reserved.

there is resistance at many levels (from the personal to the political) to adopting these measures.

Global efforts in the health realm are complicated. One reason is the sheer number of actors involved. There is the World Health Organization (WHO), but its impact is less grand than its name suggests. Established in 1948, it lacks the necessary authority, capacity, and resources to carry out its mission of fostering "the attainment by all peoples of the highest possible level of health." Besides the WHO, there is the World Bank, a number of initiatives and nongovernmental organizations often associated with particular diseases, the Gates Foundation (which by itself is responsible for the majority of all private giving for global health) and other philanthropic undertakings, pharmaceutical companies, hospitals, doctors, nurses, and an assortment of national and local health authorities. Despite the numerous individuals and groups involved, there are few procedures to determine priorities much less coordinate efforts and ensure goals are being met.

For example, the International Health Regulations, agreed to by many of the world's governments in 2005, call on countries to monitor and prepare for infectious disease outbreaks. Ideally, governments would create and support organizations within their countries modeled on the Atlanta-based Centers for Disease Control and Prevention. They would also make sure that first responders and hospitals at the local level received the necessary training, equipment, and facilities to handle outbreaks. More than a decade later, many countries, lacking expertise and resources alike, have failed to put into place such capacities.

Making matters worse, there is no consensus on priorities. The UN's Sustainable Development Goals, adopted in 2015, call for efforts against both infectious and noncommunicable diseases. But the overwhelming share of the resources devoted to global health continues to focus on fighting known infectious diseases such as HIV/AIDS, malaria, and tuberculosis, or on meeting the special health demands of mothers, newborns, and children. NCDs, by contrast, receive only a few cents on the dollar, even though they have emerged as a much greater cause of illness and death. In 2017, for example, twice as many premature deaths were from NCDs than from infectious diseases. This emphasis has remained in place despite the progress made against infectious diseases or in reducing maternal and infant mortality and the increasing number of older people in many societies. NCDs lack the urgency or the sense of crisis associated with infectious disease outbreaks, and thus it is more difficult to galvanize a response to them.

These factors—a lack of consensus on priorities and policies, the absence of an organized governance framework, a shortfall in resources, the continuing threat of infectious diseases, and the emergence of an epidemic in NCDs—add up to two realities: health around the globe has improved dramatically, yet the future of global health remains uncertain and the health of any society remains vulnerable due to its interconnectedness to the health of others.

Trade and Investment

Trade at the international level is the exchange (buying and selling) of manufactured goods, agricultural products, and services (including such things as insurance, banking, and legal work) across borders. It is a necessity, because no country is self-sufficient in raw materials, grows all the food it needs, has enough domestic demand for all it produces, and manufactures all that it wants to consume.

All things being equal, trade is a good thing, although it can also eliminate certain jobs and hurt some firms and workers. On balance, though, trade creates jobs and boosts the overall welfare of a country. Imagine a country of 100 million people. That is a country with 100 million potential consumers. But there are close to 8 billion people in the world. Trade dramatically expands the size of the potential market that producers can reach. It is thus a boon for those who work for companies that export, with statistics showing that export-oriented jobs tend to be relatively high paying. As a company sells to a larger market, its average cost of production decreases, and the company can then sell its products more cheaply. Trade can be an engine of increased productivity, economic growth, development, and poverty reduction.

Trade also broadens the array of goods that consumers can purchase. Barely any coffee or tea is grown in the United States, but

THE GROWTH OF TRADE

Total global trade as a percentage of world GDP

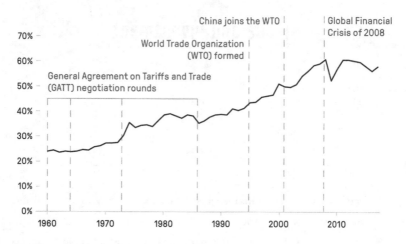

Sources: World Bank; World Trade Organization.

Americans wake up to these drinks because of trade. Trade gives people access to the most innovative and highest-quality goods and services produced around the world. Trade also allows consumers to purchase things at lower prices if those goods come from countries able to produce them more cheaply due to lower labor costs (whether stemming from greater efficiencies, the incorporation of advanced technology, and/or lower wages) or greater access to raw materials. Imports can also stimulate innovation because they expose domestic producers to new ideas and products that they can incorporate and build on. Competition from abroad also motivates domestic producers to improve their products or prices.

Underpinning these ideas is what is known as the theory of comparative advantage, introduced two centuries ago by the British political economist David Ricardo. The theory posits that international trade allows a country to specialize in producing those things it can make more cheaply and import those it cannot. The Germans thus export chemicals, the Saudis oil, the Swiss watches, the Canadians timber, the Japanese cars, the Americans machinery, and the Chinese textiles. The idea is that trade works best when every country does what it does best. Those things it cannot make or cannot make well, it imports from others.

Countries that participate in international trade run either a trade surplus (if the value of their exports is greater than the value of their imports) or a trade deficit (if the value of imports exceeds the value of exports). That is their trade balance. It is impossible for every country to run a surplus because overall trade in the world must balance out. Some countries will run overall deficits. They will also likely run bilateral deficits with some countries and bilateral surpluses with others. Deficits tend to reflect the relative strengths of currencies (a strong currency makes imports cheaper and exports more expensive, leading to a deficit) and the extent to which people in a country have access to money and prefer to spend (which adds to the consumption of imports) rather than save. Not surprisingly, trade deficits get bigger following tax cuts that tend to stimulate spending and discourage saving. None of this matters so long as a deficit is not the result of unfair trade practices or currency manipulation and the country can pay for what it imports with a currency that others will accept. If not, then it will have to cut back on imports or increase the value of its exports.

One additional complication needs to be inserted here. It is increasingly difficult to measure exports and imports, because few items are made entirely in one country. Instead, the production process is fragmenting, with components and raw materials coming from around the world and assembly taking place in multiple countries. This is the case for everything from automobiles to iPhones. A good may cross one or more international boundaries (even the same one) several times during production. This phenomenon is known as a global supply chain (sometimes called a value chain in that the value of the good or service increases at each stage of the process). In fact, the buying of unfinished goods or services that contribute to production currently accounts for three-quarters of international trade.

Most official statistics fail to capture the complex reality of global supply chains, in the process making trade surpluses and deficits appear starker than they are. Depending on the sequence of steps in the manufacturing process, a country may get 100 percent of the "credit" for producing a good—in other words, the final value of the good is logged as an export—when in fact it only carried out its final assembly and received merely a fraction of the final sale price. There is research indicating that on average close to one-third of global exports are accounted for by importing foreign goods and using them in the production process. This reality has among other things real implications for statistics: the U.S. trade deficit with China may be in the realm of 30 percent lower than what is reported due to the fact that many of China's exports to the United States include elements from third countries.

The rise of global supply chains also has policy implications. After all, while imposing tariffs (import fees) may protect some industries from competition, it will make the importation of goods used to produce other goods more expensive and thus make domestic products more expensive and less competitive. Also, government actions designed to weaken the home currency and create a competitive advantage for exporters have the side effect of making essential imports (of raw materials or components) more expensive for domestic producers. Finally, while there is growing talk in Washington about "decoupling" the American economy from the Chinese one, the existence of complex global supply chains makes this easier to talk about than to bring about. While there may be significant decoupling in strategic sectors that have implications for national security, such as 5G and semiconductors, it is

THE GLOBAL SUPPLY CHAIN OF A BOEING 787

Component parts by country of origin

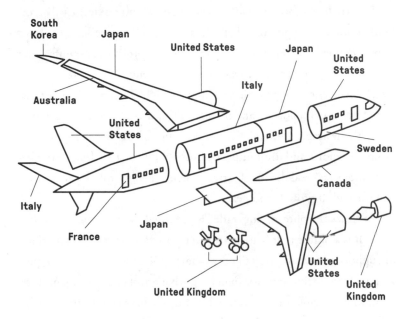

Source: Boeing; *The Wall Street Journal.*

unlikely that the world's two largest economies can be separated to a significant extent.

The benefits of trade are not just economic. Trade can serve strategic ends—for example, by bolstering alliances. But trade can also be good for ties with potential adversaries. Countries that trade together may think twice before going to war with each other or doing other things that might disrupt mutually beneficial trade. Trade among European countries and across the Atlantic clearly failed to prevent the outbreak of World War I, but there is reason to believe interdependence can be a factor that encourages restraint. Japan's behavior in the run-up to World War II, when it lacked mutually beneficial trade ties with adversaries, supports this line of thinking. Such interdependence constitutes one rationale for U.S.-China trade.

Free trade is a form of trade in which goods and services easily cross borders and can be purchased at a "market price" that reflects the costs of production and transit along with whatever profit the manufacturer seeks. The principal alternatives to free trade tend to be protectionism, which involves erecting barriers to imports to shield domestic producers from foreign competition, and mercantilism, which sees trade surpluses as highly desirable and embraces policies including protectionism that promote exports and limit imports. Both will ultimately lead to retaliation and the breakdown of arrangements meant to promote trade and through it growth and peace.

At times the phrase "fair trade" is proposed as an alternative to free trade. It is a phrase that is attractive on the surface because it is hard not to support something described as "fair." Often the term is coupled with calls for reciprocity, for matching what another government does. Again, in principle this is reasonable. But fairness should not be confused with outcomes; trade need not be balanced to be fair so long as what is done is consistent with obligations under relevant trade laws and commitments. Otherwise, fair trade can become a euphemism for both protectionism and mercantilism if it is used to advantage exports or discourage imports.

UNFREE TRADE

There are a number of barriers to free trade. The oldest and most common instrument is tariffs, a tax added to the price of a product when it enters a country. The "tax" is paid directly by the importing business (and collected by the importing government) and then is normally passed on to consumers in the importing country in the form of higher prices. The tariff is not paid by the exporting country, but it will make the exports in question more expensive and less competitive. When goods are affected by a tariff, the volume of exports and the profit from exports will likely fall.

A tariff makes something more expensive and thus less attractive to would-be consumers, who will either buy something similar at a lower price—be it made by a domestic producer or another foreign producer—or forgo the purchase. Tariffs can be put in place for many reasons, be it to protect firms that could otherwise not hold their own against imports, to retaliate against other countries that use tariffs or other tools to protect their companies, to bring about a change in the overall balance of trade, or as a kind of sanction in response to disliked policies that have nothing to do with trade. Tariffs were a mainstay of U.S. policy in the 1930s when the Smoot-Hawley law was passed and have become a common tool under the Trump administration starting in 2017. The danger, of course, is that tariffs can simply raise prices and reduce the volume of trade, slowing economic growth and poisoning political relationships in the process.

There are also "nontariff barriers," which, as the phrase suggests, make it difficult for goods produced in one country to reach another. Quotas—ceilings on the amount of a specific item (for example, cars)—on goods allowed to be imported from another country are one such nontariff barrier. Nontariff barriers need not be quantitative. Europe has put into place rules that limit or preclude imports of genetically modified foods. For a time, Japan refused to import metal baseball bats, citing baseless safety considerations. Bureaucracies can put into place all sorts of regulations and procedures that make it difficult for products to reach their intended destinations. There can also be rules stipulating that domestically produced components make up a certain percentage of a final product. Again, the idea is to limit the degree to which imports can reach the market, in the process protecting jobs in competing industries in the home country. The problem is that consumers will have to pay a higher price or accept lower quality or both. Exporting countries often live with such obstacles because it is better to have some exports reach consumers than none. But exporting countries have also been known to retaliate, reducing access to their markets as a consequence. In such circumstances, everybody loses.

There are other less obvious or visible barriers to free trade. One is subsidies, essentially economic grants, low-cost loans, or purchases made by governments to or from domestic companies or industries that offset part of their costs of production and thereby allow them to set lower prices than they normally could. This pricing ability allows them to compete more effectively domestically (against imports) and abroad (where they are competing for market share). For a long time, Airbus was a beneficiary of subsidies, a practice that contributed to its emergence as a serious competitor to Boeing. China's large firms (so-called state-owned enterprises) depend on extensive government subsidies to a degree that distinguishes them from practices elsewhere.

Another device used to tilt the playing field in favor of a country's exports and to penalize imports is currency manipulation. Steps by a government's central bank (which controls the amount of money in circulation and the costs of borrowing through interest rates) to decrease the relative value of its currency against the value of the currencies of its trading partners will make imports more expensive to would-be consumers (thereby reducing demand) and its exports cheaper to potential consumers in other countries. China practiced currency manipulation when it was entering world markets and pushing to expand its exports.

Currency manipulation that drives the value of a currency down can boost exports and reduce imports. This is the goal of mercantilist practices. But there is a price to be paid for such behavior, because it will likely make citizens unhappy if they can no longer afford to buy preferred goods made outside their country. And currency manipulation invites currency manipulation by others (leaving everyone no better and arguably worse off as trade slows, which in turn slows economic growth) or leads to other forms of retaliation, such as tariffs. This, too, happened in the run-up to World War II.

Dumping is yet another behavior inconsistent with free trade. Dumping occurs when a country exports something at a price below what it would sell for at home. It might even be below what it costs to produce. The motive for engaging in such "irrational" behavior is to gain market share in a foreign country, after which it may be possible to raise prices without losing out. Dumping can also be used to keep workers working in order to skirt domestic political problems caused by unemployment. In such cases, there is normally a hidden government subsidy. Members of the General Agreement on Tariffs and Trade (GATT) agreed to the first Antidumping Code in 1979 and expanded it in 1994 with the creation of the World Trade Organization (WTO).

Trade also requires that patents and copyrights be respected, that rights be paid for, and that technology and work not be stolen. Companies that spend money on research and development and introduce new techniques and products deserve to make a profit on the basis of their efforts. If they do not make a profit, they may lack the funds for further investment or the incentive to continue to innovate. The same holds for individuals who produce creative work. Such protection has become more difficult in the internet age. China, in particular, has stolen valuable intellectual property, and its companies have then introduced it into their own products that are sold at home and abroad.

One last barrier to free trade is fundamentally different. It comes about when exports are blocked not by the would-be importing country but by the exporting country. Such export controls are put into place for national security reasons, to keep certain technologies with military or intelligence applications out of the hands of trading partners who are viewed as potential or actual adversaries. Export controls used for legitimate reasons of national security are thus a necessary exception to free trade. The danger, of course, is that national security can be used illegitimately as a cover for protectionism.

TRADE TALKS

Trade does not just happen. Mostly it is the result of painstaking negotiations that reduce tariffs and other obstacles to the free movement of goods and services across national borders. Such negotiations can be global, regional, multilateral in just about every imaginable configuration, or bilateral (between just two countries). Trade agreements are becoming increasingly broad, setting standards for things like working conditions and environmental practices. Many agreements also come with a process for resolving inevitable disputes that emerge when one country judges the behavior of another to be inconsistent with the terms of the agreement.

Modern trade pacts can be traced back to the post–World War II period, when, in 1947, twenty-three countries signed the General Agreement on Tariffs and Trade. GATT's emphasis was on reducing tariffs inhibiting the flow of manufactured goods, and in that the organization succeeded: the average global import tariff on goods has more than halved, falling from more than 20 percent in 1947 to 9 percent in 2018. Roughly two and a half decades later, GATT was superseded by the World Trade Organization, which now counts 164 members and has a broader mandate that in principle empowers it to promote free trade not just in manufacturing but also in agriculture and services and to protect intellectual property, including patents, copyrights, and select technologies. The WTO also includes a dispute settlement system, which is often referred to as the organization's "crown jewel" because it allows trade complaints to be brought before an appellate body that determines whether WTO rules are being violated and issues rulings to the parties. Altogether there have been nine rounds of global trade talks, the most recent of which, the Doha Round launched in 2001, ended without agreement, largely because it was impossible to reach consensus on how agricultural products would be handled.

Global trade negotiations have been most effective in reducing tariffs on manufactured goods. All members of GATT—and now the WTO—must provide other members with most favored nation (MFN) status, which reduces tariffs on their products to the lowest level offered to any other country with MFN status. Tariffs were then essentially cut through negotiated bargains, either sector by sector or through "formula" cuts, which were across-the-board reductions. Lower tariffs facilitate trade, and average tariffs have fallen sharply over the decades. Dumping is much less prevalent. The volume of world trade increased from just over $120 billion in 1960 to $6.5 trillion in 2000, a principal reason the world economy increased fivefold in those same forty years. International merchandise trade as a percentage of global GDP rose from just under 20 percent fifty years ago to around 45 percent today. World merchandise trade volume is now in the range of $20 trillion, three times what it was in 2000 and hundreds of times what it was in the aftermath of World War II. International trade continues to grow, although the rate of growth has slowed.

Global trade pacts have not been as effective at reducing barriers to trade in agricultural goods or in services, which includes such fields as construction, finance, accounting, health care, and transportation. Nor have global trade agreements done much to reduce trade distorting practices such as government subsidies, currency manipulation, and theft of intellectual property.

One consequence of the difficulty in achieving a new global trade accord has been the proliferation of regional and other "narrower" trade pacts between or among two or several countries. The number of regional trade agreements reported to the WTO has increased fifteen-fold over the past thirty years, from just over twenty in 1990 to around three hundred in early 2019. The European Union can be understood in part as a regional free trade accord for its members. The United States, Canada, and Mexico entered into the North American Free Trade Agreement in 1994, which reduced tariffs, facilitated investment flows, and protected intellectual property rights. The result was a major expansion in regional trade and investment to the overall benefit of all three countries. Mexico's economy grew at a much faster pace, increasing the number of jobs available at home and reducing the flow of would-be immigrants to the United States. NAFTA was partly renegotiated in 2018, resulting in a new pact rebranded the United States-Mexico-Canada Agreement by the U.S. government and signed into law in early 2020.

Eleven countries in the Americas and Asia created the Comprehensive and Progressive Agreement for Trans-Pacific Partnership (CPTPP, once known as the Trans-Pacific Partnership) in 2018 to expand their trade and raise labor and environmental standards in their respective regions. The impact of CPTPP was weakened by the decision in 2017 by the United States (which had negotiated and signed the agreement under the Obama administration, although it had not yet been brought before Congress for approval) not to join the new trade group, one that among other things reduces tariff and select nontariff barriers, provides greater protection to intellectual property, and creates new mechanisms to resolve disputes over trade and investment. In so doing, the United States lost an opportunity to create a common front that could pressure China to modify its trade practices and raise its standards or risk being excluded from important markets. Increasingly, agreements such as CPTPP have become the laboratories for developing new trade arrangements that cover an expanding range of practices.

Trade can be good for importing countries because it increases choice and lowers costs. But even if trade is good for a society overall, it may jeopardize specific companies and the jobs of those who work for them if imports become so popular that domestic workers are laid off and factories are closed. One potential response is protectionism and the use of tariffs, but as already noted, this can be costly to the society because it raises prices for imports, be they finished goods or raw materials that end up in (and raise the cost of) other products. Tariffs can also trigger a trade war in which other governments retaliate for the imposition of tariffs on their goods by placing tariffs on the other country's exports. In such scenarios, there are rarely winners.

One alternative to protectionism when firms close and workers lose their jobs is government and private-sector programs that provide temporary financial support to laid-off workers along with opportunities to train workers for new jobs. Such programs, known as trade adjustment assistance, are increasingly necessary when companies must close and jobs disappear not because of foreign competition and cheap imports but because of new technologies that increase productivity and require fewer workers to achieve the same—or even higher—outputs. The arrival of artificial intelligence, robotics, autonomous vehicles, and other new technologies suggests that it will be more important than ever for governments and firms to train employees so that they are ready to transition to newly created jobs as their previous jobs are eliminated. It will also be necessary to make sure funds for health care and retirement are portable so that workers can retain them when they switch jobs.

INVESTMENT

Cross-border investment, like trade, has increased sharply over the decades, with international flows of capital (money) increasing substantially in the decades prior to the Global Financial Crisis before stagnating in the decade since. Foreign direct investment flows increased more than one hundred times from 1970 to 2018. Foreign investment can take the form of building a manufacturing plant in another country or purchasing foreign companies. Investment can prove beneficial for both sides, although, in practice, investment can be a complicated source of friction. For the country being invested in, foreign investment can be a welcome source of capital that helps businesses to grow. Depending on the terms of the investment, it can also be a means for foreign investors to gain access to desired technologies. Those making the investment can then produce goods more efficiently that can be exported anywhere, allowing access to a desired foreign market. There is no equivalent of the WTO to regulate foreign investment. There are, however, various bilateral and multilateral compacts that set terms meant to encourage investment, mostly by protecting the rights and interests of investors.

What might matter most are local conditions: investors are understandably wary of investing in situations where they cannot be confident of physical security, political stability, and legal protections. My former boss at the State Department, Secretary of State Colin Powell, was fond of saying that capital is a coward. Potential investors are often scared off by widespread corruption, the absence of an independent central bank, high taxes, requirements that they share or transfer important technologies, and restrictions on their ability to repatriate (send home) profits. The educational level of the workforce and physical infrastructure also matter.

Countries wanting to attract investment need to compete in these areas. At the same time, governments have the right to restrict investment in their countries for reasons of national security, to avoid foreign ownership of critical companies and industries to ensure their independence, and to protect their intellectual and technological properties. Some have also put into place controls that limit the ability of outsiders to move in and out of markets at short notice in a manner that could contribute to financial turmoil.

LOOKING AHEAD

Trade and investment have been areas of great progress for some seventy years now. The volume of both has grown steadily and markedly, at once both a contributor to global growth and a reflection of it. The problem ahead is that the barriers to further progress are complex and addressing them will prove more difficult. New agreements will need to be negotiated and enforced. Another problem is a familiar one: how to help those workers who lose out because of foreign competition or, as increasingly will be the case, because of new, more productive technologies that eliminate existing jobs. The answer lies in educating and training workers (and in making it possible for them to navigate the inevitable transitions) so they can step into new jobs. Identifying the answer is the easy part; putting it into practice so that people can continue to work will be the challenge.

Currency and Monetary Policy

oney is basic to the functioning of any economy. It allows goods and services (including work) of every kind to be paid for and sold in an efficient manner. All the alternatives, such as barter or exchanging one good or service for another, would be extremely inefficient given that there may not be a match either in what is sought or in value. This is true for trade between and within countries alike. Money is also essential for investment, for providing credit for business and personal uses or mortgages to buy homes. Money allows for savings.

A question arises, though, as to what money is to be used. The United States uses dollars, Japan yen, much of Europe euros, Russia rubles, China yuan, Mexico pesos, and so on. There is no global currency, because there is no global central bank or printing press. Most governments want to have maximum control over their own economies, something that argues for having their own currencies. In this way they can decide how much of it to put in circulation so that they can achieve maximum levels of economic growth and employment without causing severe inflation that would undermine the value of the currency. The effect of severe inflation is to wipe out savings and make normal business activity all but impossible, in the process undermining political stability. This was what happened in Germany in the 1920s, when hyperinflation caused the price level to increase billions (yes, billions) of times in a span of two years, paving the way for Hitler to come to power. It is what happened in Zimbabwe beginning in 2007 and Venezuela more recently. Governments also want to keep control over their monetary policies in order to avoid the opposite danger, that of deflation, which would cause their economies to shrink, leading to a rise in unemployment and a reduced standard of living.

Central banks are tasked with managing the money supply, which in turn should affect their currency's value and inflation. To expand the money supply, most advanced countries buy their own bonds and give the seller currency, and to reduce the money supply, they sell their bonds and pull currency out of circulation. Interest rates can also be adjusted in order to influence inflation and other economic targets. All of this is known as monetary policy. The lower interest rates are, the more people and businesses tend to borrow, invest, and spend, all of which increases the pace of economic activity and growth. The risk, though, is that an overheated economy will lead to inflation, in which people and businesses begin to lose confidence in the value of the currency, especially if the larger supply of money is not backed by increased economic activity. Such a loss of confidence gets in the way of trade and investment. Higher rates can be necessary to limit inflation, but they also have the effect of reducing borrowing and slowing economic activity. Fewer jobs will be created, and fewer homes will be built. Getting the balance right is easier said than done; this is one reason why central banks should be independent, seeking to do what is best for the long-term health of the economy rather than promoting short-term political goals. Making the task even harder is that other factors such as government spending and tax policy (together known as fiscal policy) as well as trade policy can and do affect the pace of economic activity but are outside the purview of central banks and are determined by executives and legislatures.

The World Bank (more formally, the International Bank for Reconstruction and Development) is not the world's central bank, as its name suggests, but rather a global organization devoted to promoting economic development in poorer countries. The International Monetary Fund (IMF), one of the institutions created at the 1944 Bretton Woods Conference that was convened to plan for the post–World War II global economy, operates in the domain of currencies and monetary policy but with a limited mandate. One of its roles is to assess and advise governments on their financial health. Another is to assist countries that find themselves overextended financially and in need of loans, in which case the IMF gives the government a loan and in return gets the recipient to commit to change its fiscal and monetary policies and undertake broader reforms. Its prescriptions generally include decreasing public spending and increasing taxation. The IMF has little leverage and hence little influence over countries that run sustained trade and payments surpluses, however, even if those surpluses are the result of fiscal, monetary, and currency policies that encourage exports and discourage imports and domestic consumption. This was the case with Japan decades ago and applies today to countries such as Germany and China.

While there is no worldwide central bank, national currencies can be exchanged for one another. For most countries, the exchange rate—how many pesos or euros for how many dollars, for example—is largely determined by markets, by realities of supply and demand. Some countries do peg their currencies to another one—promising to hold its value stable. But governments' efforts to determine the rates of their currencies tend to fail over time because sooner or later currencies will come to reflect underlying economic conditions. In practice, the choice for most countries is not really between a completely market-driven exchange rate and a hard peg, because countries can and do intervene in the market to try to influence the market value of their currency. There are, however, differences in emphasis and degree.

THE ERA OF THE DOLLAR

The dollar remains the currency of choice for conducting international trade and the closest thing to an international currency. What this means in practice is that the price of Chinese goods is generally quoted in dollars, and even if a Brazilian company is importing those goods, it will usually pay the Chinese company in dollars. Once the Chinese company receives the dollars, it will exchange them at a bank for the local currency or sell them to private investors who want to invest in the United States due to an attractive return on U.S. assets or a perceived measure of safety in investing in the United States. Those countries that sell more goods and services internationally than they buy also end up accumulating large amounts of dollars; this is the case with Japan and China. This is not a problem as long as they come about it honestly (and not through unfair trade or currency practices) and are content to do so, whether because of their confidence in the dollar or the lack of any real alternatives. If there was no widely accepted reserve currency, the world could not have the same level of international trade and investment that it currently does, and the world would be a poorer place.

The dollar's role reflects the reality of American political stability along with the sheer size of the American economy and its relative openness. It also reflects people's confidence that the value of a dollar won't dramatically change and that the U.S. Treasury won't default on its debts. Central banks around the world want to hold the U.S. dollar, to ensure their ability to purchase imports, to enable them to pay their debts to foreigners, and to act as an insurance policy for when financial crises strike. According to the IMF, as of early 2019 the U.S. dollar constituted more than 60 percent of the official foreign exchange reserves held by the world's central banks, while the euro, the second most widely held reserve currency, accounted for just 20 percent.

THE U.S. DOLLAR IS THE MOST WIDELY HELD RESERVE CURRENCY

Share of allocated global reserves, Q1 2019

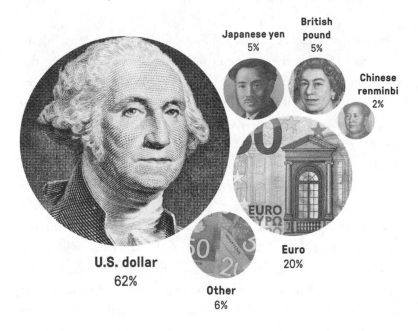

Japanese yen 5%

British pound 5%

Chinese renminbi 2%

U.S. dollar 62%

Euro 20%

Other 6%

Source: International Monetary Fund.

After World War II, all currencies in the world were fixed to the dollar, which in turn was backed by gold. In principle, anyone holding dollars could exchange them for gold. This didn't last given the chronic, large trade surpluses run in the 1960s by export-dependent countries such as Japan, then the emerging world power in trade much as China is today. In 1971, the U.S. government "closed the gold window" and ceased offering to convert dollars for gold because it simply did not have enough of the mineral to cover the world's dollar holdings.

The bottom line is that the world moved to a situation in which the dollar was valuable not because of the gold it could be exchanged for but because people were prepared to accept dollars in exchange for goods and services they sold to Americans and others. This situation is one described by economists as "fiat currencies," in that the currency is worth what markets say it is worth.

For a brief time, the world's major economies tried to keep their exchange rates fixed even without the link to gold. Every currency was set or locked in compared with the dollar and as a result with one another. This system was adopted because it provided greater predictability to governments and businesses than "floating" (constantly adjusting) rates; one could enter a deal knowing in advance just what it would cost in the local currency months or years later.

Fixed currencies did not prove to be steadier and more predictable in practice, because markets had their own views about the relative worth of currencies. When markets lost confidence in a currency, governments that wanted to maintain the fixed exchange rate were forced to spend their currency reserves (usually dollars) to purchase their own currency. At some point, however, the government would run out of reserves, the difference would become unsustainable, and the government would be forced to "devalue" its currency, essentially acknowledging the lower value set by markets. Such moves proved to be economically disruptive and politically damaging to the governments in question. And on the other side of the ledger, the United States grew frustrated that some countries with chronic surpluses didn't want to "revalue"— change the value of their currencies up—a move that would have made their exports more expensive and imports cheaper, outcomes that would have reduced their trade surplus, helped producers and exporters elsewhere, and limited their dollar holdings.

After the end of a global system of fixed exchange rates based on the dollar, countries were left free to pick their own currency and monetary system. Most countries have come to forgo fixed rates and accept the market price. Letting the market set the value of your currency also frees a country's central bank to set monetary policy as it sees fit. But not everyone has chosen to let the market set the value of their currency. The countries of Europe, for example, moved toward a system where their currencies were anchored first to the German mark and then to the euro, when they entered into the monetary and currency union that created it. And even governments that mostly let the market set the value of their currency do not, however, necessarily adopt a completely "hands-off" posture; they sometimes intervene in currency markets to buy or sell their own currency in an effort to moderate fluctuations. Such a situation is often described as a "managed float" as opposed to a purely floating rate.

The United States continues to run a trade deficit, importing considerably more than it exports in the way of goods and services. Again, the rest of the world is content with this so long as it is confident that the value of the dollar will remain relatively steady and the U.S. economy will remain healthy and able to buy their exports. The net outflow of dollars associated with the trade deficit is a source of useful liquidity (funds) to the world, enabling it to grow faster than it otherwise would. But it could become a source of instability if excessive trade deficits cause a loss of confidence in the health of the dollar and reduce the willingness of others to accept it as the de facto global currency. If that were to happen, the U.S. central bank (the Federal Reserve) could find itself having to raise interest rates even as unemployment was rising. The need to stabilize the dollar would take precedence over economic growth.

For now and for the foreseeable future, the dollar is both the national currency of the United States and the de facto international currency of the world. This is mostly good for the United States, because it leaves it with control over its own economic fate and means that when it must borrow, it does so in its own currency and does not have to worry that the amount it owes increases because of shifts in relative currency values. Because demand for the dollar pushes down interest rates, the U.S. government, companies, and households can also borrow at cheaper rates. France's minister of finance in the 1960s Valéry Giscard d'Estaing famously called this an "exorbitant privilege."

Some see a dollar-dominated world as a mixed blessing. The rest of the world is affected by U.S. monetary policy but has little influence over it. The Federal Reserve, or the Fed, is responsible for setting U.S. monetary policy in response to conditions in the United States, not in response to the needs of the global economy. But the adjustment of interest rates by the Federal Reserve for the purpose of managing inflation or maximizing employment in the United States affects other economies as well, especially those that still fix their exchange rate to the dollar or have accumulated debt in dollars.

At least in principle, the dollar could be replaced by another currency, a number of them (a basket), a new international currency, a cryptocurrency, or some combination. It is remarkable that even during the global financial crisis of 2008–2009, which started in the United States, the dollar rallied and remained the favored currency for investors. There is no other country with an economy of sufficient size and with a currency that can be traded freely anywhere in the world that enjoys the requisite amount of confidence. Japan is too small; the future of the euro is too uncertain. China, the world's second-largest economy, is not prepared to allow its currency to float, preferring the greater predictability of a managed exchange rate, and it continues to want to control the flow of money into—and out of—the country. A basket of currencies requires a degree of coordination that doesn't exist, although it could emerge if enough governments lost confidence in the United States. There is no independent world central bank, so an international currency is not a serious option, although the IMF issues a limited amount of special drawing rights that are used to bolster the financial reserves of member countries and some argue could one day evolve into an international currency. The world is a long way away from such a point, however. The dollar is not perfect, but in the land of the blind the one-eyed man is king, and for now the dollar is the proverbial one-eyed man.

What could change things? As other economies grow and become more open, they may be both willing and able to take on the role of a reserve currency. China obviously comes to mind here. Change could also come about if the world comes to have concerns over the health or management of the U.S. economy. The large and growing pool of U.S. debt, now above $22 trillion and increasing at around $1 trillion a year, could dilute confidence in the dollar. And there is the increasing U.S. propensity to "weaponize" international financial transactions to sanction select governments and individuals, a practice that could well hasten a move to dollar alternatives. For instance, after the United States withdrew from the Iran nuclear agreement, European countries tried, so far unsuccessfully, to build a parallel international financial system that would have allowed them to process financial transactions with Iran while avoiding U.S. sanctions.

There are additional arrangements that contribute to the smooth functioning of the global economy. There is a large degree of interconnectedness to the world, and there are several groups (the Basel Committee on Banking Supervision, the Financial Stability Board, and others) that set standards for banking practices to reduce the chances that a crisis within an individual country will spread across borders. The 2008 global financial crisis was primarily triggered by economic mismanagement in the United States, but it affected every other country in the world given the centrality of the American economy.

All of which brings us back to where this chapter began: there is a global economy, a degree of global coordination, and a de facto global currency, but there is no global central bank or common understanding on monetary arrangements. This reality has mostly worked well; economic growth, investment and trade flows, gains in development—all are a testament to a "system" that has been, for the most part, effective. At the same time, the system remains vulnerable not just to the effects of national policies in the United States but, because of interconnectedness (globalization) and the potential for what is known as contagion, to the knock-on effects of a financial crisis in any country of scale. This situation is best understood as a condition to be managed rather than a problem to be solved because governments will not be willing to give up control of their own economies to some international authority.

Development

Development is a widely used term that reflects more than economic growth. It also captures the degree to which a country's wealth has kept up with or, better yet, surpassed population increases, how well any increased wealth is distributed throughout the population, and measures reflecting the quality of life. Development is most often associated with the economic condition of relatively poor countries (variously described as "underdeveloped," "least developed," or "developing").

There is no clear line separating developing countries from developed ones. The World Bank has rejected the distinction as overly simplistic and separates countries according to per capita income (a measure of the value of what a country produces in a single year divided by the number of people living there), a good approximation of an average citizen's standard of living. Countries are then determined to be either low income, lower middle income, upper middle income, or high income. GDP per capita ranges from above $160,000 in Monaco and $80,000 in Switzerland to under $500 in Burundi, South Sudan, Malawi, Niger, Madagascar, Mozambique, and Somalia. Although the American economy is not quite twice the size of China's, GDP per capita in the United States ($60,000) is six times that of China because the American population is but one-fourth that of China's.

. . .

There is now agreement that any assessment of development must reflect a range of social factors, with the favored measure being the Human Development Index (HDI), which ranks countries according to an overall assessment of per capita wealth, educational attainment, and life expectancy. According to the latest HDI rankings, Norway enjoys the highest human development, while the United States comes in at number 13, China at 86, and Niger last. Human development has improved all over the world: between 1990 and 2015, the number of countries classified as having low human development fell from sixty-two to forty-one, while those classified as having very high human development rose from eleven to fifty-one. At the same time, progress has slowed since 2010.

The term "development" first gained currency after World War II, initially in regard to European countries that had been ravaged by the war and faced the challenge of getting back on their feet. Indeed, the formal name of the World Bank (created in 1944, before the war had even come to an end) is the International Bank for Reconstruction and Development. Over time, the notion of development became less associated with European countries, because many of them recovered fairly quickly thanks to the massive economic assistance that was provided by the United States under the Marshall Plan, their own efforts, and the emergence of what began as the European Coal and Steel Community and would later evolve into the European Community and eventually the European Union. Development came to be associated much more with poor countries in Africa, Asia, the Middle East, and Latin America. Many of these countries found themselves newly independent following the demise of the colonial era, and they were unprepared for the demands that independence brought with it.

Why did development become such an important issue, and why does it remain so today? Humanitarian concerns are a substantial factor; the quality of the lives of billions of men, women, and children are

HUMAN DEVELOPMENT INDEX, 2017

○ Education index   ▲ Income index   ■ Life expectancy index

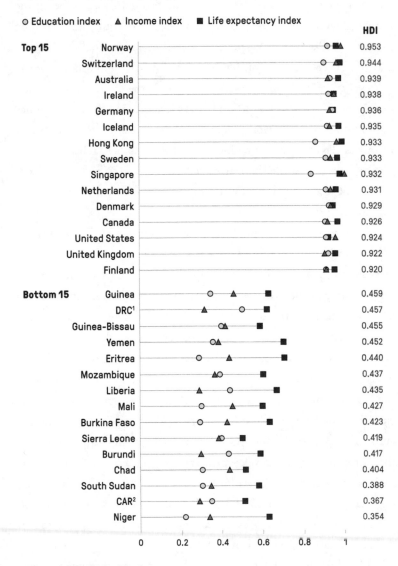

	HDI
Top 15	
Norway	0.953
Switzerland	0.944
Australia	0.939
Ireland	0.938
Germany	0.936
Iceland	0.935
Hong Kong	0.933
Sweden	0.933
Singapore	0.932
Netherlands	0.931
Denmark	0.929
Canada	0.926
United States	0.924
United Kingdom	0.922
Finland	0.920
Bottom 15	
Guinea	0.459
DRC[1]	0.457
Guinea-Bissau	0.455
Yemen	0.452
Eritrea	0.440
Mozambique	0.437
Liberia	0.435
Mali	0.427
Burkina Faso	0.423
Sierra Leone	0.419
Burundi	0.417
Chad	0.404
South Sudan	0.388
CAR[2]	0.367
Niger	0.354

1. Democratic Republic of the Congo

2. Central African Republic

Source: United Nations Development Programme.

at stake. There is also an economic interest, in that billions of people in developing countries are potential consumers and producers. National security is a factor as well, in that a lack of development can create venues where terrorists or criminals or pirates can put down roots, where radicalism can flourish, and where infectious disease can spring up and spread. A lack of development can also produce conditions that generate refugees, who in turn can overwhelm the capacity of neighbors, in the process creating additional weak states.

National security issues caused development to get caught up in the Cold War competition between the United States and the Soviet Union. The United States saw development as essential in order to prevent disaffected populations from turning to local Communists who would in turn look to the Soviet Union for assistance. Showing that market-oriented approaches to development were superior to central, government-dominated planning was part of the competitive struggle between systems that was central to the Cold War. The Soviet Union did much the same, although it emphasized centrally planned economies much like its own. Both superpowers dispatched a good deal of foreign aid to countries to either keep them in their camp or woo them to their side.

Considerable development took place in the decades after World War II and, more recently, following the end of the Cold War. The proportion of people living in extreme poverty (defined as those living on less than $1.90 per day) is down from 40–50 percent of the world's population fifty years ago and more than one-third of the population as recently as 1990 to under 10 percent today. Nearly 1.1 billion people have moved out of extreme poverty since 1990. China's economic boom has driven much of this improvement, because its extreme poverty rate plummeted from 66 percent in 1990 to less than 1 percent in 2015.

Two centuries ago, less than 20 percent of the world's people were literate, but now more than 85 percent of the world's people can read and write, with adult male literacy rates a few points higher than that and adult female rates a few points lower. The percentage of those who are undernourished worldwide is also down, while life expectancy has improved by some twenty-five years on average compared with seventy years ago. As a result, the gap between the expected duration of the average life in developed countries and the average life in the developing ones has narrowed markedly. The average number of years of education that people receive in the developing world more than tripled between 1950 and 2010. Access to improved sanitation and clean drinking water is up, while child and maternal mortality is down.

New technologies have the potential to foster development. By the end of 2018, there were more than 7.5 billion mobile cellular subscriptions, averaging just over one for every person on the planet. The number of internet users reached 1 billion in 2005 and is now estimated to stand at 3.9 billion, or just over half the people on the planet. Such technologies can provide access to education and health care, connect farmers and small manufacturers with useful market data, and enable banking. Eighty percent of those in developed countries use the internet, as do 45 percent of those in developing countries. This latter number is growing fast: in 2005, only 15 million Africans had access to the internet, but by 2016 this number had climbed to nearly 200 million.

At the same time, much remains to be done before development is a reality for many. Approximately ten percent of the world's population still lives in extreme poverty, is undernourished, is illiterate, and lacks access to electricity. Almost everyone in the wealthier developed countries can read and write, but two in five African adults cannot, which nevertheless represents gains in literacy there. Nearly 900 million people still practice open defecation. Many girls and women still face discrimination and a host of barriers to realizing their full potential. Projected rapid increases in population in South Asia and sub-Saharan Africa could dilute any progress that comes to pass. For instance, while the proportion of Africans living in extreme poverty has declined, due to rapid population growth the number of Africans living in extreme poverty has increased by over 100 million over the past quarter century. Climate change will be an added burden. The bottom line is that nearly one billion people still live in a situation assessed to be one of low human development.

In addition, inequality has increased both between and within many countries given differences in how both economies and populations have grown. In the world as a whole, the top 10 percent holds 85 percent of global wealth. Further, overall gains in living standards do not mean that everyone has achieved the basics.

Despite considerable progress, development remains a pressing issue. Many debates surround the policies designed to promote development. The most basic is the question of the appropriate role of the state and whether it is better to embrace a directed, top-down approach to development or to take a bottom-up approach in which the state takes a backseat to market forces and private interests. This debate has survived the end of the Cold War and continues to this day, between those taking a more market-oriented and democratic path (for example, India) and those favoring a large government role, which can bring with it more economic progress but less personal freedom. China is most often held out as the exemplar of this latter approach.

In truth, the choices are less stark than they may appear because most countries combine elements of both approaches. Still, there are clear differences of degree. Those countries favoring a large role for the government do so for economic and political reasons alike. The government can name priorities and choose where investment goes, rewarding constituents or allies. Economic control tends to translate into political control. Some (but not all) of the uncertainties associated with markets can be reduced.

There are many paths available to countries regardless of their level of development. In some cases, the government may choose to close off selected areas of its market to imports in order to nurture homegrown industries not ready to compete successfully with foreign producers, something known as "import substitution" or the "infant industry argument." Such protectionist policies can provide time and space for domestic industries and agriculture to gain strength so that they can compete successfully with imports and hold their own as exporters. The danger is that because local producers are shielded from foreign competition, they can be costly, generate products of lesser quality, and be prone to corruption. There is also the reality that this approach may not be sustainable, because others are likely to tire of one-sided trading relationships in which their exports do not enjoy the same sort of access to the market of the developing country—especially if the developing country turns into a manufacturing and exporting superpower as has China.

Another way governments can foster development is by providing subsidies to select industries and agriculture, something that can give them huge advantages when it comes to competing with those who must pay for capital, raw materials, or labor at market prices. The beneficiaries of subsidies are often state-owned enterprises that enjoy actual or near-monopoly power. Governments can also help domestic producers by limiting foreign investment (again to shield locals from competition). And governments can require foreign companies that do invest to transfer their technology to local firms in ways that will eventually make the host country more competitive.

An alternative approach to economic development emphasizes reduced government subsidies, the privatization of state-owned enterprises, provision of incentives to foreign investors, a sound currency to promote investment and savings, reasonable tax policies that provide a mix of incentives for individuals and businesses, safeguards against corruption and out-of-control public spending often associated with government subsidy, and defined property rights so land and buildings can attract investment and be collateral for loans.

Again, trade can be an engine of development, but in a way that involves less government protection, be it through tariffs, other barriers, or limits on foreign investment. Openness to trade can both generate high-quality jobs tied to exports and provide consumers access to the best products produced elsewhere, a value both in and of itself and as a stimulus to modernize and improve. Trade is also less prone to corruption and misallocation than assistance. Poorer countries often have a built-in advantage of lower labor costs, something that makes their products less expensive and hence more competitive. To be viable, however, trade requires access to foreign markets (and sometimes favored access, for example, by increasing quotas or reducing tariffs), something that often cannot be achieved unless it is explicitly negotiated.

There is no right or wrong approach to development. China has done remarkably well thus far, but at the cost of political freedom, environmental damage, creating a society (through enforced limits on family size) in which there will be insufficient working-age men and women to support the elderly, large inefficiencies that have wasted great sums of money, and widespread corruption. Other countries such as South Korea have done well by following a more market-oriented path. They have been willing to live with greater uncertainty and the ups and downs of economic cycles in order to achieve high growth rates, limit the political reach of the government, and reduce both the chance of massive corruption and the inefficiencies stemming from misguided central planning.

There are long-standing debates about the utility of foreign aid (sometimes called foreign assistance) as a development tool. Here it is necessary to distinguish among aid for development purposes, aid designed to meet humanitarian needs—be it to help a country recover from a natural disaster, care for refugees, provide basic health care, or donate food to ward off hunger—and aid provided to allies deemed to be strategically critical for general foreign policy purposes, which can consist of military training, arms transfers, or general budgetary support.

Development aid or assistance tends to be focused on providing funds either for specific projects or for helping people directly. What we do know is that aid targeting education pays off, especially when it is focused on the education of girls and women, where reductions in illiteracy and the development of skills can reduce pregnancies, improve the health of children, and lead to productive small-scale economic activity. Studies also show that aid aimed at improving health and increasing access to energy is useful. Specific channeling of aid to such basic needs coupled with careful monitoring appears to be the best approach. Insufficiently targeted aid can perpetuate inefficiencies and lead to corruption and tends to be wasted on expensive vanity projects.

Some things are true of all successful countries. Predictability matters. Companies need to feel confident that their assets will not arbitrarily be seized, that they will be able to market and sell what they produce, and that they can bring a reasonable share of the profits back home. It is no less true that development can only take place (or advance at a meaningful rate) in a context of stability. This translates into both political stability (along with good governance) and physical security, because economic development struggles in their absence. People need to be able to go to school, to work, and to shops. Conflicts will interrupt economic activity and scare off investment and tourists. It is noteworthy that two countries whose HDI ratings have dropped the most in recent years, Syria and Libya, are experiencing serious, prolonged armed conflict.

While there are multiple paths to developing a nation, there are some strategies that have clearly been useful. The introduction of new technologies and training of skilled laborers can translate to increases in productivity. Foreign trade and inbound investments can be a real engine for these improvements. Countries that shift their economic focus away from small-scale agriculture into manufacturing, a change that goes hand in hand with increased urbanization, have also seen boosts to their development. Enforcing the rule of law, property rights protections, and access to capital are vital. Citizens need opportunities, and eliminating barriers to them, especially ones rooted in discrimination based on gender, religion, or ethnicity, is a boon to a country's quality of life. Investments in education and infrastructure pay dividends. And nations are rewarded for a gradual integration with the rest of the world—as opposed to a rapid integration early in the development process. Countries should look to diversify their economic activities so they can employ more people and provide alternatives to dependence on individual commodities. Relying on commodities such as oil can look good statistically (in terms of the GDP per capita) but in reality can be counterproductive because it lends itself to corruption and can discourage employment-generating economic activity.

In recent decades, countries of the world have joined together in the United Nations to set goals for development. The first set of goals, the Millennium Development Goals, were adopted by the United Nations in 2000. The specific objectives were to eradicate extreme poverty and hunger; achieve universal primary education; promote gender equality and empower women; reduce child mortality; improve maternal health; combat HIV/AIDS, malaria, and other diseases; and adopt better and more sustainable environmental practices. The intention was to achieve these goals or at least meaningful progress toward them by 2015. As might be expected, the record was mixed. Percentages of extreme poverty, malnourishment, and maternal and child mortality all came down, but the overall number of those in extreme poverty stayed high given population increases. Gender bias and inequality persisted, the number of displaced persons and refugees ballooned, and the effects of climate change grew more severe. And even where there was progress (such as in the dramatic reduction of extreme poverty in China), foreign aid played a negligible role.

The subsequent set of goals, adopted in 2015, are the seventeen Sustainable Development Goals. These cover all of the concerns of the previous goals but with added emphasis on reducing hunger and inequality, protecting people from violent crime and sex trafficking, and ensuring growth does not come at the expense of climate-related concerns. Progress will require concerted effort on the part of governments, international agencies, foundations, businesses, and NGOs. The aim is to see real progress by or before 2030. The expectation is that the record will be uneven, underscoring the reality that development is not just a historical phenomenon but a continuing one.

Part IV

○—————○

ORDER
AND
DISORDER

istory can be understood as an ongoing narrative of world orders materializing, breaking down, and reemerging in another form. At its core, world order is a description and a measure of the world's condition at a particular moment or over a specified period of time. World order is a matter of degree and trend, akin to an assessment of an individual's health in that it reflects a mix of positive and negative elements and can be understood either as a snapshot or as a moving picture.

Order tends to reflect the degree to which there are widely accepted rules as to how international relations ought to be carried out and the degree to which there is a balance of power to buttress those rules so that those who disagree with them are not tempted to violate them or are likely to fail if in fact they do. Any measure of order necessarily includes elements of both order and disorder and the balance between them. There is never total peace, much less complete justice and equality in the world.

All this raises a fundamental question: Why does world order matter as much as it does? When it is in short supply between countries, and in particular the major powers of the day, the loss of life and the absorption of resources can be enormous and the threat to prosperity and freedom substantial. This is the lesson of the two world wars that defined the first half of the twentieth century. This is why world order is so basic, because its existence or absence translates into benefits or costs for everyone given how interconnected the world now is. It is the international relations equivalent of oxygen: with it cooperation on virtually every front becomes possible, while without it prospects for progress fade.

The Australian academic Hedley Bull, in his seminal book *The Anarchical Society*, writes about international *systems* and international *society*. It is a distinction with a difference. An international system is what exists absent any policy decisions; countries and other entities along with various forces simply interact with and affect one another. There is little or nothing in the way of choice or regulation or principles or rules. What distinguishes an international society from a system is that a society reflects a degree of buy-in on the part of its participants, including an acceptance of limits on what is either sought or discouraged, how it is to be sought or discouraged, or both. Elements of a society exist when governments do not use force to resolve disputes, instead turning to diplomacy, or, more positively, when they observe established rules on trade and band together to address climate change, refugees, proliferation, and terrorism.

In the international sphere, the notion of "society" as described by Bull has specific meaning. First, the principal "citizens" of this society are countries. Second, a founding principle of this society is that the governments and leaders who oversee the countries are essentially free to act as they wish within their own borders. How those individuals come to occupy positions of authority, be it by birth, revolution, elections, or some other means, matters not. Third, the members of this international society respect and accept this freedom of action on the part of others (in exchange for others in turn accepting that they can act as they wish within their own borders) and also the existence of other members of this society. It is not far off to describe this approach to international relations as a "live and let live" cross-border understanding.

The title of *The Anarchical Society* captures the essence of the book, namely, that at any moment in history there are forces promoting anarchy in the world and forces promoting society. The words "chaos" and "disorder" could be substituted for "anarchy," and "order" for "society," but whatever the choice of words, the idea could not be clearer. What gives any moment or era of history its character is the balance between these forces. Indeed, it is akin to the balance sheet of a business, but instead of revenues and expenses, or assets and liabilities, what is at issue is the combined strength of those forces tearing the world apart as opposed to those bringing it together.

The framing works for all three previous sections of this book. Each of the four historical eras covered can be understood through the lens of order. The emergence of the modern notion of sovereignty, along with trade, increased order, but the rise of nationalism and the erosion of the balance of power ultimately overwhelmed it and resulted in World War I. Similarly, World War II came about through failures of diplomacy, the reemergence of strident nationalism, the rise of protectionism, and a failure to maintain a balance of power. By contrast, the Cold War stayed cold because forces of order, including diplomacy, arms control, nuclear deterrence, and the NATO alliance, more than offset competing ideologies, proxy wars, a nuclear arms race, the division of Germany and Europe, and more. And as discussed, the character of the post–Cold War era is still being determined, although it is not difficult to identify numerous elements of what Bull terms anarchy and I describe as disarray in my previous book.

This framing can also work at the regional level. The Middle East is the way it is because of the preponderance of forces of anarchy and the relative paucity of those promoting order. In Asia the balance is or at least was markedly different, which goes a long way to explaining why the region has been so successful over the past few decades. What makes Europe worrisome is the erosion on that continent of the main elements of what Bull described as society and the rise of new sources of anarchy. Both Latin America and Africa are characterized by order between countries but in many instances disorder and at times something much worse within them.

And at the global level, what we have seen is that in each domain there are again elements of order and disorder, but that in most of these areas the gap between the two is growing, as the result of governments and others falling short in their willingness or ability to contend with challenges. This reality holds for many of globalization's realms, in particular those of climate change and cyberspace.

The specifics of what goes into any balance sheet obviously change. The approach of this final section, then, is to discuss order and disorder in a manner that is likely to prove useful no matter what happens with the particulars. It will thus focus on enduring features of both order and disorder to give you the tools you need to understand both the state of play and the trends at the regional and global levels.

Sovereignty, Self-Determination, and Balance of Power

The bedrock of world order, since the Treaty of Westphalia that ended the Thirty Years' War in Europe in the mid-seventeenth century, has been respect for sovereignty and the idea that borders ought not to be changed forcibly. This has become the closest there is to a universal principle promoting order in the world. Only countries, sometimes referred to as states, nations, or nation-states, can claim sovereignty.

Sovereignty is closely tied to the supremacy of governmental authority within a country's given borders. This applies to all who live or happen to be present there regardless of the form of government. Individuals and other entities such as corporations have rights, but on most issues they must respect the ultimate authority of the national government and those who act in its name unless the constitution or law of the country provides otherwise. The specifics are for the government and in some cases people of particular countries to decide.

Sovereignty also has an international dimension. Unlike the domestic definition, sovereignty in the international context connotes equality. All countries, no matter what their size or population or power or wealth, are equal in their rights, above all in the notion that their borders are to be respected by other states. Noninterference in the internal affairs of another country is a hallmark of sovereignty and the current world order.

A political entity qualifies as a sovereign country if it possesses supreme political authority and, to paraphrase the nineteenth-century German sociologist Max Weber's famous conception, a monopoly on the legitimate use of force within its borders. In other words, it can enforce its laws and punish those who break them, and its citizens recognize the government's authority to do so. The government is supposed to be able to control its borders and regulate all that enters and leaves its territory, from goods to people. In return, a country has the ability to adopt the domestic policies of its choosing. Finally, a country is one recognized by its peers, that is, other sovereign countries. Normally, this recognition manifests itself in the establishment of embassies, the exchange of ambassadors, and diplomatic interactions such as concluding treaties. The UN General Assembly is composed only of entities, that is to say countries, that meet or at their time of entry were thought to meet these criteria. The United Nations currently recognizes 193 countries in the world.

Sovereignty is widely considered near but not quite absolute. An ongoing debate is tied to the question of whether there ought to be legitimate grounds for intervening (including with military force) in the internal affairs of other countries, for example, to prevent genocide, defined as the purposeful destruction of a group of people based on their race, religion, ethnicity, or national identity. Central to this debate is whether order ought to reflect more than relations between countries and take into account what goes on within them.

In recent years, there has been an effort to rebalance the rights of the state and the rights of the individual away from the former and toward the latter. Under this line of thinking, sovereignty is something of a contract between a government and both its citizens and other governments, and when a government is unable or unwilling to live up to its responsibilities, it forfeits some of the rights that normally come with being sovereign. One of these rights is the presumption of noninterference and a free hand for it to do what it wants at home. Eleven years after the civil war and genocide that took place in Rwanda in 1994, the world embraced the Responsibility to Protect doctrine (commonly referred to as R2P), which in principle provides a basis for interventions by other countries or regional or global organizations (be it with words, sanctions, or even military force) in situations in which a government carries out or fails to prevent mass atrocities against people living in its territory.

In practice, the R2P doctrine has not fared well. The United States and its NATO allies invoked R2P to justify their intervention in Libya in 2011, but several governments (above all China and Russia) came to view the doctrine with suspicion when what began as a humanitarian effort to deter attacks against civilians morphed into an effort to oust the ruling regime. It also turns out that R2P can be extraordinarily difficult and costly to carry out, something that helps to explain why the world did little when some 500,000 Syrians lost their lives and a majority of the population was made homeless because of a conflict in Syria that its government has played a central role in. There is also the reality that many governments, including China, Russia, and India, tend to resist any exception to the notion of absolute sovereignty out of concern that a precedent could be established that might be used to constrain what it is they do or would like to do within their own borders.

In addition, when a government allows a terrorist group to operate freely in its territory, it cannot expect its borders to be respected by actual or would-be victims of that terrorism. This was the case with the Taliban-led Afghan government, which saw its sovereign rights violated after it allowed al-Qaeda to use Afghanistan as a base from which to carry out the September 11, 2001, terrorist attacks against the United States. Similarly, when one country violates the sovereignty of another country directly, be it with military force or cyberattacks, it legitimizes retaliation against it either in kind or with other means chosen by the victim.

Russia merits special mention given much of the above. On the one hand, its belief in sovereignty is near absolute lest others "interfere" with what goes on politically in Russia. At the same time, Russia has intervened militarily in Ukraine, seizing Crimea and undermining the government's authority in other parts of the country. In addition, Russia employed various tools in the domain of cyberspace and social media in order to influence the outcome of the 2016 presidential election in the United States. What all this reveals is that respect for even the most basic of international rules is far from universal.

It should be added that sovereignty can also be voluntarily constrained or even ceded or delegated. This, for example, is what countries do inside the European Union, where they pool their sovereignty, allowing the EU's various organs to make decisions that affect them. Other countries do something similar in the World Trade Organization. In all such cases, governments do so out of the belief that on balance their interests are better served by engaging in collective decision making even if occasionally decisions are made that they disagree with. What is critical in all these cases is that the transfer of sovereignty is partial and voluntary and can be rescinded at any time.

Sovereign states and their governments are not the only pieces on the chessboard in the international system. There are also corporations, nongovernmental organizations such as Amnesty International, Doctors Without Borders, and Greenpeace, foundations, members of the media, religious authorities, governors and mayors, and regional and global organizations—not to mention terrorists, drug cartels, and pirates. The reality is that while countries usually wield more power and influence than other actors, they are not alone in their ability to do so, and they are not always in a position to prevent others from asserting themselves. The result is a world defined more by the principle that state sovereignty is dominant than by the reality.

SELF-DETERMINATION

One issue tied to sovereignty is that of self-determination, or the notion that people have the right to choose whether they want a country of their own. Many countries contain within them people with different religions, languages, and, in some cases, tribes or other associations. The question naturally arises as to what criteria should be used to determine which groups or territories get to become independent countries and who should decide these criteria. No international consensus exists on the answer to either question. For instance, Taiwan fits all of the criteria of a sovereign state. Its governing authorities command a monopoly on the use of force, and it has its own military, central bank, and independent political system. Yet fewer than two dozen countries recognize it as a sovereign country due to China's claim over the island. In addition, although the United States and more than one hundred other countries recognize Kosovo as an independent country, dozens of countries including China, Russia, and its neighbor Serbia have not granted it recognition. In other words, sovereignty lies in the eyes of the beholder. This is less central than it was after World War II, when much of the Middle East, Africa, and South Asia was colonized by European countries. But the issue has not gone away, because there are groups that want, but do not have, a country of their own and areas within countries that wish to be independent.

What self-determination means in the current context is unclear. The phrase "respect for the principle of equal rights and self-determination of peoples" can be found more than once in the UN Charter, but it was one thing for self-determination to be a widely embraced principle in the colonial era and something else altogether for it to apply in a world in which there are already more than 190 countries. There is no easy solution for how to determine the appropriate stance of governments toward situations in which a group of people push for a state of their own. A good start, though, would be to amend the concept of self-determination and replace it with the notion that statehood is something to be granted as well as asserted. Given that the impact of a group seeking independence can ripple across the region in question or even the globe, too many people are affected by these decisions to allow statehood to be determined solely by the party seeking it.

In the future, support for what has been called self-determination is likely to be less common than was the case in the era of decolonization. That said, existing governments should agree to consider bids for statehood in cases where there is historical justification, a compelling rationale, support from the population in question, and a viable territory for the new state. The impact on the country that would give up a portion of its territory and population should be weighed. Governments should agree to consult with one another before reaching a decision as well as with the parties involved. One useful precedent here is the 1978 Camp David Accords between Egypt and Israel, which did not extend the principle of self-determination to the Palestinians but rather supported the notion that "representatives of the Palestinian people should participate in negotiations on the resolution of the Palestinian problem in all its aspects."

BALANCE OF POWER AND DETERRENCE

Order cannot be based on support for the principle of sovereignty alone. It must also be grounded in a balance of power, which means that those who oppose the order are not able to overturn it through armed force.

It is unrealistic to base order on the hope or expectation that countries will demonstrate restraint or respect toward others out of goodwill. Ideally, the balance of power would be such that they are not even tempted to try to alter the status quo through force, calculating that any such attempt would fail or at least that its costs would outweigh its benefits. This is the essence of deterrence. What is critical for deterrence to work, though, is both sufficient military capability and the perceived willingness to use it. This is true whether one is talking about major powers at the global level or medium powers at the regional level.

Order and the balance of power buttressing it can take many forms. There can be a single dominant country or empire, which is then referred to as a hegemon; this tends to be described as either a unipolar world (for example, the status of the United States just after the end of the Cold War) or an imperial order, as was the case in parts of the ancient world. Order can also be based on having two major powers; this was the case during the four decades of the Cold War in which the United States and the Soviet Union dominated a bipolar world. Other periods of history (early and mid-nineteenth-century Europe comes to mind) have been characterized by an order based on several major powers operating in a multipolar world. We may be moving in the direction of such a world.

Alliances and Coalitions

Whatever the number of powers, order can be either strengthened or undermined by alliances. An alliance is a collection of countries that have come together to promote what they see as their common security interests. All alliances enshrine a formal commitment or obligation to provide military—and possibly other kinds of—support if any member of the alliance is attacked or faces the immediate likelihood of being attacked. Alliances can involve the provision of assistance (be it military, economic, or intelligence), joint exercises, and at least some coordination of decision making both to prepare for potential contingencies and to help to deter them. What alliances require is the capability and the will to meet a commitment; an alliance cannot succeed if either is absent.

The decision to form or join an alliance normally represents a judgment that the benefits of membership outweigh the costs and obligations and are preferable to standing alone. As Winston Churchill once quipped, "There is only one thing worse than fighting with allies, and that is fighting without them."

Alliances are not good or bad per se. They can be a grouping designed to balance or offset a threat (be it a single country or a rival alliance) or to overthrow the existing order and replace it with another.

Alliances, depending on their composition and aims, can either contribute to world order or detract from it. Each country need not be in a position to deter or defeat aggression from every potential adversary. That said, countries that wish to join forces to overturn the existing order can also form alliances to help them do so. As is often the case, what matters most are the purposes to which arrangements are put, not the arrangements themselves.

Alliances are as old as international relations. Alliances were prevalent in ancient Greece and in medieval Europe. Somewhat more recently, alliances were central to both the outbreak of and fighting in World Wars I and II.

A good deal of history is determined by strong countries that threaten or use armed force to assert their will over weaker neighbors. When this happens, weaker countries may enter into an alliance with one or more stronger countries so that the threatening neighbor no longer enjoys an advantage. Or they can defer to the stronger country, essentially giving up some of their freedom of choice and action in order to stay on its good side and avoid the costs of conflict.

Such deference goes by many terms. It is sometimes described as *droit de regard*—a French term literally meaning a right of inspection—which involves giving another government a large say in one's own decisions. During the Cold War, the phrase "Finlandization" was in vogue, something that derived from Finland's careful relationship with its much more powerful neighbor, the Soviet Union. In the run-up to World War II, "appeasement" was the term used to describe how the Western democracies tried (unsuccessfully) to limit Nazi Germany's ambitions by giving it some of what it sought in the hope that its ambitions could be satisfied. The great advantage of entering into an alliance is that it provides weaker countries with an option other than going it alone militarily or, more realistically, submitting to the wishes of a stronger neighbor.

Alliances played a major role in shaping international relations in the aftermath of World War II. What was fundamentally different during this period was that the United States and a group of eleven other countries opted for a peacetime alliance. As discussed earlier in the context of the history of modern Europe, the North Atlantic Alliance, more formally known as the North Atlantic Treaty Organization, was created in 1949 at the outset of the Cold War in response to a perceived threat emanating from the Soviet Union. Membership was extended to those countries that shared this outlook and embraced core democratic values. The opposing bloc, the Warsaw Pact, was founded in 1955 and included the Soviet Union and seven "satellite" countries that had little choice but to follow Moscow's lead.

Alliances have multiple purposes. The most fundamental is to deter and if need be defend against external foes. For a weaker state, joining with others (and in particular with one or more strong partners) can constitute the only realistic path to sustaining security and true independence if it is faced with a powerful and potentially hostile neighbor. Strategic independence or autonomy is for most countries not a sustainable proposition. The cost of joining an alliance is to accept the reality that the stronger partner will have significant influence over the weaker partner's decisions and potentially reduce its autonomy.

For strong countries, alliances provide a means for bolstering the ability to deter or wage war or to pursue other objectives. Allies can be a force multiplier, something that has provided and continues to provide the United States a big advantage over both Russia and China, which mostly act on their own in the world and cannot expect to receive assistance from others should they need it. An alliance can provide a channel for enhancing influence or even control, imposing some restraint on the foreign policies of its members. And the provision of guarantees can reduce the incentive for member states to develop certain capabilities of their own, such as nuclear weapons. For example,

America's alliances with countries such as Japan and South Korea reduce the need for them to develop or acquire nuclear weapons of their own. An alliance also gives them confidence so that they need not be intimidated by strong countries seeking to pressure or threaten them. No matter how strong an alliance is, the weaker partner is always worried to some degree that it will be left to fend for itself in a time of crisis. The French leader Charles de Gaulle often voiced his skepticism that the United States would risk the destruction of New York in order to save Paris, a concern that led France beginning in the 1950s to develop its own nuclear force.

But even for a strong country an alliance involves risks and costs. It can find itself pushed into or worse yet trapped in situations not of its own choosing by the actions of an alliance member. It can also find itself constrained on occasion by what allies are not prepared to support or do. And even if such situations do not arise, alliances can require expensive military investments by the strongest member if the alliance as a whole is to be credible.

For weak and strong countries alike, alliances constitute a major commitment of resources and involve potentially far-reaching obligations and consequences. NATO, for example, explicitly states in Article 5 of its charter that an attack on one is an attack on all, meaning that all will respond militarily regardless of whether they themselves are directly attacked. An alliance is only as credible as its members make it. It is essential that there be clarity as to what triggers the obligations central to the alliance and what those obligations are.

The inequality between what members of an alliance bring to it can be a source of tension. "Burden sharing" is never equal; it is not just that each member possesses different military and economic capacity but that each has its domestic politics that often limit what it is able to contribute. NATO has often been roiled by American frustrations over the failure of most European members to meet the agreed goal of spending at least 2 percent of their GDP on defense. This can be overdone because what matters more than such calculations is how money is spent and whether the benefits derived from the alliance outweigh the costs, however unevenly they may be borne, which has been the case both here and for the United States in Asia.

Alliances are creatures of their context. When that context changes—in particular, when the situation that triggered the building of an alliance fades or disappears—there are several options. First, the alliance can cease, a victim of its own success. This was the case after both world wars for the victorious alliances.

An alliance can also disappear when it is defeated and is no longer permitted to exist by the victors or desired by its members. This was the case with the alliance among Germany, Japan, and Italy after World War II and then again with the Soviet-dominated Warsaw Pact after the conclusion of the Cold War.

A successful alliance (one that has prevailed in some struggle) has additional options. It can remain in existence but ratchet down what it does or prepares to do. Another option is to find new and different things to do, and if it happens to be an alliance with geographic limits, it can change those limits and find new places to be active. In the aftermath of the Cold War, for example, NATO decided not just to continue but to expand its membership and take on missions outside the area for which it was originally constituted.

There are any number of alternatives to alliances, from acting alone (unilateralism) to forming less formal but still collective "coalitions of the willing." These can be informal "start-ups" focused on a narrow, particular mission or something more general. Another alternative is to work through regional and global organizations, although in practice such an approach tends to lead to a more diluted response or inaction given the differing views of members of such broad groupings and, in some cases, the requirement for consensus or unanimity as a precondition to taking action. This is a principal reason why standing regional bodies as well as the United Nations often disappoint. All such groupings constitute versions of collective action or multilateralism, something not to be confused with multipolarity, which is simply a description of the distribution of power in the world, one that indicates there are multiple centers of power.

One final caution. Terms like "alliance" and "ally" are thrown around casually, often as synonyms for a friendly country. But these terms should be saved for those circumstances in which fundamental security obligations exist. Countries can be friends, even close partners, but allies have a solemn obligation to come to one another's defense.

International Society

As discussed earlier, a society is something more than a system. A balance of power is necessary but not sufficient for a society to emerge and operate. Alliances can either add to or detract from order. Here we look at four additional factors—the prevalence of democracy, the degree of economic interdependence, the extent of global governance, and respect for international law—that determine whether one can speak of an international system, society, or something in between.

DEMOCRACY

One factor that tends to contribute to world order is the extent to which countries are democracies. Or, to be more precise, mature or robust democracies. Democracies can be headed by a separately elected president (as is the case in the United States and France) or a prime minister who leads the largest party in the parliament, as is the case in much of Europe. What democracies have in common, though, is not just free and fair elections but also checks and balances that limit the power of government officials and that protect the basic rights of individuals.

More than 40 percent of the world's countries and roughly the same percentage of the world's people live in countries classified as free and democratic. India is the world's most populous democracy, the United States the world's second largest. Approximately one-third of the world's people live in countries (including China) that are decidedly unfree and undemocratic. The rest (roughly a quarter) live in countries such as the Philippines and Mexico that fall somewhere in between. There are more robust democracies now than there were half a century ago, but there have been some notable counterexamples to the advance of democracy in the second decade of this century.

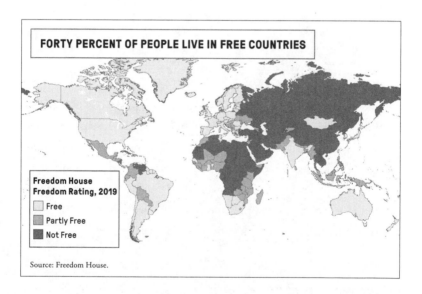

FORTY PERCENT OF PEOPLE LIVE IN FREE COUNTRIES

Freedom House
Freedom Rating, 2019

☐ Free
▨ Partly Free
■ Not Free

Source: Freedom House.

There is considerable evidence that mature democracies, that is, those countries with strong constitutions, meaningful checks and balances on the exercise of power, and extensive individual rights, tend not to attack other democracies. This is often referred to as the "democratic peace" theory. History suggests this is true, but immature or illiberal democracies—that is, those lacking in many of the features that make

THE NUMBER OF DEMOCRACIES HAS INCREASED SINCE WORLD WAR II

Note: Only includes countries with a population of 500,000 or more.

Source: Polity IV Project, Center for Systemic Peace; *The Economist*.

a democracy strong or robust—show no such constraint and, to the contrary, are particularly vulnerable to being hijacked by extreme nationalist appeals. Turkey, the Philippines, Poland, and Hungary all come to mind here. What's more, mature democracies—nations where power is truly checked and balanced—tend to be relatively rare and extraordinarily difficult to bring about, something that makes the democratic peace theory more of a concept than a reality.

ECONOMIC INTERDEPENDENCE

Economic interdependence is also viewed as something that can bolster peace. The argument is that the more that countries have a stake in mutually beneficial economic dealings—such as trade or investment flows—the more they will act with restraint so as not to upset conditions that serve their interests. While this may be true in certain situations, amid crisis other calculations can trump "rational" economic concerns, something demonstrated by the outbreak of World War I. Security concerns tend to outweigh economic ones. Leaders often feel the need to sacrifice long-term considerations for the immediate lest they lose power in the short term as a result of being seen as not having done enough on behalf of a vital national interest. A crisis over Taiwan could provide a test for this theory, because circumstances could arise in which China (which has demonstrated considerable restraint in its foreign policy until recently so it would not disrupt economic ties essential for its development) could have to make a choice between its long-term political goal of bringing Taiwan under its control (something that would risk conflict with the United States) and its immediate economic self-interest (which would argue for not doing anything that would disrupt beneficial trade and investment).

GLOBAL GOVERNANCE

The degree of global governance reflects how much the most powerful countries in the world accept existing political and economic arrangements, the rules governing international relations, and how these rules are to be set, modified, and enforced. It also reflects the extent to which these countries are prepared to endorse new rules and arrangements for dealing with emerging challenges, in particular those associated with globalization. As discussed elsewhere in this book, governance in the realm of globalization has fallen short in every domain, and in several critical areas such as climate change and cyberspace the gap between the international challenge and the desired collective response is widening.

There are a good many institutions and frameworks in place to promote global governance. The most prominent is the United Nations, an institution created to advance order and to prevent or, failing that, to resolve international disputes. It was designed during World War II and came into being in its wake. Its aim was to encourage countries to settle their inevitable differences and disputes peacefully—and to discourage governments from resorting to military action unless it was specifically endorsed by the UN. On occasion it has provided a useful forum for debate; as Winston Churchill once remarked, "Meeting jaw to jaw is better than war." More broadly, the UN was built to avoid yet another world war, something the League of Nations, the UN's predecessor created in the wake of World War I, failed to do. The UN can authorize the use of military force, something that can add to order if it is necessary to restore stability. UN authorization also adds an important dimension of legitimacy to the undertaking.

In reality, though, the UN's contribution to international order has been and is likely to remain quite limited. Institutions are never more influential than the degree to which their principal members are prepared to agree and act in collaboration. The UN is no exception; most authority is to be found in the Security Council, a body of fifteen members, ten of whom rotate off after a period of two years and five of whom (the United States, China, Russia, France, and the United Kingdom) have permanent seats and possess a veto that can be used to prevent the UN from acting or endorsing an action. When these five major powers agree, as they did in 1990 in the aftermath of Iraq's invasion and occupation of Kuwait, the UN Security Council can bestow considerable legitimacy on an undertaking and make it easier to rally international support on its behalf.

On most occasions, however, such consensus is impossible to bring about, which means the UN either prevents collective action or is sidelined. Countries are understandably unwilling to defer to the UN on questions involving their vital national interests and their perceived security. The UN is further weakened by the reality that the Security

THE UNITED NATIONS SECURITY COUNCIL

Council no longer represents the balance of power in the world; if it did, Japan, India, and Germany (or the European Union) would have a permanent seat. Bringing about such change is close to impossible because there is no agreement among the five permanent members of the Security Council to do so. The UN General Assembly, a body where each country has one vote regardless of its size, wealth, or military might, has little authority and little influence.

Order can also be promoted by organizations other than those that are formal and have a membership that is universal or close to it. Indeed, multilateralism (essentially defined as collective efforts to tackle a specific problem or set of problems) is increasingly to be found in more selective groupings of countries that have relevant capabilities and are like-minded. NATO, for example, provided multilateral support for military intervention in the former Yugoslavia in the early 1990s when Russia blocked UN Security Council endorsement. There are groups such as the G8 (the United States, the United Kingdom, France, Germany, Italy, Canada, Japan, and Russia) that have been meeting at least once a year since the early 1970s to coordinate responses to a range of common and often global economic and sometimes political challenges. (To be precise, Russia joined what was the G7 in 1998, but its membership was later suspended.) There is also the G20, a larger grouping that includes China, Russia, and a number of medium powers, that has met annually since 1999 and also tries to deal with global challenges. And there are any number of small groupings formed for narrower purposes. All contribute something to the world's order even if the world remains something other than orderly.

INTERNATIONAL LAW

International law touches on many aspects of international relations and is another source of order in the world. Perhaps most significantly, it lays out those circumstances in which the use of force is warranted or justified, such as in self-defense. It also establishes principles as to whether and how military force should be used (for example, it is meant to be proportionate to the provocation and only used against enemy combatants rather than civilians). It also makes clear that the use of certain kinds of weapons (for example, chemical weapons) can never be justified.

The problem, of course, is that the world as it exists is not to be confused with a society within a country. There is no global court of law with real authority over matters of war and peace; the World Court (more formally the International Court of Justice) located in The

Hague is in reality much more modest and technical in its scope. The International Criminal Court (ICC) has a narrow writ to try those accused of war crimes; in principle, such a capacity will help discourage individuals and governments from committing atrocities in the first place. The court is weakened by the reality that it often cannot arrest alleged criminals and even more by the fact that the United States is not a party to it out of concern the ICC could order the arrest and prosecution of American soldiers and diplomats. More generally, there is no global police force with the right to intervene wherever it deems it necessary to keep the peace. And there is no global "prison" or assured penalties for those who violate many of the rules that have been set out.

There is a large body of law designed to limit the frequency and violence of war and to strengthen world order. One focus of these laws is when a war can be justified, what is technically known by the Latin phrase *jus ad bellum* (right to war). The most widely shared principle is that wars fought in self-defense (whether by the attacked or invaded country or on its behalf) are legitimate, certainly as long as the goal is to liberate conquered territory or to stop an attack already under way. This principle is embedded in the United Nations Charter.

Other principles associated with the decision to wage war are that it be undertaken on behalf of a just cause, that there be a probability of success, that it be a last resort after other remedies have been exhausted, and that it be legitimized by a proper authority. This line of thinking is valuable, not so much as a formal constraint on when a war can be initiated—no one needs a license from an international body to start a war—as because it may discourage actions that will alienate others and because it provides a framework for individual citizens and governments to judge whether a war makes sense.

Another focus of international law is how a war should be fought. (The Latin phrase for this is *jus in bello*, or "law in war.") Here the considerations include a sense of proportionality in the amount of force used, that civilians (noncombatants) not be intentionally attacked, and that certain weapons that cause indiscriminate mass casualties not be employed.

There is a third set of considerations regarding law and war that does not enjoy the standing of the first two but that is gaining some traction; it is known by the Latin phrase *jus post bellum*, or "law after war." It has to do with post-conflict situations and deals with such considerations as when it is right to go beyond restoring the status quo ante (what existed before the attack) in terms of territorial adjustments or imposed limits on militaries, the prosecution of war crimes, the imposition of sanctions, and requirements for compensation. These laws do not give a clear list of dos and don'ts that dictate behavior and are not universally observed. But they are valuable because they provide a set of important questions to be considered before policy is undertaken by a government or supported by a citizen.

International law also promotes order in less dramatic ways. It sets out rules and procedures for diplomatic recognition and the treatment of diplomats, for the negotiation of treaties and other agreements, for the governance of seas, airspace, and outer space, and for litigation and immunities from prosecution. The demarcation of what seas fall under the jurisdiction of countries—generally, the first twelve nautical miles from the shore that are viewed as an extension of a country's territory and the first two hundred nautical miles that are known as the country's exclusive economic zone, which gives it certain rights over resources like oil reserves and fish—is especially important. All of this smooths the day-to-day interactions between countries, reducing the chance for conflict and facilitating diplomacy, trade, and investment.

Treaties and other international agreements can make these rules formal and create mechanisms for managing disagreements. But such agreements only come about when there is consensus among the necessary parties, something that is often lacking or present only in a diluted form. The act of joining a treaty is a sovereign right that governments can either take or refuse to take, as is the option of complying with a treaty or withdrawing from one. Thus, a number of countries have refused to endorse the Treaty on the Non-Proliferation of Nuclear Weapons, and one (North Korea) withdrew years after signing it and also violating it. The United States has signed, but never ratified, the United Nations Convention on the Law of the Sea, or UNCLOS. More recently, the United States under President Donald Trump has withdrawn from (or stated its intention to do so) several international agreements and treaties entered into by his predecessors, including a nuclear arms control agreement with Russia, a nuclear agreement with Iran, a trade pact involving a dozen Asian and Pacific countries, and the Paris climate accord.

War Between Countries

Wars between countries are the most obvious sign that order has broken down. Such wars can be and are different in motive, purposes, means, duration, scale, cost, and scope. Feeding into this dynamic—and on occasion serving as a trigger of war in its own right—is both the rise and the fall of countries and empires. Countries, such as Nazi Germany and imperial Japan, can rise up to challenge existing orders as they did in the run-up to World War II, while fading empires (the Austro-Hungarian Empire before World War I, the Ottoman Empire after World War I, the former Yugoslavia in the 1990s) can give way to disorder when central authority breaks down and outsiders are tempted to enter the fray.

The challenge is to find a way to accommodate rising powers on terms they and existing powers can all accept and to plan for and manage the unraveling of weak empires and countries. There is nothing new in this: writing over two thousand years ago, the ancient Greek historian Thucydides opined that the Peloponnesian War was in the end inevitable because of "the growth of Athenian power and the fear which this caused in Sparta." Some observers would argue that this is a good description of the challenge the world faces today in light of the rise of China.

One need not travel so far back in time to find examples of wars between countries. In 1990, Iraq attacked and swallowed up all of neighboring Kuwait; it took an international coalition led by the United States and military action to liberate Kuwait and restore its government along with its independence. More recently, Russia used armed force to invade and occupy portions of Georgia and Ukraine, and it has annexed Ukraine's region of Crimea.

War provides the most basic evidence that order has broken down. Wars can be global, regional, or local. They can be fought for territory or resources, out of fear or ambition. They can be fought by entities other than countries, such as terrorist groups, militias, or guerrilla forces associated with some movement. They can be waged to overthrow a government and replace it with another, or to preserve a regime that is being challenged by internal or external forces.

Not every armed encounter counts as a war. Some experts argue that scale matters, that the violence must claim at least one thousand lives before it can be classified as a war rather than as an incident or something less. This is clearly arbitrary. Also arbitrary is whether to call something a war, a conflict, or an armed conflict. The word "war" tends to be used to describe an event of scale that has a protracted nature. Defining something as a "war" may bring with it certain legal implications, especially as regards the rights of combatants. An intervention (if it is armed) reflects what one party does; it only turns into a conflict or a war if it is resisted in kind or if there is retaliation. It should be added that certain armed interventions (peacekeeping for one) can actually end or discourage wars.

I am not aware of any minimum time requirement for a war to be judged a war. Wars have been known to last decades (the Thirty Years' War in the early seventeenth century and, more recently, the war in Afghanistan come to mind) and as short as six days in the case of the June 1967 Middle East conflict.

All wars are costly, some much more than others. Some nine million soldiers were killed during World War I and nearly twice that many during World War II. Several times that number of soldiers were wounded in those wars, and the number of civilians killed or wounded also numbered in the tens of millions. The economic cost is near impossible to tabulate.

Traditionally, war is defined as involving the use of military force. But wars can be fought with other instruments, including economic penalties (sanctions and tariffs come to mind) and cyberattacks. Even when military forces are involved, shots need not be fired; an embargo, in which ships and planes are used to deny a country the ability to transport goods or people, is an act of war. Military forces can also be positioned coercively, in a threatening manner, in order to bring about a desired response. This is often referred to as "gunboat diplomacy," and while such actions do not constitute a war, they threaten one and can lead to a war if the response is judged inadequate.

CAUSES AND TYPES OF WAR

The great early nineteenth-century Prussian general and strategist Carl von Clausewitz described war as the continuation of politics by other means. Wars between countries can be started for a host of reasons including ambition, greed, ideology, to redress some past grievance, to save lives, to block an adversary from rising, or to prevent adversaries from acquiring or using some capability. Throughout history, territorial disputes have been a common trigger for interstate war. And wars can be a means of satisfying domestic political pressures or a tactic to distract a population's attention away from internal frustrations and failures.

Wars can be distinguished by type. The two world wars of the twentieth century were total wars, in that any and all resources and weapons were brought to bear while much of the world's peoples and territory were caught up in it. Most wars, though, are limited, be it in purpose or means, although it should be pointed out that it takes two or more antagonists to keep wars limited, and just because a war is initiated with a limited purpose in mind or with limited means, there is no guarantee that it will stay that way.

Wars are sometimes described as being either conventional or unconventional. The former can mean a war fought between opposing armies (as well as air forces and navies) wearing uniforms and under the control of governmental authority. Most of the fighting in a conventional war tends to take place on battlefields away from large numbers of civilians and noncombatants. In contrast, an unconventional war tends to refer to wars fought by soldiers of an entity other than a state, often by troops who mimic the tactics of more organized forces. Such soldiers tend not to wear uniforms and often attempt to blend into civilian populations. The battlefields for such wars may be urban areas. An unconventional war can also mean a war in which what are termed unconventional munitions—nuclear, chemical, or biological—are used. Cyberattacks are also becoming more common, either alone or as part of a larger military effort, further blurring not only the line between conventional and unconventional war, but also between war and peace. Increasingly, unconventional wars are becoming the norm.

One specific type of war is *preventive* war, undertaken against a gathering threat or what is perceived to be a gathering threat. The threat can be general, such as the rise of a country seen as a rival—or more specifically, the feared development or acquisition by a rival of a new military capability. In either case, a preventive war is a calculated action undertaken to block the emergence of a perceived threat before it is fully formed. The Soviet Union considered a preventive war against China in the late 1960s to prevent it from acquiring a nuclear capability. Israel successfully carried out preventive attacks against nuclear facilities being built in Iraq (in 1981) and Syria (in 2007). The United States has more than once considered a preventive war against North Korea given its efforts to develop missiles that could carry nuclear warheads and hit American soil. Both Israel and the United States have considered undertaking preventive attacks on Iran's nuclear facilities and might again one day if Iran appears to be developing nuclear weapons.

A preventive strike or war is not without its drawbacks. To begin with, it is an act of war and thus represents a calculation that such a blow to order is preferable to the threat to order that would develop if a rival's rise or acquisition of a new military capability were allowed to continue. But such a calculation is impossible to make with precision, because there is no way to know in advance exactly how the country attacked will respond or how it would act if it were not attacked and allowed to grow stronger. Assuming the worst about a country's intentions can all too easily bring about the worst in outcomes. There are also alternatives to mounting a preventive strike, including sanctions, deterrence, improving defenses, and diplomacy designed to curb the quality and quantity of a capability.

Preventive war is also potentially destabilizing in a more general sense, in that threat is in the eyes of the beholder and a world in which preventive strikes became commonplace would become a world of non-stop violence. It is for this reason that preventive war has little or no standing in international law and little or no political backing.

A *preemptive* strike or war is something quite different. Whereas a preventive use of force targets a gathering threat, a preemptive action targets an imminent threat. Preemptive attacks are the equivalent of throwing the first punch as the other side is about to punch you. As a result, it is widely considered legitimate and lawful, something understood as an anticipatory act of self-defense. Israel's attack on Egyptian forces at the start of what became the June 1967 Middle East war is judged by some to be a preemptive strike. Unfortunately, the terms "preventive" and "preemptive" are often confused and used interchangeably when in fact they are very different in their legal basis and in their implications for order. The United States termed its attack on Iraq in 2003 a preemptive war when in reality it was preventive. This difference helps to explain just why it was so controversial to many around the world.

Obviously, those undertaking preemptive action must be able to demonstrate that the target possesses such means and is about to use them. This is easier said than done because intelligence is rarely so clear. And even genuine preemptive strikes are not risk-free, because just like preventive strikes they can lead to retaliation, including actions that use the very systems that were attacked but managed to survive.

PREVALENCE OF WAR AND LOOKING AHEAD

Wars between countries have become less common in recent decades. There are no great-power conflicts at the moment, something that marks a welcome departure from previous centuries, in particular the last one. But there are a good many wars (or conflicts as they are often called) all the same, including those going on in Syria, Yemen, Afghanistan, Libya, Ukraine, and Sudan. The absence of wars among the great powers should not be taken to mean the major powers are on the sidelines, because the United States has been heavily involved in Afghanistan for nearly two decades and Russian forces have directly intervened in both Ukraine and Syria. In addition, these wars may not involve one major power pitted against another, but they are costly all the same; the conflict in Syria alone has claimed some 500,000 lives and displaced more than half the country's population since it began in 2011.

MOST WARS ARE CIVIL WARS

Number of conflicts

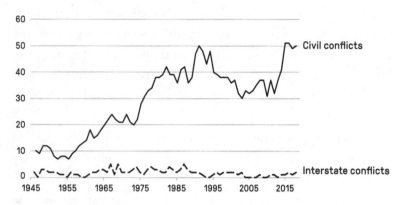

Note: Only includes civil and interstate conflicts in which at least one side was the government of a country. Civil conflicts may include foreign state intervention.

Source: UCDP/PRIO Armed Conflict Dataset version 19.1; Pettersson, Therese, Stina Högbladh, and Magnus Öberg, 2019. "Organized violence, 1989–2018 and Peace Agreements," *Journal of Peace Research* 56, no. 4; Gleditsch, Nils Petter, Peter Wallensteen, Mikael Eriksson, Margareta Sollenberg, and Håvard Strand (2002). "Armed Conflict 1946–2001: A New Dataset," *Journal of Peace Research* 39, no. 5.

And even though the major powers are not at war with one another, military spending continues to increase. In other words, nations continue to prepare for potentially large wars. The world spends slightly less than $2 trillion each year on maintaining and arming militaries. One-third is spent by the United States alone, a number that is larger than the combined defense spending of the next seven countries but reflects America's unique set of global interests. Other major military spenders include China, Saudi Arabia, Russia, India, France, the U.K., Japan, and Germany.

Thus it is not clear whether the absence of wars involving the great powers is an enduring trend or something of an aberration. Some judge this trend as likely to last, arguing wars between countries have become less common because actual or potential costs have gone up, especially in those instances in which nuclear weapons could be introduced. Other themes raised by those who argue that war has become less frequent include the prevalence of democratic societies disinclined to bear such costs. Leaders of these countries are accountable to voters and the substantial economic interdependence between nations raises the indirect costs of war because trade and investments will be hampered.

I am less sanguine and believe that wars between countries have become less common only because policies that have prevented them were adopted, including creating robust alliances and maintaining conditions of credible deterrence. If these policies were neglected or altered, wars could occur with greater frequency. In addition, the outbreak of World War I suggests the need to be skeptical that commerce can be a trustworthy bulwark against wars. And as was the case in the run-up to both World War I and World War II, neither democratic societies nor those ruled by authoritarian leaders are immune to the passions of nationalism that could lead to war. Despite hopes to the contrary, there is little reason to believe that war is a relic of the past. It is all too easy to imagine a war between the United States and China triggered over events involving Taiwan, between NATO and Russia caused by the latter's aggression in Europe, between the United States and either North Korea or Iran as a result of their nuclear programs, between India and Pakistan, or between Saudi Arabia and Iran. Human nature has not changed, and the motives that have led rulers and peoples to undertake wars have not disappeared.

Internal Instability and War
Within Countries

Developments within countries can also pose a threat to world order. A lack of order can provide space for terrorists to train, prepare for, and carry out their attacks. It can also create conditions where infectious diseases break out on their way to going global. Civil wars can generate large flows of refugees that can in turn cause instability in neighboring countries. Internal instability within a given country can also be a magnet for regional and global powers that seek advantage in promoting a particular outcome. Although a good deal of history is the result of the behavior of strong countries, it is clear, too, that weak, failing, and failed countries—countries where the government is unable or unwilling to perform the tasks expected of it, above all maintaining internal security—can cause serious problems for order beyond their borders.

There is no evidence suggesting that wars within countries are becoming obsolete; there has been an average of twenty internal conflicts a year around the world since the end of the Cold War in 1989. Many countries at some point in their histories face a challenge from secessionist movements that seek to break away and establish a country of their own. What these secessionists seek is not an alternative to sovereignty but rather a sovereign country of their own. South Sudan broke away from Sudan in 2011, and there is an effort in the Catalonia region of Spain to create a new country for those living in that area. Meanwhile, some governments are facing challenges from terrorist organizations, drug cartels, and pirates whose goal is not so much a country of their own as the ability to ignore the government and carry out activities that advance their own political or financial agendas. Violent internal struggles that involve a country's own forces, as well as militias, terrorist groups, and armed forces from both neighboring nations and farther afield, have become something of a staple in the Middle East and to a lesser extent in other parts of the world. Internal conflicts are far more common than conflicts between countries. They also tend to last longer and, after they conclude, are more likely to flare up again.

It is essential here to distinguish between one country being in a position of *relative* weakness vis-à-vis another and a situation in which a country finds itself in a position of *absolute* weakness. What makes a country weak in absolute terms (also commonly referred to as a fragile state) is its inability to control what takes place within its borders or to make available to its citizens what they require to lead a normal life. This is not an isolated phenomenon: more than one in five people in the world—on the order of 1.5 billion—live in fragile states. While such a state may have a seat at the United Nations, sign international treaties, and maintain embassies abroad, it is unable to perform the basic duties of what we expect from governments, be it maintaining internal security, collecting taxes, issuing and supporting a viable currency, building infrastructure, offering a basic education, regulating food and product safety, or providing the basics for retirement and health care.

Weak states often lead to the emergence of large areas of territory (sometimes called ungoverned spaces) that are outside the effective control of the government. What separates a weak state from a failed state is a matter of degree, with failed states simply describing a weak government that has lost control over most of its territory and stands little or no chance of regaining it. In other words, weak states are salvageable so long as they receive and make good use of some external assistance, while failed states would require enormous effort spanning years or even decades before they are able to effectively govern their territory. Somalia is the prototypical failed state, with little chance of becoming a functioning country anytime soon. The same holds true for Yemen, and perhaps Syria and Venezuela. Pakistan and Mexico are examples of present-day weak states.

CAUSES OF INTERNAL INSTABILITY AND STATE FAILURE

What conditions are most associated with a state's weakening or collapse? Vulnerable countries tend to be those that lack a commitment to the rule of law, whether because of corruption, leaders with too much power, or some combination of the two. This in turn reduces incentives to own private property or invest in the country, which stymies economic growth. After all, why would someone buy property, create a company, or build a factory in a place where the government may one day arbitrarily decide to take it? Discrimination tends to be high in weak states, usually blocking the way forward for minorities and women, leading to poor economic performance. Public services such as education and mass transportation are inadequate.

On the political side, countries ripe for internal instability tend to be characterized by high concentrations of power in merely a few hands. There tends to be little oversight of these leaders and little inclination on their part to learn from mistakes. The government may be seen as having lost its legitimacy and right to rule by a significant share of the population. Constitutions—and checks and balances on the arbitrary exercise of power—either are inadequate or are inadequately enforced. On the economic side, countries that are primed to fail often suffer from rampant corruption, which impedes economic growth by forcing people to spend time and money making payoffs rather than focusing on their businesses. Government capacity is low, so taxes are rarely collected, and when they are, they are collected unevenly. Police forces and courts are too weak or too corrupt to enforce the law. Inequality is high, and upward mobility is limited or nonexistent. Elites tend to perpetuate themselves; special interests dominate anything associated with the general interest.

Civil wars are another source of instability within countries. These wars are most often wars of *secession* in which part of the population with a common identity or geography seeks to break away and form a country of its own. This was the case with the American Civil War. Following the end of the Cold War, a number of wars of secession were waged amid the weakening of central control in what was Yugoslavia.

A different sort of internal war is better understood as a war of *succession*, in that the goal is to oust the current ruling authority and replace it with another that would rule in a very different way over the country's entire territory. This is the case with revolutionary wars and wars of national liberation; it may well characterize the winner-take-all war in Afghanistan between the government and the Taliban. Either way, what ensues is a conflict between internal forces not controlled by the government (or ruling authority) and government forces.

Internal conflicts can break out for any number of reasons. After World War II, such struggles were relatively commonplace as colonies sought independence. In recent years, they have become common in the Middle East, often breaking out for internal reasons (for instance, disputes between a minority or a political movement and the government) but continuing in part because other governments intervene directly or indirectly on behalf of one or more of the protagonists. Iraq, Syria, Yemen, and Libya to varying degrees reflect this pattern. Also adding fuel to the fire are recruits and arms entering from outside the country.

Not surprisingly, civil wars are more frequent in societies that are not homogeneous but rather contain one or more sizable minorities. Such conflicts are less likely when there is a robust democracy, which protects minorities and grants large degrees of political and cultural autonomy, thereby diluting any enthusiasm for total separation. Nations governed by something close to a dictatorship may also be insulated from internal conflict, because there is little opportunity to start or maintain effective resistance. Instead, it is in situations that fall in between these two extremes where civil wars are most likely.

Other traits that suggest a greater likelihood of civil war breaking out include low education levels (especially for boys and men), lower levels of GDP per capita, and an outsized economic reliance on a resource like oil, which tends to lead to corruption and few real jobs. The phenomenon of the "oil curse," where countries "blessed" with large amounts of oil tend to fail to develop a diverse economy and a middle class, is often observed.

POLICY RESPONSES

There is a range of tools available for dealing with challenges to order within borders. Some of these tools can best be understood as preventive, in that they are designed to reduce the odds countries will grow weak or become venues of civil war. Such tools include diplomacy to resolve disputes and various forms of aid to promote economic growth and increase a country's ability to cope with military and physical threats to order. Economic incentives can be offered and sanctions threatened to influence behavior. Peacekeeping forces can help maintain or restore stability, but as the term suggests, there must first be a peace in place to keep. Such a peace also needs to be widely supported if peacekeeping forces are not to be overwhelmed. When no such peace exists, far larger and more capable military forces are required to carry out a mission of peace-making.

If prevention fails, reactive tools include diplomacy, sanctions to penalize bad behavior, and military intervention—be it to attack those working against order (as NATO aircraft did when they bombed Serbian targets in 1999 to stop government attacks on civilian populations seeking to escape Serbian rule) or to provide protection until the country does so on its own. U.S. forces did precisely this for the Kurds in northern Iraq starting in 1991 when they were threatened by the central government.

There is no magic bullet for dealing with civil wars. What works in one context may fail in another. Negotiation can lead to a peace settlement, but successful negotiations require leaders both willing and able to compromise. And even successful negotiations can, over time, breed dissatisfaction with at least some elements of the population. Not surprisingly, civil wars ended by negotiation are the most prone to resuming. Often peacekeeping forces are required. Clear victories (or, from the opposing perspective, defeats) can sow the seeds of stability, but only if the winner is prepared to act with a degree of magnanimity and the losing side is prepared to accept the outcome.

There are, however, several alternatives. Partition is one. People who cannot live together can sometimes live next to each other. This is the case for Cyprus, where peace has held now for nearly half a century following a political crisis in the early 1970s that led to the island being divided between Greek and Turkish Cypriots. The neat division of the island, however, only came about following large population shifts (favoring the Turkish Cypriot community at the expense of Greek Cypriots) and backed—to this day—by a Turkish military presence.

This is somewhat the case in Northern Ireland, where, after three decades of "the Troubles," in which more than three thousand people lost their lives, there has been relative calm made possible by a capable

British police and military presence, walls separating Protestant and Catholic neighborhoods that in turn have helped to perpetuate a largely segregated school system, and a political process that offered an alternative path forward for the Catholic minority that had been deprived of equal rights and protections. Partition, though, is not a cure-all. When the British left India in 1947, they partitioned the country, in the process creating what today is Pakistan. The relationship between India and Pakistan remains fraught; the two countries have fought multiple wars and developed nuclear weapons aimed at each other.

State weakness and failure along with civil wars will remain relatively common given the many factors that bring about intrastate conflict and violence. Somalia remains a failed state thirty years after it collapsed, while over the past decade Syria, Yemen, South Sudan, the Central African Republic, and the Democratic Republic of the Congo have all become failed states. All this has real import for the world, because it suggests that significant refugee flows will continue and that a good many governments will be unable to ensure that their territory is not used to house terrorists or criminal enterprises involved in cyberattacks or the drug trade. Additionally, weak governments will not be in a position to contribute to efforts to deal with global challenges such as climate change; in fact, they are more likely to be victims of it. And local conflicts will present opportunities for outsiders to get involved to bring about a desired outcome, be it the preservation of a particular government or its ouster. Such external intervention can determine local outcomes, as was the case when both Iran and Russia intervened in Syria. It can also lead to wars between the competing outside actors. Interestingly, it was in a "peripheral" region—Crimea, coincidentally— where the major powers in the nineteenth century found themselves in a conflict that spelled the end of their efforts to maintain a world order. The lesson for our own era is obvious.

One other form of external intervention requires mention: nation-building. The idea (sometimes also termed state-building) is controversial, in large part because it is associated with costly and unsuccessful American efforts to transform Afghanistan and Iraq into stable democracies. But nation-building worked in both Germany and Japan following World War II as well as in Colombia more recently, where a decade of sustained U.S. involvement along with economic and security-related support strengthened the government so it could defeat a terrorist insurgency and dramatically reduce drug production. Granted, the conditions that created the possibility of success in these situations do not always exist. Still, a limited, focused effort that aimed to build state capacities so that a significant degree of internal order could be maintained might well be warranted in parts of Central America and Mexico as well as in select countries in Africa and the Middle East. Again, in a global world, what happens in any country has the potential to affect us all, and there is a strong case for helping governments reach a point where they can meet their basic international obligations.

The Liberal World Order

Much has been said and written about the liberal or rules-based world order. This refers to the set of international arrangements—initially the United Nations, the International Monetary Fund, and the World Bank, and subsequently the General Agreement on Tariffs and Trade, the precursor of the World Trade Organization—created in the aftermath of World War II. These institutions were created to facilitate the peaceful resolution of disputes, promote free trade and development, and encourage cross-border investment and commerce.

This order was liberal in the classic sense (as opposed to the contemporary political usage), in that the countries participating tended to be democratic; the order was very much voluntary, rules based, and open to all countries. The balance of power and peace was maintained by the United States working with its allies in Europe and Asia, backed by both conventional military forces and nuclear weapons. Deterrence and arms control also contributed to the balance of power and successfully ensured nuclear weapons were not used. Free trade contributed to the strength of allies and also provided some incentive for would-be foes not to act disruptively.

Russia (formerly the Soviet Union) and China have occupied an unusual position in relationship to this order. Both are permanent members of the UN Security Council and members of the World Bank, the IMF, and the WTO and have been part of such groupings as the Group of Eight and the Group of Twenty. (Russia was suspended from the G8 in 2014 after its annexation of Crimea.) At the same time, they have demonstrated little or no interest in safeguarding human rights or becoming more liberal or democratic or seeing any other country evolve in that direction. Russia has violated several of the most basic elements of the liberal world order, including respect for the borders of others and the rights of noncombatants in a war zone, while China is ignoring international legal rulings regarding the South China Sea and implementing economic and trade policies that are inconsistent with what was expected of it when it was granted admission to the WTO.

This liberal world order is now fraying, the result of a decline in America's relative power and its growing unwillingness to play its traditional role in the world, a rising and increasingly assertive China, and a Russia determined to play the role of the spoiler. Authoritarianism is on the rise not just in the obvious places, such as China and Russia, but also in the Philippines, Turkey, and Eastern Europe. Global trade has grown, but recent rounds of trade talks have ended without agreement, and the WTO has proved unable to adequately deal with many of today's most pressing challenges, including tariff and nontariff barriers, government subsidies, currency manipulation, and the theft of intellectual property. Resentment over the United States' exploitation of the dollar to impose sanctions is growing, as is concern over the country's accumulation of debt. More fundamentally, America's allies are increasingly unsure whether they can rely on the United States during a time of crisis and are uneasy with its unilateralism.

The UN Security Council is of little relevance to most of the world's conflicts, and international arrangements have failed to contend with the challenges associated with globalization. The world has put itself on the record as against genocide and has asserted a right to intervene when governments fail to live up to the responsibility to protect their citizens, but the talk has not translated into action. The Nuclear Non-Proliferation Treaty allows only five states to have nuclear weapons, but there are now nine that do (and many others that could follow suit if they chose to). The world is having a difficult time regulating the acquisition and use of new technologies with military applications, from robotics to artificial intelligence to drones. The EU, by far the most significant regional arrangement, is struggling with disputes over migration, economic policy, and the division of responsibility between itself and its members. And around the world, countries are increasingly resisting U.S. primacy. For its part, the United States, divided politically and stretched militarily after prolonged wars in Iraq and Afghanistan, appears less willing to promote the liberal world order than it has at any time since World War II.

The reemergence of ethnocentric and exclusive nationalism has also undermined the current order. When nationalism morphs into hyper-patriotism that is hostile toward foreign countries and their citizens, it becomes dangerous and undermines order. Nationalism of this sort can lead to an aggressive foreign policy and an excuse for intervention on behalf of a kindred ethnic group who happen to be citizens of another country. We are seeing just this in Russian behavior toward Russian minorities in neighboring countries, most dramatically in Ukraine. It is worth pointing out that this extreme and violent nationalism developed after what was widely judged to be a national humiliation in Russia, namely, the loss of the Cold War and NATO's enlargement.

It may seem odd that this is happening at a time of powerful global forces. But therein may lie the explanation: people are asserting their national identities in the face of forces over which they feel they have little control and by which they feel threatened, be it economically, culturally, or politically. Mounting opposition to free trade, immigration, and entities ranging from the EU to the UN may be explained in part by this tension. What this underscores is that the tension between nationalism and world order was in no way resolved by the decolonization movement following World War II. To the contrary, nationalism is a force to be reckoned with, one increasingly at odds with tolerance within societies and peaceful relations across and beyond borders.

Why is all this happening? Today's world order has struggled to cope with power shifts: China's rise, the appearance of several medium powers (Iran and North Korea, in particular) that reject important aspects of the order, and the emergence of non-state actors (from drug cartels to terrorist networks) that can pose a serious threat to order within and between states. In short, power is more distributed in more hands than at any other time in history.

The technological and political context has changed in important ways too. Globalization has had destabilizing effects, ranging from climate change to the spread of technology into far more hands than ever before, including a range of groups and people intent on disrupting the order. Nationalism and populism have surged—the result of greater inequality within countries, the dislocation associated with the 2008 global financial crisis, job losses caused by trade and technology, increased flows of migrants and refugees, and the power of social media to spread hate.

Meanwhile, effective statecraft is conspicuously lacking. Institutions have failed to adapt. No one today would design a UN Security Council that looked like the current one, yet real reform is impossible, because those who would lose influence block any changes. Efforts to build effective frameworks to deal with the challenges of globalization, including climate change and cyberattacks, have come up short. Decisions by European governments or the EU have created a powerful backlash against existing governments, open borders, and the EU itself.

The United States overreached in trying to remake Afghanistan, invading Iraq, and pursuing regime change in Libya. But it has also taken a step back from maintaining global order, and in certain cases it has arguably done too little. In most instances, U.S. reluctance to act has come not over core issues affecting the balance of power in Europe or Asia but over peripheral ones that leaders wrote off as not worth the costs involved, such as the strife in Syria, where the United States failed to respond meaningfully when Syria first used chemical weapons or to do more to help anti-regime groups. This reluctance to act has increased the boldness of other nations, leading them to disregard U.S. concerns and act independently. The Saudi-led military intervention in Yemen is a case in point. Russian actions in Syria and Ukraine should also be seen in this light. There is a troubling historical echo to what has happened in Crimea; the Crimean War marked the effective end of the Concert of Europe in the nineteenth century and signaled a dramatic setback in the current order. Doubts about U.S. reliability have multiplied under the Trump administration, thanks to its withdrawal from numerous international pacts, its conditional approach to once-sacrosanct U.S. alliance commitments in Europe and Asia, its distancing from several partners in the Middle East, and the gap between its rhetoric and its actions in dealing with both North Korea and Iran.

Given these changes, resurrecting the old order will be impossible. It would also be insufficient, owing to the emergence of new challenges. Once this is acknowledged, those who have an interest in preserving the central elements of liberal order should go about strengthening these elements and supplementing them with measures that account for changing power dynamics and new global problems. The United States and its partners would work to shore up arms control and nonproliferation agreements; strengthen existing alliances; bolster weak states that cannot contend with terrorists, cartels, and gangs; and counter the interference of authoritarian powers in the democratic process. The judgment that attempts to integrate China and Russia into the existing world order have mostly failed should not be grounds for rejecting future efforts to include them in fashioning and subsequently maintaining world order, because the course of the twenty-first century will in no small part reflect how such efforts fare. Such efforts will necessarily involve a mix of compromise, incentives, and pushback. Relationships will be a blend of competition and cooperation, with the twin goals of seeing that the former does not tip over into confrontation nor preclude the latter.

Countries will also need to work together to address problems of globalization, including but not just climate change, trade, and proliferation. These will require not resurrecting the old order but building a new one. Efforts to limit, adapt to, and possibly offset climate change need to be more ambitious. The WTO must be amended to address the sorts of issues raised by China's appropriation of technology, its provision of subsidies to domestic firms, and its use of nontariff barriers to trade. And rules of the road are needed to regulate cyberspace and outer space. Together, these challenges call for a modern-day concert. Such a call is ambitious but necessary.

The United States will need to show restraint and recapture a degree of respect in order to regain its reputation as a benign actor. This will require some sharp departures from the way U.S. foreign policy has been practiced in recent years: to start, it must be more prudent in using military force or weaponizing U.S. economic policy through the overuse of sanctions and tariffs. But more than anything else, the current reflexive opposition to internationalism and multilateralism needs to be rethought. It is one thing for a world order to unravel slowly; it is quite another for the country that had a large hand in designing and building it to take the lead in dismantling it.

All of this also requires that the United States get its own house in order—reducing government debt, rebuilding infrastructure, improving public education, investing more in basic research, adapting the social safety net, adopting a smart immigration system that allows talented foreigners to come and stay, tackling political dysfunction by making it less difficult to vote, and undoing gerrymandering. The United States cannot be an example to others around the world nor can it effectively promote order abroad if it is divided at home, distracted by domestic problems, and lacking in resources. The good news for Americans is that their country has the means to do all this and still maintain an active or even leading role in the world, one that reflects the fundamental truth that in a global era what happens beyond a country's borders affects what happens within those same borders. Evidence for this view stems from the four decades of Cold War experience, when defense spending constituted a far higher percentage of GDP than it does today without detracting from the nation's economic vitality.

The major alternatives to a modernized world order supported by the United States appear unlikely and unappealing. A Chinese-led order, for example, would be an illiberal one, characterized by authoritarian domestic political systems and statist economies that place a premium on maintaining domestic stability. There would be a return to spheres of influence, with China attempting to dominate its region, likely resulting in clashes with other regional powers, such as India, Japan, and Vietnam, which may build up their conventional or even nuclear forces in response.

A new democratic, rules-based order fashioned and led by medium powers in Europe and Asia, as well as Canada, however attractive a concept, would simply lack the military capacity and domestic political will to get very far. A more likely alternative is a world with little order—a world of deeper disarray. Protectionism, nationalism, and populism would gain ground, and democracy would recede. Conflict within and across borders would become more common, and rivalry between great powers would increase. Cooperation on global challenges would be all but precluded. If this picture sounds familiar, that is because it increasingly corresponds to the world of today.

History is replete with governments and leaders who viewed the existing world order as illegitimate because it did not protect what they saw as their vital interests or accord them a place in the world that they judged commensurate with their power or ambitions. Napoleon, Bismarck, and Hitler would surely fit here. History also teaches that order is not the natural state of international affairs and does not just emerge or continue automatically; to the contrary, it requires commitment and concerted effort by governments and others who are willing and able to put aside their differences in an effort to sustain it. The question is whether the governments and those who choose them in this era are prepared to make such a commitment. The answer to this question will tell us whether the past seventy-five years since World War II have been an aberration, and the world will come to resemble more what existed in the century before, or whether the liberal world order and its many benefits will endure.

ACKNOWLEDGMENTS

Close to fifty years ago, when I was a student at Oberlin College, I somehow found the courage to ask my religion professor, Thomas Frank, how long it took him to prepare the extraordinary lecture he had just delivered. He studied me through squinted eyes, rolled up his left sleeve, looked at his watch, sighed, and answered. "I'd say about thirty years and thirty minutes."

The process of writing a book is quite similar. One of the questions I get asked most frequently when I talk about one of my books is how long it took me to write it. The answer is not as simple as you might think. Take this book. It would be accurate to say that I began it in late 2017, as that is when I first put pen to paper or, more accurately, fingers to keyboard. A first full draft was completed by early spring 2019. Rewriting and editing took up the late spring through the summer and early fall. But the writing of this book actually took considerably longer if one counts the time I devoted to thinking through what to include in and how to structure this one.

As is my pattern, after finishing the first draft I asked people to read it. Given the nature of the book, I asked more people than usual for their reactions, in part to increase the odds I got the substance right, but also to make sure it worked for people of various backgrounds, be they young or old, students or non-students, experts or generalists. Some read and reacted to the entire manuscript, others to a single chapter. But all of them—Ted

Alden, Alyssa Ayres, Tom Bollyky, Marie Brenner, Dan Caldwell, John Campbell, Steven Cook, Trish Dorff, Sam Haass, Bruce Hoffman, Martin Indyk, Amy Jaffe, Charlie Kupchan, Dan Kurtz-Phelan, Lee Levison, Jim Lindsay, Susan Mercandetti, Caroline Netchvolodoff, Shannon O'Neil, Stewart Patrick, Richard Plepler, Gideon Rose, Adam Segal, Brad Setser, Stan Shuman, Sam Vinograd, and Iva Zoric—added value by way of suggestions, criticism, and corrections. Any remaining shortcomings should be laid at the feet of the author.

I also want to give shout-outs to the people at Penguin, above all Scott Moyers and Christopher Richards. This is the second book I have done with them, and I will simply say it is a true and valued relationship, at least from my end. And speaking of relationships, let me not neglect my agent, Andrew Wylie, who continued to weigh in on the project as it moved along.

There are quite a few maps and graphs in this book. I owe a big thanks to Katherine Vidal, Will Merrow, Michael Bricknell, and Joyce Chen, all of whom work here at CFR. I also owe a great deal to the team at Penguin, including interior designers Lucia Bernard and Claire Vaccaro, production editor Carlynn Chironna, copy editor Ingrid Sterner, production director Gloria Arminio, and cover designer Oliver Munday.

I want to single out David Sacks, my research assistant, for all he did to make this book both possible and better. The research load was heavier than usual given the wide range of subjects covered. David has the gift of being able to produce prodigious amounts of quality work at warp speed. All that along with the fact he was not shy about voicing his own informed views about what I had written made him an indispensable partner throughout the writing and editing process alike.

I wrote the bulk of this book in early mornings and on weekends, as I have a day job here at the Council on Foreign Relations, which I have been fortunate to lead for seventeen years. I want to thank my colleagues here, above all Doreen Bonnami, Nicholas Weigel, Alyssa Goessler, and Jeff Reinke, who not only commented on the manuscript but helped structure my life and protect my time so I could do my job and produce this book. I also want to salute the talented and dedicated staff at CFR who have produced hundreds of backgrounders and video explainers, a classroom simulation of the National Security Council and the United Nations called Model Diplomacy, and a curriculum, World 101, that anyone can benefit from. All are of high quality, available for free on the Council's website, cfr.org, and like this book intended to help Americans and others better understand the world that for better and for worse will shape their lives in fundamental ways.

Speaking of the Council on Foreign Relations, I need to remind readers that it is an independent, nonpartisan membership organization, think tank, publisher, and educator. Its mission is to be a resource that improves the quality of the debate in this country and around the world about the foreign policy choices facing governments and citizens. It does not, however, take positions of its own on matters of policy, and what is contained in these pages represents my thinking and not the institution's.

One last (but definitely not least) item. This book is dedicated to my family: my wife, Susan, and our two children, Sam and Francesca. We are living not just in history but in difficult, often stressful times, and I am fortunate and then some to have a family that provides the ultimate sanctuary, one filled with conversation, laughter, love, and yes, constructive criticism.

WHERE TO GO FOR MORE

The central aim of this book has been to provide you with a foundation to better make sense of and prepare for a world that will shape your life. Ideally, though, it has whetted your appetite to learn more and to follow international events and foreign policy debates more closely.

But how? There is no substitute for reading a quality newspaper that has substantial international coverage. Those with the most value have teams of journalists on the ground where events unfold or policy is made, along with editors whose job it is to ensure accuracy. The best papers also tend to limit opinions to the editorial pages. A good list to choose from would include *The New York Times*, *The Wall Street Journal*, *The Washington Post*, and the *Financial Times*, although there are many other newspapers well worth reading that are published in other American cities and in major world capitals.

There are also a number of magazines worth reading regularly. The best weekly that combines coverage of the news with analysis (and at times a large dose of opinion) is *The Economist* (which has the added advantage of being written with flair). Other general interest magazines that often contain important international coverage include *The New Yorker* and *The Atlantic*.

Slightly more specialized are those magazines and websites devoted to international issues and the foreign policy of the United

States and others. These tend to provide not news but analysis and in some cases recommendations for what should be done. The best of these magazines or journals is *Foreign Affairs*, published six times a year by the Council on Foreign Relations, where I happen to be president. Equally valuable is its website, ForeignAffairs.com, which publishes shorter pieces more closely tied to the news. Despite my obvious bias, *Foreign Affairs* is the authoritative magazine devoted to the subject and is incomparably more readable and understandable than academic and policy journals, which with few exceptions (including *The American Interest, International Security, The National Interest,* and *Survival*) are often difficult to read and understand.

Another place to go for background, analysis, and suggested policy are the websites of the various think tanks. Again, I am biased, and think the best is that of the Council on Foreign Relations (cfr.org). What makes it special is the effort to include explainers and background information and analysis for nonexperts as well as experts. Other sites worth visiting include those of the American Enterprise Institute, the Brookings Institution, the Carnegie Endowment for International Peace, the Center for Strategic and International Studies, and the Rand Corporation. Some non-American institutions also have excellent sites, including Chatham House (U.K.), IFRI (France), the Lowy Institute (Australia), the SDP (Germany), and the International Institute for Strategic Studies, or IISS, which, while London based, is international in its orientation. (Full disclosure: I worked there for several years when I was in my twenties. It was so long ago that it was just the ISS, because it had yet to become fully international. And because I am disclosing, I should add that I also worked for a time at both the Carnegie Endowment and the Brookings Institution.)

There are as well the sites of more specialized institutions, such as the Inter-American Dialogue, the Peterson Institute for International Economics, the Washington Institute for Near East Policy, Human Rights Watch, Freedom House, and the International Crisis Group. And speaking of websites, there are a few devoted to international subjects that I would recommend, including War on the Rocks and

Foreign Policy. I apologize for omitting many quality organizations and sites, but my point is simply that there are many valuable resources online for those interested.

There are also a large number of reference books, many of which are available online. Among these are *The Military Balance* (published annually by the IISS), the *SIPRI Yearbook* (which includes texts of arms control pacts and is published by the Stockholm-based SIPRI), and various publications from the UN, IMF, WTO, OECD, and World Bank. In particular, I would note the twice-yearly IMF World Economic Outlook reports, the World Bank's Global Economic Prospects, and the WTO World Trade Report.

U.S. government departments and agencies such as the Office of the U.S. Trade Representative and the Commerce Department publish a wide range of valuable statistics and data in areas that fall under their purview. *The CIA World Factbook* is particularly useful. I also recommend the annual unclassified threat assessment issued by the U.S. director of national intelligence, the *Global Trends* survey published every four years by the National Intelligence Council, and analyses published regularly by the Congressional Budget Office and the Congressional Research Service.

Television offers relatively little in the way of serious coverage of international and foreign-policy-related issues—and certainly much less than was the case just a few decades ago. There are, though, important exceptions, including the *PBS NewsHour*, various shows on MSNBC (including *Morning Joe*, where I appear with some regularity), on occasion *CBS Sunday Morning* and *60 Minutes*, and *Fareed Zakaria GPS*, which airs on Sundays on CNN and is arguably the best television show devoted to international subjects. PBS's *Frontline* produces quality documentaries on international subjects, as do HBO and others from time to time.

The best coverage of the world on radio is to be found on National Public Radio (NPR) and NPR affiliates. Such NPR shows as *Morning Edition, All Things Considered*, and *Weekend Edition* regularly feature serious international coverage and conversation. Regional radio shows on NPR affiliates can be especially good, in particular Michael Krasny's *Forum* on KQED out of San Francisco and Brian Lehrer's talk show out of WNYC in New York. Podcasts are also coming on strong but tend to come and go too rapidly to be listed here. That said, I would be remiss and disloyal if I did not mention three that we do at the Council on Foreign Relations—*The President's Inbox, The World Next Week*, and *Why It Matters.*

I confess I spend some time on social media, Twitter in particular. I find it useful as a way to share thoughts, disseminate what I and others have written, and learn about things. I invariably come across some article or video of some speech or event that I did not know about and am glad to look at. All that said, I feel compelled to issue a warning at this point, akin to what one finds on medicines. Twitter and the internet more broadly can be dangerous places for information. There are often no editors, no one to verify that what is there is either accurate in what it states or accurate in what it represents; that is, what it says can be true but possibly represents merely 10 percent of the picture. In this way, something posted can be accurate and inaccurate at one and the same time. It is also the case that social media promotes narrowcasting, allowing users to follow only others who share a similar worldview. In such instances, users come across only information that confirms their existing beliefs and are not challenged to hear the opposing side and grapple with new or different information. So if you do spend time on Twitter, consider following individuals or organizations who speak to international issues and embrace ideas different from your own.

I would hope that some of you reading this book will be persuaded to undertake a more formal study of international affairs. I would simply add that you need not take a formal international relations course (not that I would discourage it) to learn something of real value. Offerings in history, science, economics, politics, regional studies, comparative religion, and more can all be valuable, especially if you are fortunate enough to come across a good teacher who makes the subject come alive. My own interest in the field that has kept me interested and occupied for close to five decades began with a professor of religion in college. I went off to do my junior year abroad (in the Middle East), and as they say, one thing led to another that led to another.

Enrolling in a formal classroom setting is not the only path. There are a growing number of online academic options, many of which are not just high quality but free. Here again I want to point out one associated with my own institution, the Council on Foreign Relations. Called World 101, it is in many ways an online companion to this book, one made of modules with videos, graphics, interviews, and more on many of the same subjects.

Because this is a book, though, I want to end with books. If this was the first book you have read about the world, I hope it is not your last. I would argue for history, memoirs, and biography above all else. Some of the books that have most influenced me include Hedley Bull's *The Anarchical Society*, which will be overly theoretical for many readers but nonetheless provides a useful framing for thinking about and assessing world order; Henry Kissinger's *A World Restored*, which is not just a brilliant history of the Congress of Vienna but a primer on statecraft; and a book written by two of my former Harvard colleagues, Richard Neustadt and Ernest May, *Thinking in Time: The Uses of History for Decision-Makers*, which, as the subtitle suggests, offers tips for how best to use history for guidance.

For those especially interested in the current post–Cold War era, I would highlight G. John Ikenberry's *Liberal Leviathan*, Robert Kagan's *The Jungle Grows Back*, Henry Kissinger's *World Order*, Charles Kupchan's *No One's World*, Joseph Nye's *Is the American Century Over?*, Hal Brands's *Making the Unipolar Moment*, Ian Bremmer's *Every Nation for Itself*, and Fareed Zakaria's *The Post-American World*. To this list I would immodestly add my own *A World in Disarray*. These and literally hundreds of other books and articles are mentioned in the notes that follow. The notes include not just source material for this book but also additional readings relating to every chapter for those who wish to delve deeper and wider.

NOTES

Preface

xv   **a rudimentary understanding of the world:** The American Council of Trustees and Alumni analyzed more than eleven hundred colleges and universities, with a combined enrollment of nearly eight million students, and found that less than half of the schools surveyed require the study of literature (34 percent), a foreign language (12 percent), U.S. government or history (17 percent), or economics (3 percent). Only 33 percent of the schools surveyed received a grade of A or B from the council, while the remaining 67 percent received a C, D, or F. See American Council of Trustees and Alumni, *What Will They Learn? 2018–2019: A Survey of Core Requirements at Our Nation's Colleges and Universities,* www .goacta.org/images/download/what-will-they-learn-2018-19.pdf.

xvi   **less than a third required history majors:** The American Council of Trustees and Alumni studied the requirements of history majors at seventy-six of America's leading colleges and universities and found that only twenty-three programs—or 30 percent—require a course on American history. American Council of Trustees and Alumni, *No U.S. History? How College History Departments Leave the United States out of the Major* (2016), 4, www.goacta.org/images /download/no_u_s_history.pdf.

xvii   **one-third of Americans:** According to the latest data from the Bureau of Labor Statistics, in October 2018, 69.1 percent of 2018 high school graduates were enrolled in colleges or universities. Bureau of Labor Statistics, "Economic News Release: College Enrollment and Work Activity of Recent High School and College Graduates Summary," April 25, 2019, www.bls.gov/news.release/hsgec.nr0.htm.

xvii   **40 percent who do achieve a degree:** According to the latest data from the U.S. Census Bureau, 77 million Americans have attained either a bachelor's degree

(48.2 million), a master's degree (21 million), a professional degree (3.2 million), or a doctoral degree (4.5 million). Given that there are 215 million Americans twenty-five years of age or older, only 36 percent of Americans have attained a bachelor's degree or higher. See www.census.gov/topics/education/educational -attainment/data.html.

xvii **85 percent of adults:** The United Nations Educational, Scientific and Cultural Organization tracks literacy rates around the globe and found that 86 percent of adults (those aged fifteen years and older) are literate, while 750 million are not. UNESCO Institute for Statistics, "Fact Sheet No. 45: Literacy Rates Continue to Rise from One Generation to the Next" (September 2017), uis .unesco.org/sites/default/files/documents/fs45-literacy-rates-continue-rise -generation-to-next-en-2017_0.pdf.

xix **one out of twenty people:** As of July 2019, the U.S. Census Bureau estimated the U.S. population at 329.3 million, and a world population of 7.6 billion, meaning that the United States has 4.3 percent of the people in the world—or roughly 1 out of 23. See www.census.gov/popclock/.

xix **on the order of 25 percent:** In 2018, the United States had an output (gross domestic product, or GDP) of $20.5 trillion, which is 24 percent of the global total of $84.7 trillion. International Monetary Fund, "World Economic Out- look Database" (April 2019).

PART I: THE ESSENTIAL HISTORY

From the Thirty Years' War to the Outbreak of World War I *(1618–1914)*

5 **Thirty Years' War:** For the best history of the Thirty Years' War, see Peter H. Wilson, *The Thirty Years War: Europe's Tragedy* (Cambridge, Mass.: Belknap Press of Harvard University Press, 2011).

6 **Treaty of Westphalia:** For an excellent discussion of the Treaty of Westphalia, see Henry Kissinger, *World Order* (New York: Penguin Books, 2014), 20–41.

7 **Congress of Vienna:** The best books on the Congress of Vienna and the Concert of Europe are Henry Kissinger, *A World Restored: Metternich, Castlereagh, and the Problems of Peace, 1812–22* (Boston: Houghton Mifflin, 1957); and Harold Nicholson, *The Congress of Vienna* (New York: Harcourt Brace Jovanovich, 1946).

7 **Concert of Europe:** For more on the Concert of Europe, see René Albrecht- Carrié, *The Concert of Europe* (London: Macmillan, 1968).

8 **I would argue for:** I expanded on this in my essay "How a World Order Ends: And What Comes in Its Wake," *Foreign Affairs*, January/February 2019.

8 Otto von Bismarck: For more on Bismarck, see Henry Kissinger, "The White Revolutionary: Reflections on Bismarck," *Daedalus* 97, no. 3 (Summer 1968): 888–924; and Jonathan Steinberg, *Bismarck: A Life* (Oxford: Oxford University Press, 2011).

9 For China, the nineteenth century: For those interested in this period of Chinese history, the best one-volume work is Jonathan D. Spence, *The Search for Modern China* (New York: W. W. Norton, 1990).

10 the Meiji Restoration: For more on this era of Japanese history, see Donald Keene, *Emperor of Japan: Meiji and His World, 1852–1912* (New York: Columbia University Press, 2002).

11 This primacy arguably lasted: For an account of Britain's relative decline, see Aaron L. Friedberg, *The Weary Titan: Britain and the Experience of Relative Decline, 1895–1905* (Princeton, N.J.: Princeton University Press, 1988).

12 Exactly why World War I broke out: Of this vast literature, I would recommend Christopher Clark, *The Sleepwalkers: How Europe Went to War in 1914* (New York: HarperCollins, 2012); Barbara W. Tuchman, *The Guns of August* (New York: Ballantine Books, 1962); and Margaret MacMillan, *The War That Ended Peace: The Road to 1914* (New York: Random House, 2013).

12 One influential history: See Clark, *Sleepwalkers*.

12 "Fifty years were spent": B. H. Liddell Hart, *History of the First World War* (London: Pan Books, 1970), 1.

From World War I Through World War II (1914–1945)

14 War came in the summer of 1914: One of the best histories of World War I is Michael Howard, *The First World War* (Oxford: Oxford University Press, 2002).

14 The leaders who plunged: The kaiser told German soldiers they would return home, victorious, before the autumn leaves fell. David Blackbourn, *History of Germany, 1780–1918* (Malden, Mass.: Blackwell, 2003), 349. The German crown prince anticipated "a jolly little war." John Merriman, *A History of Modern Europe: From the Renaissance to the Present* (New York: W. W. Norton, 2010), 888.

14 farewell address of 1796: President George Washington, "Washington's Farewell Address 1796," https://avalon.law.yale.edu/18th_century/washing.asp.

14 Secretary of State explained: John Quincy Adams, "Speech to the U.S. House of Representatives on Foreign Policy," July 4, 1821, https://millercenter.org/the-presidency/presidential-speeches/july-4-1821-speech-us-house-representatives-foreign-policy.

15 **What brought the Americans:** Michael Beschloss, *Presidents of War* (New York: Crown, 2018), 310–14.

15 **It is possible:** Barbara W. Tuchman, *The Zimmermann Telegram: America Enters the War, 1917–1918* (New York: Macmillan, 1958). See also Beschloss, *Presidents of War*, 310–16.

16 **As many as 200,000:** Merriman, *History of Modern Europe*, 902–4.

16 **"Men marched asleep":** Wilfred Owen, "Dulce et Decorum Est," in *The Collected Poems of Wilfred Owen*, ed. C. Day Lewis (London: Chatto & Windus, 1963).

16 **nine million soldiers:** Ian Kershaw, *To Hell and Back: Europe, 1914–1949* (New York: Viking, 2015), 91.

16 **twenty-one million were wounded:** Merriman, *History of Modern Europe*, 923.

16 **millions or even tens of millions:** Merriman, *History of Modern Europe*, 923.

17 **the last of his Fourteen Points:** The fourteenth point stated, "A general association of nations must be formed under specific covenants for the purpose of affording mutual guarantees of political independence and territorial integrity to great and small states alike." The full text of Wilson's Fourteen Points address is available at avalon.law.yale.edu/20th_century/wilson14.asp.

19 **idealism over realism:** For more on this school of thought, see Hans J. Morgenthau, *Politics Among Nations* (New York: Alfred A. Knopf, 1948).

20 **Nationalism often gains momentum:** For a lengthier discussion of nationalism, see E. J. Hobsbawm's *Nations and Nationalism Since 1780: Programme, Myth, Reality* (Cambridge, U.K.: Cambridge University Press, 1990) and Ernest Gellner's *Nations and Nationalism* (Ithaca, N.Y.: Cornell University Press, 1983).

20 **the League failed:** For a history of the League of Nations, see Ruth B. Henig, ed., *The League of Nations* (Edinburgh: Oliver & Boyd, 1973).

21 **the Kellogg-Briand Pact:** The signatories agreed to "condemn recourse to war for the solution of international controversies, and renounce it, as an instrument of national policy in their relations with one another." The full text of the Kellogg-Briand Pact can be found at avalon.law.yale.edu/20th_century/kb pact.asp.

21 **seen by many observers:** Mario J. Crucini and James A. Kahn, "Tariffs and the Great Depression Revisited," FRB NY Staff Report No. 172 (September 2003); Douglas A. Irwin, "The Smoot-Hawley Tariff: A Quantitative Assessment," *Review of Economics and Statistics* 80, no. 2 (May 1998): 326–34.

21 **One school of thought:** Norman Angell, *The Great Illusion: A Study of the Relation of Military Power in Nations to Their Economic and Social Advantage* (New

York: G. P. Putnam's, 1912); Edward D. Mansfield, *Power, Trade, and War* (Princeton, N.J.: Princeton University Press, 1994).

23 **came to be known as appeasement:** Tim Bouverie, *Appeasement: Chamberlain, Hitler, Churchill, and the Road to War* (New York: Tim Duggan Books, 2019).

24 **"lend-lease" program:** On December 17, 1940, President Franklin D. Roosevelt introduced the idea of lend-lease in a press conference and followed it up with a "fireside chat" on December 29 in which he declared America "must be the great arsenal of democracy." For more on lend-lease, including the text of the press conference and "fireside chat," see www.fdrlibrary.org/lend-lease.

25 **Hitler turned on the Soviet Union:** For a riveting recounting of this decision, see Stephen Kotkin, "When Stalin Faced Hitler: Who Fooled Whom?," *Foreign Affairs*, November/December 2017.

25 **an act of folly:** Barbara Tuchman, *The March of Folly: From Troy to Vietnam* (New York: Alfred A. Knopf, 1984).

26 **a scathing book in 1919:** John Maynard Keynes, *The Economic Consequences of the Peace* (London: Macmillan, 1919).

26 **clause that placed the responsibility:** Article 231 of the Treaty of Versailles, often termed the "War Guilt Clause," stated, "The Allied and Associated Governments affirm and Germany accepts the responsibility of Germany and her allies for causing all the loss and damage to which the Allied and Associated Governments and their nationals have been subjected as a consequence of the war imposed upon them by the aggression of Germany and her allies." The full text of the Treaty of Versailles is available at www.loc.gov/law/help/us-treaties /bevans/m-ust000002-0043.pdf.

26 **isolationism, which gained traction:** A February 1937 poll revealed 95 percent of Americans agreed that the United States should not participate in any future war. George C. Herring, *From Colony to Superpower: U.S. Foreign Relations Since 1776* (Oxford: Oxford University Press, 2008), 504. For more on this isolationist tradition in U.S. foreign policy and a history of U.S. foreign policy, see Robert Kagan, *Dangerous Nation: America's Foreign Policy from Its Earliest Days to the Dawn of the Twentieth Century* (New York: Alfred A. Knopf, 2006). Another worthwhile book that looks back on the various schools of thought running through U.S. foreign policy is Walter Russell Mead, *Special Providence: American Foreign Policy and How It Changed the World* (New York: Routledge, 2002).

26 **a decline in U.S. military readiness:** Following World War I, the United States maintained a small regular army of 140,000. The U.S. Army grew to 174,000 in mid-1939 and ballooned to 1.5 million two years later. By 1945, more than 12.1

million men and women were members of the U.S. military. Herring, *From Colony to Superpower*, 439–541.

28 **More than 15 million soldiers:** Merriman, *History of Modern Europe*, 1102.

28 **far larger number of civilians:** Of the estimated sixty million people who were killed in World War II, forty-five million were civilians. Herring, *From Colony to Superpower*, 595.

28 **6 million Jews in the Holocaust:** For this statistic and additional information on the Holocaust, visit the Holocaust Encyclopedia maintained by the U.S. Holocaust Memorial Museum, available at encyclopedia.ushmm.org/en.

28 **Germany lost around 7 million people:** Kershaw, *To Hell and Back*, 346.

28 **Japan almost 3 million:** Herring, *From Colony to Superpower*, 596.

28 **The Soviet Union lost as many:** Herring, *From Colony to Superpower*, 595–96.

28 **400,000 soldiers killed:** Nese F. DeBruyne, "American War and Military Operations Casualties: Lists and Statistics," Congressional Research Service, September 14, 2018, 2.

28 **Both were transformed into robust democracies:** The best book on Japan's transformation is John Dower, *Embracing Defeat: Japan in the Wake of World War II* (New York: W. W. Norton, 1999).

The Cold War (1945–1989)

29 **The Cold War:** For an accessible history of the Cold War, see John Lewis Gaddis, *The Cold War: A New History* (New York: Penguin Books, 2005). For a slightly lengthier treatment with more emphasis on the global dimension of the Cold War, see Odd Arne Westad, *The Cold War: A World History* (New York: Basic Books, 2017).

31 **momentum that brought about the Cold War:** The best study of the Cold War's origins is John Lewis Gaddis, *The United States and the Origins of the Cold War, 1941–1947* (New York: Columbia University Press, 1972). Few political memoirs are worth reading, but one exception to this rule is Dean Acheson's *Present at the Creation: My Years in the State Department*, in which he discusses the formation of the post–World War II world order and the opening of the Cold War. For the revisionist perspective on the origins of the Cold War that places more of the blame on the United States—not a view I subscribe to—see William Appleman Williams, *The Tragedy of American Diplomacy* (Cleveland: World, 1959).

31 **The Truman Doctrine:** President Truman articulated what would become known as the Truman Doctrine in a speech before a joint session of Congress on

March 12, 1947. The full text of the speech is available at https://avalon.law.yale .edu/20th_century/trudoc.asp.

31 **The Marshall Plan:** For a riveting history of the Marshall Plan, see Benn Steil, *The Marshall Plan: Dawn of the Cold War* (New York: Simon & Schuster, 2018).

32 **"long-term, patient but firm":** Kennan proposed this approach in an eight-thousand-word telegram—that became known as the "long telegram"—sent from the U.S. embassy in Moscow, where he was posted as the deputy chief of mission, to Washington. He later published his analysis anonymously as "X" in a famous article in the July 1947 issue of *Foreign Affairs* titled "The Sources of Soviet Conduct."

33 **"iron curtain":** Winston Churchill delivered the speech, titled "The Sinews of Peace," on March 5, 1946. He stated, "From Stettin in the Baltic to Trieste in the Adriatic, an iron curtain has descended across the Continent. Behind that line lie all the capitals of the ancient states of Central and Eastern Europe. War-saw, Berlin, Prague, Vienna, Budapest, Belgrade, Bucharest and Sofia, all these famous cities and the populations around them lie in what I must call the Soviet sphere, and all are subject in one form or another, not only to Soviet influence but to a very high and, in many cases, increasing measure of control from Mos-cow." The full text can be found at winstonchurchill.org/resources/speeches /1946-1963-elder-statesman/the-sinews-of-peace/.

34 **invaded South Korea:** For a history of the Korean War, see David Halberstam, *The Coldest Winter: America and the Korean War* (New York: Hyperion, 2007).

34 **outside the U.S. defense perimeter:** Acheson made this comment in a speech at the National Press Club on January 12, 1950. In the speech, he defined the U.S. "defensive perimeter" as running through Japan, the Ryukyus, and the Philippines—thereby excluding South Korea and the Republic of China (Tai-wan). The full speech can be found at www.cia.gov/library/readingroom/docs /1950-01-12.pdf.

34 **in particular Vietnam:** The best single-volume histories of the conflict are Stan-ley Karnow, *Vietnam: A History* (New York: Viking, 1983); and Fredrik Lo-gevall, *Embers of War: The Fall of an Empire and the Making of America's Vietnam* (New York: Random House, 2012).

35 **bought time for several of Vietnam's neighbors:** Michael Lind made this argument in his book *The Necessary War: A Reinterpretation of America's Most Disastrous Military Conflict* (New York: Touchstone, 2002), xv. After listening to scholars condemn President Lyndon Johnson for escalating the conflict in Vietnam at a dinner party in 1968, Singapore's prime minister and founding father, Lee Kuan Yew, explained that countries such as Singapore would have

fallen without America's intervention in Vietnam. Michael J. Green, *By More Than Providence: Grand Strategy and American Power in the Asia Pacific Since 1783* (New York: Columbia University Press, 2017), 317.

35 **thirteen days of the crisis:** Transcripts of the meetings between President John F. Kennedy and his senior advisers during these thirteen days when the world literally could have ended can be found at microsites.jfklibrary.org/cmc/oct16 /index.html. The best academic study of the Cuban Missile Crisis, and also great reading, is Graham Allison and Philip Zelikow's *Essence of Decision: Explaining the Cuban Missile Crisis* (New York: Longman, 1999).

36 **The basic bargain of membership:** Article 5 of the North Atlantic Treaty, concluded on April 4, 1949, states, "The Parties agree that an armed attack against one or more of them in Europe or North America shall be considered an attack against them all and consequently they agree that, if such an armed attack occurs, each of them, in exercise of the right of individual or collective self-defence recognised by Article 51 of the Charter of the United Nations, will assist the Party or Parties so attacked by taking forthwith, individually and in concert with the other Parties, such action as it deems necessary, including the use of armed force, to restore and maintain the security of the North Atlantic area." The full text of the treaty is available at www.nato.int/cps/en/natohq/official _texts_17120.htm.

38 **A sphere of influence:** For more on U.S. strategy during the Cold War, see John Lewis Gaddis, *Strategies of Containment: A Critical Appraisal of American National Security Policy During the Cold War* (Oxford: Oxford University Press, 2005).

41 **arguing that a principal reason:** Paul Kennedy, *The Rise and Fall of the Great Powers: Economic Change and Military Conflict from 1500 to 2000* (New York: Random House, 1987).

42 **Bush has been criticized:** President George H. W. Bush and his national security adviser, Brent Scowcroft, write about this criticism in their memoir, *A World Transformed* (New York: Vintage Books, 1998).

The Post–Cold War Era (1989–Present)

44 **an additional fourteen countries:** In addition to Russia, the Soviet Union dissolved into Armenia, Azerbaijan, Belarus, Estonia, Georgia, Kazakhstan, Kyrgyzstan, Latvia, Lithuania, Moldova, Tajikistan, Turkmenistan, Ukraine, and Uzbekistan.

44 **from sixteen countries in 1989 to twenty-nine:** In 1989, the following countries were members of NATO: Belgium, Canada, Denmark, France, Germany, Greece, Iceland, Italy, Luxembourg, the Netherlands, Norway, Portugal, Spain,

Turkey, the United Kingdom, and the United States. There are currently twenty-nine members of NATO, with the following thirteen countries having joined the organization since 1989: Albania, Bulgaria, Croatia, the Czech Republic, Estonia, Hungary, Latvia, Lithuania, Montenegro, Poland, Romania, Slovakia, and Slovenia.

44 **The rationale was to preserve:** For instance, Deputy Secretary of State—and Russia expert—Strobe Talbott listed these reasons in a 1995 article and concluded, "Freezing NATO in its cold war configuration would itself be a huge mistake, a major setback both for the democratic nations that hope to join the Alliance and for the American interest in supporting democratic institutions. By contrast, enlarging NATO in a way that encourages European integration and enhances European security—the policy the administration is determined to pursue—will benefit all the peoples of the continent, and the larger transatlantic community as well." Strobe Talbott, "Why NATO Should Grow," *New York Review of Books*, August 10, 1995, www.nybooks.com/articles/1995/08/10/why-nato-should-grow/#fn-2.

44 **The downside of this adaptation:** At the time, George Kennan, Michael Mandelbaum, and Thomas L. Friedman were among the prominent intellectuals and commentators who advised against NATO enlargement. Michael Mandelbaum, "Preserving the New Peace," *Foreign Affairs*, May/June 1995; Thomas L. Friedman, "Foreign Affairs; Now a Word from X," *New York Times*, May 2, 1998.

44 **subsequent alienation of Russia:** For instance, in his famous 2007 speech before the Munich Conference on Security Policy, the Russian president, Vladimir Putin, stated, "I think it is obvious that NATO expansion does not have any relation with the modernization of the Alliance itself or with ensuring security in Europe. On the contrary, it represents a serious provocation that reduces the level of mutual trust. And we have the right to ask: against whom is this expansion intended? And what happened to the assurances our western partners made after the dissolution of the Warsaw Pact? Where are those declarations today?" Vladimir Putin, "Speech and the Following Discussion at the Munich Conference on Security Policy," February 10, 2007, en.kremlin.ru/events/president/transcripts/24034.

45 **Some predicted or hoped:** Francis Fukuyama, "The End of History?," *National Interest* (Summer 1989).

45 **Others were more skeptical:** Samuel P. Huntington, "The Clash of Civilizations?," *Foreign Affairs* (Summer 1993).

45 **met President George H. W. Bush on the South Lawn:** I recount this scene in greater detail in my book *War of Necessity, War of Choice* (New York: Simon & Schuster, 2009), 60–72.

46 **"This will not stand":** George H. W. Bush, "Remarks and an Exchange with Reporters on the Iraqi Invasion of Kuwait," August 5, 1990, bushlibrary.tamu.edu/research/papers/1990/90080502.html.

46 **the Rwandan genocide:** For more on the Rwandan genocide and an examination of the conundrum such genocides faced U.S. policy makers with, see Samantha Power, *"A Problem from Hell": America and the Age of Genocide* (New York: Harper Perennial, 2007).

46 **800,000 men, women, and children lost their lives:** United Nations, "Report of the Independent Inquiry into the Actions of the United Nations During the 1994 Genocide in Rwanda," December 15, 1999, 3, www.securitycouncilreport.org/atf/cf/%7B65BFCF9B-6D27-4E9C-8CD3-CF6E4FF96FF9%7D/POC%20S19991257.pdf.

47 **R2P doctrine was discredited:** The Russian president, Vladimir Putin, argued NATO forces "frankly violated the UN Security Council resolution on Libya, when instead of imposing the so-called no-fly zone over it they started bombing it too." The Russian foreign minister, Sergey Lavrov, explained that as a result, in Syria, Russia "would never allow the Security Council to authorize anything similar to what happened in Libya." Alan J. Kuperman, "Obama's Libya Debacle: How a Well-Meaning Intervention Ended in Failure," *Foreign Affairs,* March/April 2015.

47 **grew warier of the costs:** An excellent discussion of the decision to intervene in Libya and the spillover effects the intervention had on other issues, mainly Syria, can be found in Evan Osnos's profile of Samantha Power, President Obama's ambassador to the United Nations. Osnos quotes a senior Obama administration official as stating, "For many in the government—including the President—Libya didn't go so well. If Libya had been a great success, that would've created more momentum on the Syria debate. And it wasn't." Evan Osnos, "In the Land of the Possible: Samantha Power Has the President's Ear. To What End?," *New Yorker,* December 15, 2014.

47 **September 11, 2001:** For those interested in learning more on the background of the September 11, 2001, attacks, see Lawrence Wright, *The Looming Tower: Al-Qaeda and the Road to 9/11* (New York: Alfred A. Knopf, 2006).

48 **A second crisis was economic:** For an accessible account of what led to the global financial crisis, see Michael Lewis, *The Big Short: Inside the Doomsday Machine* (New York: W. W. Norton, 2010). For a look at the crisis's long-term consequences, which continue to be felt, see Adam Tooze, *Crashed: How a Decade of Financial Crises Changed the World* (New York: Penguin Books, 2018).

49 **deterioration in U.S.-Russia relations:** For an overview of U.S.-Russia relations from the end of the Cold War through 2013, see Angela Stent, *The Limits of*

Partnership: U.S.-Russian Relations in the Twenty-first Century (Princeton, N.J.: Princeton University Press, 2014). For a look at Russia's relations with the United States in the recent past and the challenges going forward, see Andrew Monaghan, *Dealing with the Russians* (Cambridge, U.K.: Polity Press, 2019).

49 **manipulate the U.S. 2016 presidential election:** In an Intelligence Community Assessment released by the Office of the Director of National Intelligence, the U.S. intelligence agency assessed with high confidence that "Russian President Vladimir Putin ordered an influence campaign in 2016 aimed at the U.S. presidential election." The report further stated, "Russia's intelligence services conducted cyber operations against targets associated with the 2016 US presidential election, including targets associated with both major US political parties." Office of the Director of National Intelligence, "Assessing Russian Activities and Intentions in Recent US Elections," January 6, 2017, www.dni.gov /files/documents/ICA_2017_01.pdf.

50 **concern that China is forging ahead:** Council on Foreign Relations, *Innovation and National Security: Keeping Our Edge* (New York: Council on Foreign Relations, 2019).

50 **international tribunal's ruling to the contrary:** Jane Perlez, "Tribunal Rejects Beijing's Claims in South China Sea," *New York Times*, July 12, 2016.

51 **openly raise the prospect of a cold war:** Niall Ferguson, "The New Cold War? It's With China, and It Has Already Begun," *New York Times*, December 2, 2019; Odd Arne Westad, "The Sources of Chinese Conduct: Are Washington and Beijing Fighting a New Cold War?," *Foreign Affairs*, September/October 2019.

53 **2,000 active satellites:** Stewart Patrick and Kyle L. Evanoff, "The Right Way to Achieve Security in Space: The U.S. Needs to Champion International Cooperation," ForeignAffairs.com, September 17, 2018, www.foreignaffairs.com/articles /space/2018-09-17/right-way-to-achieve-security-space.

55 **drove millions of people out:** As of June 2019, the United Nations High Commissioner for Refugees (UNHCR) estimated that the number of refugees and migrants from Venezuela had reached four million. UNHCR, "Refugees and Migrants from Venezuela Top 4 Million," June 7, 2019.

56 **democracy has slowed or even reversed:** For a book-length treatment of this phenomenon, see Larry Diamond, *Ill Winds: Saving Democracy from Russian Rage, Chinese Ambition, and American Complacency* (New York: Penguin Press, 2019). The subtitle of Freedom House's 2018 report on the state of freedom in the world was "Democracy in Crisis" and the report began, "Political rights and civil liberties around the world deteriorated to their lowest point in more than a decade in 2017, extending a period characterized by emboldened autocrats,

beleaguered democracies, and the United States' withdrawal from its leadership role in the global struggle for human freedom." The report continued, "For the 12th consecutive year . . . countries that suffered democratic setbacks outnumbered those that registered gains." Freedom House, *Freedom in the World 2018: Democracy in Crisis*, 1.

56 **Inequality has increased:** Income inequality within countries continues to increase, while some estimates show that inequality between countries has narrowed because the incomes of developing and developed countries have been converging (that is, developing countries are growing more rapidly than developed countries). Relative global inequality has declined over the past few decades, from a relative Gini coefficient of 0.74 in 1975 to 0.63 in 2010. Absolute inequality, however, has increased dramatically since the mid-1970s. Since 2000, 50 percent of the increase in global wealth benefited only the wealthiest 1 percent of the world's population. The poorest 50 percent of the world's population, by contrast, received only 1 percent of the increase. The wealthiest 1 percent of the population had 32 percent of global wealth in 2000 and 46 percent in 2010. United Nations Development Programme, *Human Development Report 2016: Human Development for Everyone*, 30–31.

56 **number of civil wars has increased:** Scholars define interstate conflict or civil wars differently and use varying thresholds to determine when violence reaches the threshold where it should be counted in the data set, which means that people cite different data. I recommend using the Uppsala Conflict Data Program (UCDP) tables, charts, and graphs. According to two scholars affiliated with the UCDP project, "Non-state conflict concurrently [use of armed force between two organized groups, such as rebel groups or ethnic groups, neither of which is the government of a state] has increased: a new peak of 82 active non-state conflicts was recorded in 2017 and fatalities have increased." Forty-nine state-based conflicts (violence where at least one of the parties is the government of a state, that is, violence between two states and violence between the government and a rebel group) were active in 2017, down from fifty-three in 2016, the peak year of the entire 1946–2017 period. Of the forty-nine conflicts in 2017, only one was fought between states, while the remainder involved the government fighting a rebel group. Therése Pettersson and Kristine Eck, "Organized Violence, 1989–2017," *Journal of Peace Research* 55, no. 4 (2018): 535–47.

56 **number of displaced persons and refugees:** The United Nations High Commissioner for Refugees tracks the number of displaced persons and refugees, and noted in its annual report on global trends, "The global population of forcibly displaced increased by 2.3 million people in 2018. By the end of the year, almost 70.8 million individuals were forcibly displaced worldwide as a result of persecu-

tion, conflict, violence, or human rights violations. As a result, the world's forcibly displaced population remained yet again at a record high." United Nations High Commissioner for Refugees, *Global Trends: Forced Displacement in 2018*, 2.

56 **biased by what they are focusing on:** Steven Pinker, *The Better Angels of Our Nature: Why Violence Has Declined* (New York: Penguin Books, 2011).

57 **era of deterioration:** Richard Haass, *A World in Disarray: American Foreign Policy and the Crisis of the Old Order* (New York: Penguin Press, 2017).

PART II: REGIONS OF THE WORLD

62 **Bangladesh, in particular, faces:** Gardiner Harris, "Borrowed Time on Disappearing Land," *New York Times*, March 28, 2014.

63 **No religion claims a majority:** Pew Research Center, "The Changing Global Religious Landscape" (April 2017), 8–10.

63 **age distribution across countries:** United Nations Population Division, "2019 Revision of World Population Prospects," with graphs and maps available at population.un.org/wpp/.

64 **no single language is spoken:** According to *Ethnologue*, 1.132 billion people in the world speak English. See www.ethnologue.com/language/eng. The World Bank estimates a global population of 7.594 billion, meaning that 1 out of every 6.7 people in the world speak English. While 1.116 billion people in the world speak Mandarin Chinese, 1.082 billion (or 97 percent) of those who speak Mandarin Chinese live in China. See www.ethnologue.com/language/cmn.

Europe

67 **Europe's economy is slightly larger:** The countries included in this region had a combined output (GDP) of roughly $22.7 trillion in 2018, compared with a GDP of $20.5 trillion for the United States. Given global GDP of $84.7 trillion, Europe accounts for 26.8 percent of total output. See International Monetary Fund, "World Economic Outlook Database" (April 2019).

67 **region's fifty countries:** For the purposes of this chapter, Europe includes fifty countries: Albania, Andorra, Armenia, Austria, Azerbaijan, Belarus, Belgium, Bosnia and Herzegovina, Bulgaria, Croatia, Cyprus, the Czech Republic, Denmark, Estonia, Finland, France, Georgia, Germany, Greece, Holy See, Hungary, Iceland, Ireland, Italy, Kosovo, Latvia, Liechtenstein, Lithuania, Luxembourg, Macedonia, Malta, Moldova, Monaco, Montenegro, the Netherlands, Norway, Poland, Portugal, Romania, Russia, San Marino, Serbia, Slovakia, Slovenia, Spain, Sweden, Switzerland, Turkey, Ukraine, and the United Kingdom.

69 **second half of the nineteenth century:** For those interested in this period of European history, see James Joll, *Europe Since 1870: An International History* (New York: Penguin, 1973); L. C. B. Seaman, *From Vienna to Versailles* (New York: Harper & Row, 1955); and A. J. P. Taylor, *The Struggle for Mastery in Europe, 1848–1918* (Oxford: Oxford University Press, 1971).

69 **begin a consideration of today's Europe:** For those interested in post–World War II European history, see Tony Judt, *Postwar: A History of Europe Since 1945* (New York: Penguin Books, 2005).

70 **"keep the Soviet Union out":** Lord Hastings Lionel Ismay, NATO's first secretary-general, made this remark earlier in his political career. NATO Leaders: www.nato.int/cps/en/natohq/declassified_137930.htm.

70–71 **known as the Marshall Plan:** Steil, *Marshall Plan*.

71 **French statesman Robert Schuman:** Merriman, *History of Modern Europe*, 1123.

72 **the Warsaw Pact:** The organization's original members were Albania, Bulgaria, Czechoslovakia, East Germany, Hungary, Poland, Romania, and the Soviet Union.

73 **UN peacekeepers still deployed:** The UN Security Council in 1999 authorized the UN secretary-general to establish an international civil presence in Kosovo—the United Nations Interim Administration Mission in Kosovo (UN-MIK). As of March 2019, 351 total personnel were deployed to Kosovo as part of this mission. UNMIK Fact Sheet, peacekeeping.un.org/en/mission/unmik.

74 **One difference between the EC and the EU:** The Maastricht Treaty, known formally as the Treaty on European Union, declared, "A common foreign and security policy is hereby established." Treaty on European Union, Title V, "Provisions on a Common Foreign and Security Policy." The full treaty is available at europa.eu/european-union/sites/europaeu/files/docs/body/treaty _on_european_union_en.pdf.

74 **expanded its membership:** The twelve founding members of the EU were Belgium, Denmark, France, Germany, Greece, Ireland, Italy, Luxembourg, the Netherlands, Portugal, Spain, and the United Kingdom. In 1995, Austria, Finland, and Sweden joined. In 2004, Cyprus, the Czech Republic, Estonia, Hungary, Latvia, Lithuania, Malta, Poland, Slovakia, and Slovenia joined. In 2007, Bulgaria and Romania joined, followed by Croatia in 2013.

75 **rejected a new European constitution:** Elaine Sciolino, "French Voters Soundly Reject European Union Constitution," *New York Times*, May 30, 2005; Marlise Simons, "Dutch Voters Solidly Reject New European Constitution," *New York Times*, June 2, 2005.

75 **slim majority of British voters:** Fifty-two percent of voters opted to leave the EU, while 48 percent voted to remain in the bloc. Steven Erlanger, "Britain Votes to Leave E.U.; Cameron Plans to Step Down," *New York Times*, June 23, 2016.

76 **nineteen countries in the eurozone:** The following countries are members of the eurozone and therefore use the euro as their national currency: Austria, Belgium, Cyprus, Estonia, Finland, France, Germany, Greece, Ireland, Italy, Latvia, Lithuania, Luxembourg, Malta, the Netherlands, Portugal, Slovakia, Slovenia, and Spain.

76 **no European banking mechanism:** For a fuller discussion of this and other shortcomings with the euro, see Matthias Matthijs and Mark Blyth, eds., *The Future of the Euro* (Oxford: Oxford University Press, 2015).

76 **Europe has an aging population:** The share of the population aged sixty-five years and over is increasing in every EU member state. Eurostat, "Population Structure and Ageing," July 2019, ec.europa.eu/eurostat/statistics-explained /index.php/Population_structure_and_ageing.

77 **Russian threat to Europe:** For more on Russia, its political system, and how it views the world, see Dmitri Trenin, *Russia* (Cambridge, U.K.: Polity Press, 2019); Angela Stent, *Putin's World: Russia Against the West and with the Rest* (New York: Twelve, 2019); Steven Lee Myers, *The New Tsar: The Rise and Reign of Vladimir Putin* (New York: Alfred A. Knopf, 2015); Fiona Hill and Clifford G. Gaddy, *Mr. Putin: Operative in the Kremlin* (Washington, D.C.: Brookings Institution Press, 2015); Shaun Walker, *The Long Hangover: Putin's New Russia and the Ghosts of the Past* (New York: Oxford University Press, 2018); Nina Khrushcheva and Jeffrey Tayler, *In Putin's Footsteps: Searching for the Soul of an Empire Across Russia's Eleven Time Zones* (New York: St. Martin's Press, 2019).

77 **great power more in name:** For more on Russia's economy, see Anders Aslund, *Russia's Crony Capitalism: The Path from Market Economy to Kleptocracy* (New Haven, Conn.: Yale University Press, 2019).

77 **an economy roughly the size of Canada's:** The IMF estimated the size of Russia's economy at $1.63 trillion in 2018, compared with $1.62 trillion for South Korea, $1.71 trillion for Canada, $1.87 trillion for Brazil, and $2.1 trillion for Italy. See International Monetary Fund, "World Economic Outlook Database" (April 2019).

77 **heavily dependent on energy:** According to Russia's Ministry of Finance, in 2018 oil and gas revenues accounted for 46 percent of the country's total federal budget revenues. Ministry of Finance of the Russian Federation, "Annual Report on Execution of the Federal Budget," July 11, 2019, www.minfin.ru/en /statistics/fedbud/. According to the IMF, as of 2017 Russia's oil and gas exports accounted for 54 percent of the country's total exports. International Monetary

Fund, "Russian Federation: Staff Report for the 2018 Article IV Consultation," July 17, 2018, 31.

77 **has declined for two decades:** In 1992, Russia's population stood at 148.7 million and began declining, bottoming out at 142.7 million in 2008. Recently, the population began to recover, reaching 144.5 million in 2017 before dipping again in 2018. World Bank Database, data.worldbank.org/indicator/SP.POP .TOTL?locations=RU.

77 **male life expectancy:** World Bank Database, data.worldbank.org/indicator /SP.DYN.LE00.MA.IN?locations=RU.

78 **humiliated over how the Cold War ended:** Vladimir Putin famously said, "First and foremost it is worth acknowledging that the demise of the Soviet Union was the greatest geopolitical catastrophe of the century. As for the Russian people, it became a genuine tragedy." "Putin: Soviet Collapse a 'Genuine Tragedy,'" Associated Press, April 25, 2005. For further evidence of Putin's view of the end of the Cold War, see especially his 2014 speech before the Valdai International Discussion Club. Vladimir Putin, "Meeting of the Valdai International Discussion Club," October 24, 2014, en.kremlin.ru/events/president/news/46860.

78 **NATO's enlargement as an insult and a threat:** During his 2007 speech before the Munich Conference on Security Policy, Putin argued NATO's expansion "represents a serious provocation that reduces the level of mutual trust." Putin, "Speech and the Following Discussion at the Munich Conference on Security Policy."

79 **steadily lost interest:** Of the U.S.-led liberal world order, Putin rhetorically asked, "Let's ask ourselves, how comfortable are we with this, how safe are we, how happy living in this world, and how fair and rational has it become? Maybe, we have no real reasons to worry, argue and ask awkward questions? Maybe the United States' exceptional position and the way they are carrying out their leadership really is a blessing for us all, and their meddling in events all around the world is bringing peace, prosperity, progress, growth and democracy, and we should maybe just relax and enjoy it all? Let me say that this is not the case, absolutely not the case." Putin, "Meeting of the Valdai International Discussion Club," October 24, 2014.

79 **backed by Russian soldiers:** "Putin Admits Russian Forces Were Deployed to Crimea," Reuters, April 17, 2014

79 **dismiss the referendum as a sham:** At the time, President Obama stated, "The referendum in Crimea was a clear violation of Ukrainian constitutions and international law, and it will not be recognized by the international community." White House Office of the Press Secretary, "Statement by the President on

Ukraine," March 17, 2014. On July 25, 2018, Secretary of State Michael Pompeo reiterated the U.S. stance, stating, "The United States rejects Russia's attempted annexation of Crimea and pledges to maintain this policy until Ukraine's territorial integrity is restored." Michael R. Pompeo, "Crimea Declaration," July 25, 2018.

80 **taken 13,000 lives:** Office of the United Nations High Commissioner for Human Rights, "Report on the Human Rights Situation in Ukraine, 16 November 2018 to 15 February 2019," 6, www.ohchr.org/_layouts/15/WopiFrame .aspx?sourcedoc=/Documents/Countries/UA/ReportUkraine16Nov2018-15 Feb2019.pdf.

81 **Russia worked to influence:** Office of the Director of National Intelligence, "Assessing Russian Activities and Intentions in Recent US Elections"; European Commission, "A Europe That Protects: EU Reports on Progress in Fighting Disinformation Ahead of European Council," June 14, 2019.

81 **including the vote on Brexit:** David D. Kirkpatrick, "Signs of Russian Meddling in Brexit Referendum," *New York Times*, November 15, 2017.

81 **claimed waters off Ukraine:** BBC News, "Russia-Ukraine Tensions Rise After Kerch Strait Ship Capture," November 26, 2018.

81 **history seemed to have truly ended:** Fukuyama, "End of History?" For a rebuttal of Fukuyama's essay, see Samuel P. Huntington, "No Exit: The Errors of Endism," *National Interest* (Fall 1989).

81 **something dramatically different:** I made a similar argument in a December 2018 column for *Project Syndicate*. Richard N. Haass, "Europe in Disarray," *Project Syndicate*, December 13, 2018, https://www.project-syndicate.org/com mentary/growing-threats-to-europe-democracy-security-by-richard-n--haass -2018-12.

East Asia and the Pacific

82 **Its thirty-one countries:** For the purposes of this chapter, East Asia and the Pacific includes the following countries and territories: Australia, Brunei, Cambodia, China, Fiji, Indonesia, Japan, Kiribati, North Korea, South Korea, Laos, Malaysia, Marshall Islands, Federated States of Micronesia, Mongolia, Myanmar (Burma), Nauru, New Zealand, Palau, Papua New Guinea, the Philippines, Samoa, Singapore, Solomon Islands, Taiwan, Thailand, Timor-Leste, Tonga, Tuvalu, Vanuatu, and Vietnam.

82 **nearly 1.4 billion inhabitants:** World Bank Database, data.worldbank.org/in dicator/SP.POP.TOTL?locations=CN.

82 **some 13,000 citizens:** World Bank Database, data.worldbank.org/indicator /SP.POP.TOTL?locations=NR.

82 **world's second-largest economy:** See International Monetary Fund, "World Economic Outlook Database" (April 2019).

84 **more territorial disputes:** M. Taylor Fravel, "Territorial and Maritime Boundary Disputes in Asia," in *Oxford Handbook of the International Relations in Asia*, ed. Saadia M. Pekkanen, John Ravenhill, and Rosemary Foot (New York: Oxford University Press, 2014).

84 **one-third of global output:** The region's combined output (GDP) in 2018 was $25.6 trillion, which represents 30 percent of the world's total of $84.7 trillion. See International Monetary Fund, "World Economic Outlook Database" (April 2019).

84 **Association of Southeast Asian Nations:** The following are members of ASEAN: Brunei, Cambodia, Indonesia, Laos, Malaysia, Myanmar (Burma), the Philippines, Singapore, Thailand, and Vietnam.

84 **forum for its twenty-one members:** The following are members of APEC: Australia, Brunei, Canada, Chile, China, Hong Kong, Indonesia, Japan, Malaysia, Mexico, New Zealand, Papua New Guinea, Peru, the Philippines, Russia, Singapore, South Korea, Taiwan, Thailand, United States, and Vietnam.

84 **population nearly twice that of the United States:** Indonesia, Malaysia, the Philippines, Singapore, Thailand, and Vietnam had a combined population of 571 million in 2018, compared with a U.S. population of 327 million. See International Monetary Fund, "World Economic Outlook Database" (April 2019).

84 **combined GDP on par:** Indonesia, Malaysia, the Philippines, Singapore, Thailand, and Vietnam had a combined GDP of $2.8 trillion in 2018, compared with France's $2.78 trillion, India's $2.72 trillion, and the United Kingdom's $2.83 trillion. See International Monetary Fund, "World Economic Outlook Database" (April 2019).

85 **invaded South Korea:** For a history of the Korean War, see Halberstam, *Coldest Winter*.

86 **met by Chinese "volunteers":** For the best account of how China made the decision to intervene militarily, see Chen Jian's *China's Road to the Korean War: The Making of the Sino-American Confrontation* (New York: Columbia University Press, 1994).

86 **some 37,000 American troops were killed:** The official death toll is 36,574. DeBruyne, "American War and Military Operations Casualties," 2.

86 **3.5 million Koreans were either killed or wounded:** Westad, *Cold War*, 182.

86 **war in Vietnam:** The best single-volume histories of the conflict are Karnow, *Vietnam;* and Logevall, *Embers of War.* Also worth reading are David Halberstam, *The Best and the Brightest* (New York: Ballantine Books, 1969); and Leslie H. Gelb and Richard K. Betts, *The Irony of Vietnam: The System Worked* (Washington, D.C.: Brookings Institution Press, 1979). There is also fantastic literature worth reading, including Graham Greene, *The Quiet American* (New York: Penguin Classics, 1991); Tim O'Brien, *The Things They Carried* (New York: Houghton Mifflin, 1990); and Karl Marlantes, *Matterhorn: A Novel of the Vietnam War* (New York: Atlantic Monthly Press, 2010). Finally, it is worth investing the time to watch Ken Burns's ten-part documentary on the Vietnam War, as well as Errol Morris's *Fog of War.*

88 **Fifty-eight thousand American soldiers lost their lives:** The official death toll is 58,220. DeBruyne, "American War and Military Operations Casualties," 2.

88 **more than one million Vietnamese:** Westad, *Cold War,* 331–32.

88 **The economic cost:** Stephen Daggett, "Costs of Major U.S. Wars," Congressional Research Service, June 29, 2010, 2.

88 **rose from forty-eight years in 1960:** World Bank Database, data.worldbank .org/indicator/SP.DYN.LE00.IN?locations=Z4.

88 **average annual economic growth of more than 6 percent:** Michael Sarel, "Growth in East Asia: What We Can and What We Cannot Infer" (Washington, D.C.: International Monetary Fund, 1996), 2.

88 **gross domestic product (GDP) per capita:** World Bank Database, data.world bank.org/indicator/NY.GDP.PCAP.KD?locations=Z4.

88 **investment in education:** World Bank East Asia and Pacific Regional Report, "Growing Smarter: Learning and Equitable Development in East Asia and Pacific," 2018.

90 **Japan evolved from a defeated:** Dower, *Embracing Defeat.*

90 **It became a manufacturing powerhouse:** The two classic works on Japan's economic transformation are Hugh T. Patrick and Henry Rosovsky, eds., *Asia's New Giant: How the Japanese Economy Works* (Washington, D.C.: Brookings Institution Press, 1976); and Chalmers A. Johnson, *MITI and the Japanese Miracle: The Growth of Industrial Policy, 1925–1975* (Stanford, Calif.: Stanford University Press, 1982).

90 **estimated thirty to fifty-five million deaths:** Frank Dikötter has written the most authoritative history of the famine and estimates it resulted in at least forty-five million deaths. Frank Dikötter, *Mao's Great Famine: The History of China's Most Devastating Catastrophe, 1958–1962* (London: Bloomsbury, 2010);

Yang Jisheng, *Tombstone: The Great Chinese Famine, 1958–1962* (New York: Farrar, Straus and Giroux, 2012).

90 **ruining countless lives:** Roderick MacFarquhar, *Mao's Last Revolution* (Cambridge, Mass.: Harvard University Press, 2006).

91 **balance these two relationships:** For a book on Japan's views of a rising China, see Sheila A. Smith, *Intimate Rivals: Japanese Domestic Politics and a Rising China* (New York: Columbia University Press, 2016). On Japanese strategic perspectives, see Kenneth Pyle, *Japan Rising: The Resurgence of Japanese Power and Purpose* (New York: PublicAffairs, 2007). For more on South Korean foreign policy, see Scott A. Snyder, *South Korea at the Crossroads: Autonomy and Alliance in an Era of Rival Powers* (New York: Columbia University Press, 2018).

92 **the United States would likely become involved:** President Obama affirmed that the U.S.-Japan security treaty covers the Senkaku Islands, meaning that the United States would be obligated to come to Japan's defense if China were to attack the Senkaku Islands. The White House Office of the Press Secretary, "Remarks by President Obama and Prime Minister Abe of Japan in Joint Press Conference," April 28, 2015. President Trump has reiterated this commitment. White House, "Joint Statement from President Donald J. Trump and Prime Minister Shinzo Abe," February 10, 2017.

92 **major cause of their 1962 war:** John Garver, "India, China, the United States, Tibet, and the Origins of the 1962 War," *India Review* 3, no. 2 (2004): 9–20.

93 **whether a peaceful settlement:** This is an extremely complex issue, but two books worth reading are Richard C. Bush's *Unchartered Strait: The Future of China-Taiwan Relations* (Washington, D.C.: Brookings Institution, 2013) and Nancy Bernkopf Tucker's *Strait Talk: United States–Taiwan Relations and the Crisis with China* (Cambridge, Mass.: Harvard University Press, 2009).

94 **entering its fourth phase:** I wrote about the four phases more extensively in a piece for *The Wall Street Journal*. Richard Haass, "The Crisis in U.S.-China Relations," *Wall Street Journal*, October 19, 2018.

95 **The region is aging more rapidly:** World Bank Group, "Live Long and Prosper: Aging in East Asia and Pacific" (2016), xv.

South Asia

97 **South Asia consists of eight countries:** The eight countries included in this region are Afghanistan, Bangladesh, Bhutan, India, the Maldives, Nepal, Pakistan, and Sri Lanka.

97 **25 percent of the world's population:** About 1.82 billion people—or 24 percent of the world's population of 7.59 billion—reside in this region. World Bank Database, data.worldbank.org/indicator/SP.POP.TOTL.

97 **under 4 percent of its landmass:** World Bank Database, data.worldbank.org /indicator/AG.SRF.TOTL.K2?display=graph.

97 **4 percent of its economy:** These eight countries had a combined economic output (GDP) of $3.5 trillion in 2018, which is roughly 4 percent of the global total of $84.7 trillion. International Monetary Fund, "World Economic Outlook Database" (April 2019).

97 **three of the four countries:** Pew Research Center, "The Future of World Religions: Population Growth Projections, 2010–2050," April 2, 2015, 74.

97 **80 percent of Indians are Hindu:** Pew Research Center, "Future of World Religions," 95.

97 **world's least economically integrated region:** Sanjay Kathuria, ed., "A Glass Half Full: The Promise of Regional Trade in South Asia" (Washington, D.C.: World Bank Group, 2018), 7–9.

99 **Some lump in the five countries:** For instance, the U.S. Department of State has a Bureau of South and Central Asian Affairs whose senior official oversees both South and Central Asia.

99 **Any discussion of South Asia:** For a more in-depth discussion of India, see Stephen P. Cohen, *India: Emerging Power* (Washington, D.C.: Brookings Institution Press, 2001); and Ramachandra Guha, *India After Gandhi: The History of the World's Largest Democracy*, 2nd ed. (New York: Ecco, 2019). For more on Indian foreign policy, see Alyssa Ayres, *Our Time Has Come: How India Is Making Its Place in the World* (New York: Oxford University Press, 2018).

99 **around 7 percent annually:** According to the IMF, India's economy grew by 7.4 percent in 2014, 8 percent in 2015, 8.2 percent in 2016, 7.2 percent in 2017, and 7 percent in 2018. International Monetary Fund, "World Economic Outlook Database" (April 2019).

100 **only about one-fifth the size of China's:** In 2018, China's GDP stood at $13.4 trillion, five times India's $2.7 trillion. International Monetary Fund, "World Economic Outlook Database" (April 2019).

100 **started from a similar base:** In 1969, India's GDP stood at $58.4 billion, compared with China's $79.7 billion. In 1978, at the beginning of China's program of economic reform, India's economy was $137.3 billion, compared with China's $149.5 billion. World Bank Database, data.worldbank.org/indicator/NY.GDP .MKTP.CD?end=1979&locations=IN-CN&start=1960.

100 **held back by corruption:** "Fighting Corruption in India: A Bad Boom," *Economist*, March 15, 2014.

100 **poor infrastructure:** Sheoli Pargal and Sudeshna Ghosh Banerjee, *More Power to India: The Challenge of Electricity Distribution* (Washington, D.C.: World Bank, 2014).

100 **complex political and legal bureaucracies:** "The Constant Tinkerer: Narendra Modi Is a Fine Administrator, but Not Much of a Reformer," *Economist*, June 24, 2017.

101 **GDP per capita is only around $2,000:** The IMF reported India's GDP per capita at $2,036 in 2018, putting it at number 147 in the world, lower than Nigeria, São Tomé and Príncipe, Djibouti, Nicaragua, and Ghana. International Monetary Fund, "World Economic Outlook Database" (April 2019).

101 **Life expectancy has more than doubled:** Preetika Rana and Joanna Sugden, "India's Record Since Independence," *Wall Street Journal*, August 15, 2013.

101 **Literacy has more than quadrupled:** Rana and Sugden, "India's Record Since Independence."

101 **India has made remarkable strides:** Organisation for Economic Co-operation and Development, "Promoting Strong and Inclusive Growth in India," 2017.

101 **200 million Indians:** The U.S. Energy Information Administration estimates that 19 percent of India's population (240 million people) lacked basic access to electricity in 2013. U.S. Energy Information Administration, "Country Analysis Brief: India," June 14, 2016, 2.

101 **lack access to basic sanitation or toilets:** WaterAid, "Out of Order: The State of the World's Toilets 2017," 9. In 2014, Prime Minister Narendra Modi pledged that all Indians would have sanitation coverage by October 2019, and as part of that he launched a $20 billion toilet-building campaign. P. R. Sanjai, "World's Biggest Toilet-Building Spree Is Under Way in India," *Bloomberg*, July 30, 2018.

101 **emerged as a major political force:** Ashutosh Varshney, "India's Democracy at 70: Growth, Inequality, and Nationalism," *Journal of Democracy* 28, no. 3 (July 2017): 41–51; Christophe Jaffrelot, "India's Democracy at 70: Toward a Hindu State?," *Journal of Democracy* 28, no. 3 (July 2017): 52–63; Eswaran Sridharan, "India's Democracy at 70: The Shifting Party Balance," *Journal of Democracy* 28, no. 3 (July 2017): 76–85.

102 **Pakistan, whose name:** For those interested in delving deeper into Pakistan's economic and political development, see Anatol Lieven, *Pakistan: A Hard Country* (New York: PublicAffairs, 2011); Omar Noman, *Pakistan: A Political and Economic History Since 1947* (London: Kegan Paul, 1990); Stephen P. Cohen, *The*

Idea of Pakistan (Washington, D.C.: Brookings Institution, 2004); and Ian Talbot, *Pakistan: A New History*, rev. ed. (London: Oxford University Press, 2015).

102 **barely more than one-tenth that of India's:** In 2018, Pakistan had a GDP of $312.6 billion, compared with India's $2.717 trillion, making India's economy roughly nine times the size of Pakistan's. International Monetary Fund, "World Economic Outlook Database" (April 2019).

102 **just over $1,500:** The IMF reported that Pakistan's GDP per capita stood at $1,555 in 2018. International Monetary Fund, "World Economic Outlook Database" (April 2019).

102 **Real power is held:** C. Christine Fair, "Why the Pakistan Army Is Here to Stay: Prospects for Civil Governance," *International Affairs* 87, no. 3 (May 2011): 571–88; Cohen, *Idea of Pakistan*; Husain Haqqani, *Pakistan: Between Mosque and Military* (Washington, D.C.: Carnegie Endowment, 2005).

102 **exports of ready-made garments:** Refayet Ullah Mirdha, "Bangladesh Remains the Second Biggest Apparel Exporter," *Daily Star* (Bangladesh), August 2, 2018.

102 **U.S. trade with Bangladesh:** U.S. Census Bureau, "U.S. Trade in Goods and Services: Annual Revision," June 6, 2019.

102 **Bangladesh has suffered from dysfunctional:** For more on Bangladesh, see Ali Riaz, *Bangladesh: A Political History Since Independence* (London: I. B. Tauris, 2016).

104 **The modern history of the region:** The best books on the region's modern history are John Keay, *India: A History: From the Earliest Civilisations to the Boom of the Twenty-first Century*, 2nd ed. (London: HarperPress, 2010); Ian Talbot, *A History of Modern South Asia: Politics, States, Diasporas* (New Haven, Conn.: Yale University Press, 2016); and Sugata Bose and Ayesha Jalal, *Modern South Asia: History, Culture, Political Economy*, 4th ed. (London: Routledge, 2018).

104 **one million lives:** Yasmin Khan, *The Great Partition: The Making of India and Pakistan*, 2nd ed. (New Haven, Conn.: Yale University Press, 2017). Other notable works on partition include Patrick French, *Liberty or Death: India's Journey to Independence and Division* (London: HarperCollins, 1997); and Nisid Hajari, *Midnight's Furies: The Deadly Legacy of India's Partition* (Boston: Houghton Mifflin Harcourt, 2015).

104 **did not bring stability:** On the India-Pakistan conflict, I recommend reading Myra MacDonald, *Defeat Is an Orphan: How Pakistan Lost the Great South Asian War* (London: Hurst, 2016).

105 **Kashmir was at the center:** For more on this conflict, see Stephen P. Cohen, "India, Pakistan, and Kashmir," *Journal of Strategic Studies* 25, no. 4 (2002):

32–60; International Crisis Group, "Steps Towards Peace: Putting Kashmiris First," June 3, 2010.

105 **the 1971 conflict:** For more on this war and the creation of Bangladesh, see Warren Bass, *The Blood Telegram: Nixon, Kissinger, and a Forgotten Genocide* (New York: Alfred A. Knopf, 2013), and Philip Oldenburg, "'A Place Insufficiently Imagined': Language, Belief, and the Pakistan Crisis of 1971," *Journal of Asian Studies* 44, no. 4 (August 1985): 711–33.

105 **one of the largest recipients:** Herring, *From Colony to Superpower*, 713.

105 **India first tested a nuclear device:** For more on India's nuclear program, see George Perkovich, *India's Nuclear Bomb: The Impact on Global Proliferation* (Berkeley: University of California Press, 1999).

106 **world's fastest-growing nuclear arsenal:** Gregory D. Koblentz, *Strategic Stability in the Second Nuclear Age* (New York: Council on Foreign Relations, 2014), 14–18.

106 **Afghanistan has had its own:** For more on Afghanistan, see Ahmed Rashid, *Descent into Chaos: The U.S. and the Disaster in Pakistan, Afghanistan, and Central Asia* (New York: Viking, 2008); and Ahmed Rashid, *Pakistan on the Brink: The Future of America, Pakistan, and Afghanistan* (New York: Viking, 2012). To better understand this period of history leading up to the September 11, 2001, attacks, see Steve Coll, *Ghost Wars: The Secret History of the CIA, Afghanistan, and bin Laden, from the Soviet Invasion to September 10, 2001* (New York: Penguin Books, 2004).

109 **building stronger relationships with India:** As evidenced by the U.S. Department of Defense's "Indo-Pacific Strategy Report" released on June 1, 2019, as well as the renaming of the U.S. Pacific Command to the U.S. Indo-Pacific Command.

109 **world's fourth-largest military budget:** In 2018, India's military budget stood at $66.5 billion, placing it fourth in the world behind Saudi Arabia ($67.6 billion), China ($250 billion), and the United States ($649 billion). Stockholm International Peace Research Institute, "SIPRI Military Expenditure Database, 1949–2018."

The Middle East

111 **The Middle East:** For this chapter, the following countries are included in the region: Algeria, Bahrain, Egypt, Iran, Iraq, Israel, Jordan, Kuwait, Lebanon, Libya, Morocco, Oman, Palestinian territories, Qatar, Saudi Arabia, Syria, Tunisia, United Arab Emirates, and Yemen.

112 **around 450 million:** The World Bank recorded the combined population of the countries included in this region as 449 million in 2018. World Bank Database, data.worldbank.org/indicator/SP.POP.TOTL?locations=ZQ.

113 **around $3.5 trillion:** International Monetary Fund, "World Economic Outlook Database" (April 2019).

113 **overwhelmingly dependent on revenues:** According to the World Bank, "At about 14 percent, MENA [Middle East and North Africa] has the world's lowest share of nonoil manufactured exports and the highest share of fuel exports—between 60 and 80 percent." World Bank Group, "MENA Economic Monitor: Economic Transformation" (April 2018), 11.

113 **more than half of total:** According to the World Bank, in the Middle East and North Africa fuel exports account for over 56 percent of merchandise exports, compared with a global average of under 12 percent. World Bank Database, data.worldbank.org/indicator/TX.VAL.FUEL.ZS.UN?locations=ZQ-1W& view=chart.

113 **education they receive is poor:** United Nations Development Programme, "Arab Human Development Report 2016: Youth and the Prospects for Human Development in a Changing Reality," 74–85.

113 **youth unemployment is far above:** According to the United Nations Development Programme, "High youth unemployment rates are one of the most distinctive features of Arab labour markets. They have been nearly twice as high as the rates in other global regions since the early 1990s. . . . [Y]outh unemployment will keep rising, reaching 29.1 percent in the Middle East and 30.7 percent in North Africa by 2019, whereas the peak rate in other world regions will not exceed 18 percent." United Nations Development Programme, "Arab Human Development Report 2016: Youth and the Prospects for Human Development in a Changing Reality," 80.

113 **participation by girls and women:** According to the OECD, "Despite improvements in women's education, female labor force participation remains very low—only 22%, compared to more than 50% in OECD countries." Organisation for Economic Co-operation and Development, *The Pursuit of Gender Equality: An Uphill Battle* (Paris: OECD Publishing, 2017), 238.

113 **to one degree or another autocratic:** According to Freedom House, only 5 percent of the population in the Middle East and North Africa lives in countries categorized as "free" (those who live in Israel or Tunisia), while 12 percent live in "partly free" countries and the remaining 83 percent live in "not free" countries. Only two of the region's eighteen countries are categorized as "free" by Freedom House, with the organization categorizing twelve as "not free" and

four as "partly free." Freedom House, *Freedom in the World 2018: Democracy in Crisis*, 16–17.

113 **ruled by hereditary monarchies:** Eight of the world's ten remaining ruling monarchies are in the region: Bahrain, Jordan, Kuwait, Morocco, Oman, Qatar, Saudi Arabia, and the United Arab Emirates.

114 **conjecture and controversy:** Bernard Lewis, *Islam and the West* (Oxford: Oxford University Press, 1994); Edward W. Said, *Orientalism* (New York: Pantheon Books, 1978).

114 **world's proven oil reserves:** The region accounts for 51.4 percent of the world's total proved oil reserves, 37.5 percent of the world's total oil production, and 44.7 percent of the world's total proved natural gas reserves. British Petroleum, "Statistical Review of World Energy" (2018).

115 **almost half of all terrorist attacks:** According to the United Nations Development Programme, "In 2014 alone, the region accounted for almost 45 percent of all terrorist attacks worldwide." United Nations Development Programme, "Arab Human Development Report 2016: Youth and the Prospects for Human Development in a Changing Reality," 174.

115 **Israel-Palestinian conflict:** For good introductions to the Israel-Palestinian conflict, I recommend Ari Shavit's memoir *My Promised Land: The Triumph and Tragedy of Israel* (New York: Spiegel & Grau, 2013) as well as Thomas Friedman's *From Beirut to Jerusalem* (New York: Farrar, Straus and Giroux, 1989) and David K. Shipler's, *Arab and Jew: Wounded Spirits in a Promised Land* (New York: Broadway Books, 2015).

117 **decline of the Ottoman Empire:** For those interested in the Ottoman Empire, I recommend Bernard Lewis, *The Emergence of Modern Turkey*, 3rd ed. (New York: Oxford University Press, 2002); and Feroz Ahmad, *The Making of Modern Turkey* (London: Routledge, 1993).

118 **1967 war between Israel and its Arab neighbors:** For a history of the Six-Day War, see Michael Oren, *Six Days of War: June 1967 and the Making of the Modern Middle East* (New York: Presidio Press, 2003).

120 **undertaking in Oslo:** The 1993 Oslo I Accord can be found at ecf.org.il /issues/issue/184. The 1995 Oslo II Accord can be found at ecf.org.il/media _items/624.

122 **helped to overthrow:** Stephen Kinzer, *All the Shah's Men: An American Coup and the Roots of Middle East Terror* (Hoboken, N.J.: John Wiley & Sons, 2003). For a revisionist take on this episode, see Ray Takeyh, "What Really Happened in Iran: The CIA, the Ouster of Mosaddeq, and the Restoration of the Shah," *Foreign Affairs*, July/August 2014.

122 **a revolution overthrew the Shah:** For more on the Iranian revolution, see James Buchan, *Days of God: The Revolution in Iran and Its Consequences* (New York: Simon & Schuster, 2012).

122 **instituted a unique theocratic system:** For more on contemporary Iranian politics, see Ray Takeyh, *Guardians of the Revolution: Iran and the World in the Age of the Ayatollahs* (Oxford: Oxford University Press, 2009).

123 **claimed nearly one million lives:** Westad, *Cold War*, 565.

124 **military action and liberated Kuwait:** For more on the Gulf War, see Rick Atkinson, *Crusade: The Untold Story of the Persian Gulf War* (New York: Houghton Mifflin, 1993); and Michael R. Gordon, *The Generals' War: The Inside Story of the Conflict in the Gulf* (New York: Little, Brown, 1995).

124 **There are many analyses:** Haass, *War of Necessity, War of Choice*; Michael J. Mazarr, *Leap of Faith: Hubris, Negligence, and America's Greatest Foreign Policy Tragedy* (New York: PublicAffairs, 2019).

124 **a conflict that proved expensive:** On the Iraq War and the war in Afghanistan, see Dexter Filkins, *The Forever War* (New York: Alfred A. Knopf, 2008).

124 **"war of choice that was ill-advised":** Haass, *War of Necessity, War of Choice*, 278.

125 **Dubbed the Arab Spring:** For more on these protests and the democracy movements, see Steven A. Cook, *False Dawn: Protest, Democracy, and Violence in the New Middle East* (New York: Oxford University Press, 2017).

126 **Some 500,000 Syrians have lost their lives:** Megan Specia, "How Syria's Death Toll Is Lost in the Fog of War," *New York Times*, April 13, 2018.

129 **Joint Comprehensive Plan of Action:** The full text of the agreement can be found at 2009-2017.state.gov/e/eb/tfs/spi/iran/jcpoa/.

Africa

131 **forty-nine countries:** For the purposes of this chapter, the following countries are grouped together as "Africa" or more precisely "sub-Saharan Africa": Angola, Benin, Botswana, Burkina Faso, Burundi, Cabo Verde, Cameroon, Central African Republic, Chad, Comoros, Democratic Republic of the Congo, Republic of the Congo, Côte d'Ivoire, Djibouti, Equatorial Guinea, Eritrea, Eswatini, Ethiopia, Gabon, the Gambia, Ghana, Guinea, Guinea-Bissau, Kenya, Lesotho, Liberia, Madagascar, Malawi, Mali, Mauritania, Mauritius, Mozambique, Namibia, Niger, Nigeria, Rwanda, São Tomé and Príncipe, Senegal, Seychelles, Sierra Leone, Somalia, South Africa, South Sudan, Sudan, Tanzania, Togo, Uganda, Zambia, and Zimbabwe.

131 **Africa south of the Sahara:** For broader treatments of this region, see Richard Dowden, *Africa: Altered States, Ordinary Miracles* (New York: PublicAffairs, 2009); S. N. Sangmpam, *Ethnicities and Tribes in Sub-Saharan Africa: Opening Old Wounds* (New York: Palgrave Macmillan, 2017); and Jean-François Bayart, *The State in Africa: The Politics of the Belly*, 2nd ed. (New York: Polity, 2009).

133 **before the Europeans arrived:** For more on precolonial African history, see Cheikh Anta Diop, *Precolonial Black Africa* (New York: Lawrence Hill Books, 1987).

134 **ruinous eight-year war:** Martin Evans, *Algeria: France's Undeclared War* (Oxford: Oxford University Press, 2012).

134 **establishing good governance:** Crawford Young, *The Postcolonial State in Africa: Fifty Years of Independence, 1960–2010* (Madison: University of Wisconsin Press, 2012).

134 **apartheid, or separateness:** For more on the apartheid era, see Nancy L. Clark and William H. Worger, *South Africa: The Rise and Fall of Apartheid*, 3rd ed. (New York: Routledge, 2016); Allister Sparks, *The Mind of South Africa* (New York: Alfred A. Knopf, 1990); and Joseph Lelyveld, *Move Your Shadow: South Africa, Black and White* (New York: Penguin Books, 1986). I also recommend reading Alan Paton's *Cry, the Beloved Country* (New York: Scribner, 1948), a novel that can teach just as much as a history book.

135 **political and military movements:** For more on the struggle against apartheid, see Stephen R. Davis, *The ANC's War Against Apartheid: Umkhonto we Sizwe and the Liberation of South Africa* (Bloomington: Indiana University Press, 2018).

135 **Nelson Mandela, an anti-apartheid activist:** I recommend Mandela's autobiography, *Long Walk to Freedom*, for an account of this period of South African history. Nelson Mandela, *Long Walk to Freedom: The Autobiography of Nelson Mandela* (Boston: Back Bay Books, 1995).

135 **I wrote about ripeness:** Richard N. Haass, *Conflicts Unending: The United States and Regional Disputes* (New Haven, Conn.: Yale University Press, 1990).

136 **only a few percent of the world total:** The region's combined output (GDP) in 2018 was $1.58 trillion, which represents 1.9 percent of the world's total of $84.7 trillion. See International Monetary Fund, "World Economic Outlook Database" (April 2019).

137 **absolute number of Africans:** The World Bank estimates that the *share* of the African population in extreme poverty declined from 57 percent in 1990 to 43 percent in 2012. At the same time, the World Bank estimates that from 1990 to

2012 the *number* of people living in extreme poverty in Africa increased by more than 100 million. Kathleen Beegle et al., "Poverty in a Rising Africa" (Washington, D.C.: World Bank Group, 2016), xi.

137   **400 million people:** According to the World Bank, in 2012, 389 million Africans lived on less than $1.90 a day. Beegle et al., "Poverty in a Rising Africa," 4.

137   **Half of the people:** According to the World Bank, almost 600 million of the 1.1 billion people in the world who do not have access to electricity are in sub-Saharan Africa. World Bank Group, *Africa's Pulse* 17 (April 2018): 59.

137   **Tax collection tends to be minimal:** McKinsey Global Institute, "Lions on the Move II: Realizing the Potential of Africa's Economies" (September 2016), 103–12.

137   **corruption tends to be extensive:** Thomas Isbell, "Efficacy for Fighting Corruption: Evidence from 36 African Countries," Afrobarometer Policy Paper No. 41, July 2017.

137   **Literacy has improved:** Beegle et al., "Poverty in a Rising Africa," 86–88.

138   **Intra-African trade is negligible:** According to a recent report, intra-African exports were 16.6 percent of total exports in 2017, compared with 68.1 percent in Europe, 59.4 percent in Asia, and 55.0 percent in the Americas. United Nations Conference on Trade and Development, *Economic Development in Africa Report 2019* (Geneva: United Nations, 2019), 19.

138   **Exports are largely primary commodities:** Mineral products (petroleum, ores, and so on) account for 50 percent of total exports from Africa to the rest of the world, while exports of manufactured goods account for only 20 percent. United Nations Conference on Trade and Development, *Economic Development in Africa Report 2019*, 23.

138   **Infrastructure is inadequate:** According to one recent report, "Africa currently has fewer kilometers of roads than it did 30 years ago and has the highest costs of transporting goods in the world." United Nations Conference on Trade and Development, *Economic Development in Africa Report 2019*, 6.

138   **rank among the top one hundred:** McKinsey Global Institute, "Global Flows in a Digital Age: How Trade, Finance, People, and Data Connect the World Economy," April 2014.

138   **Given visa requirements:** Africans need visas to travel to over half of the countries within the continent. McKinsey Global Institute, "Lions on the Move II," 123.

138   **now over sixty years:** The World Bank reports that life expectancy in sub-Saharan Africa is 60.8 years. World Bank Database, data.worldbank.org/indicator/SP.DYN.LE00.IN?locations=ZG.

138 **Infant and maternal mortality rates:** Beegle et al., "Poverty in a Rising Africa," 91–92. According to the World Bank, the maternal mortality ratio in sub-Saharan Africa declined from 987 (per 100,000 live births) in 1990 to 547 in 2015. World Bank Database, data.worldbank.org/indicator/SH.STA.MMRT ?locations=ZG. Similarly, the infant mortality rate in sub-Saharan Africa declined from 108 (per 1,000 live births) in 1990 to 52 in 2017. World Bank Database, data.worldbank.org/indicator/SP.DYN.IMRT.IN?loca tions=ZG.

138 **largely been brought under control:** Beegle et al., "Poverty in a Rising Africa," 91–93.

138 **noninfectious, noncommunicable diseases:** Mitchell E. Daniels Jr. and Thomas E. Donilon, *The Emerging Global Health Crisis: Noncommunicable Diseases in Low- and Middle-Income Countries* (New York: Council on Foreign Relations, 2014).

138 **It is also the youngest:** United Nations, Department of Economic and Social Affairs, Population Division, "World Population Prospects 2019: Highlights" (2019).

138 **predicted to double again:** United Nations, Department of Economic and Social Affairs, Population Division, "World Population Prospects 2019: Highlights."

138 **becoming more urbanized:** Somik Vinay Lall et al., *Africa's Cities: Opening Doors to the World* (Washington, D.C.: World Bank, 2017).

139 **Democracy is gaining ground:** For a comprehensive account of democracy on the continent, see Nic Cheeseman, *Democracy in Africa: Successes, Failures, and the Struggle for Political Reform* (New York: Cambridge University Press, 2015).

140 **More than half of all Africans:** Freedom House, *Freedom in the World 2018: Democracy in Crisis*, 17–19.

140 **Still, it is premature:** "The March of Democracy Slows," *Economist*, August 20, 2016; Larry Diamond, "Facing Up to the Democratic Recession," *Journal of Democracy* 26, no. 1 (2015): 141–55.

140 **as many as 800,000 lives:** United Nations, "Report of the Independent Inquiry into the Actions of the United Nations During the 1994 Genocide in Rwanda," December 15, 1999, 3, www.securitycouncilreport.org/atf/cf/%7B65BFCF9B -6D27-4E9C-8CD3-CF6E4FF96FF9%7D/POC%20S19991257.pdf.

140 **more than one-fifth of Africa's population:** Nigeria has a population of 196 million, and South Africa has one of 58 million. Combined, these two countries hold 23.6 percent of the region's 1.078 billion people. World Bank Database, data.worldbank.org/indicator/SP.POP.TOTL?locations=ZG-NG-ZA.

140 **more than 45 percent of its economic output:** According to the IMF, South Africa's GDP stood at $368 billion in 2018, while Nigeria's was $397 billion. Combined, the two economies accounted for 46.6 percent of total economic output in sub-Saharan Africa, which was reported to be $1.643 trillion. See International Monetary Fund, "World Economic Outlook Database" (April 2019).

140 **postapartheid South Africa:** For more on postapartheid South Africa, see John Campbell, *Morning in South Africa* (Lanham, Md.: Rowman & Littlefield, 2016).

140 **Nigeria was a British colony:** For more on Nigeria, see John Campbell, *Nigeria: Dancing on the Brink*, updated ed. (Lanham, Md.: Rowman & Littlefield, 2013); John Campbell and Matthew T. Page, *Nigeria: What Everyone Needs to Know* (New York: Oxford University Press, 2018); and Stephen Ellis, *This Present Darkness: A History of Nigerian Organized Crime* (New York: Oxford University Press, 2016).

The Americas

143 **includes thirty-eight countries:** For the purposes of this chapter, the following countries are included in the Americas: Antigua and Barbuda, Argentina, Aruba, the Bahamas, Barbados, Belize, Bolivia, Brazil, Canada, Chile, Colombia, Costa Rica, Cuba, Curacao, Dominica, Dominican Republic, Ecuador, El Salvador, Grenada, Guatemala, Guyana, Haiti, Honduras, Jamaica, Mexico, Nicaragua, Panama, Paraguay, Peru, St. Kitts and Nevis, St. Lucia, St. Maarten, St. Vincent and the Grenadines, Suriname, Trinidad and Tobago, the United States, Uruguay, and Venezuela.

143 **three-quarters of its economic output:** The IMF reported the United States had a GDP of $20.49 trillion in 2018, while the other countries in the region had a combined GDP of $6.96 trillion. Thus, the United States accounted for 75 percent of the region's total economic output. International Monetary Fund, "World Economic Outlook Database" (April 2019).

145 **three of the top ten countries:** British Petroleum, "Statistical Review of World Energy" (2018).

145 **China appears intent:** A great resource to delve into China's investments in the region is the Dialogue's China–Latin America Finance Database, which can be accessed at www.thedialogue.org/map_list/.

150 **outcome of the Falklands War:** For more on this conflict, see Lawrence D. Freedman, "Reconsiderations: The War of the Falkland Islands, 1982," *Foreign Affairs* (Fall 1982).

150 **its share of challenges:** One book to read to get a sense of the challenges facing the region is Michael Reid's *Forgotten Continent: The Battle for Latin America's Soul* (New Haven, Conn.: Yale University Press, 2009).

151 **Oil production is down:** According to the U.S. Energy Information Administration (EIA), in April 2019 Venezuela's crude oil production dropped to its lowest level since January 2003, when a nationwide strike brought operations at its state-owned oil company to a halt. U.S. EIA, "Venezuelan Crude Oil Production Falls to Lowest Level Since January 2003," May 20, 2019.

151 **Hyperinflation rages:** The IMF reports Venezuela's inflation rate stands at 10,000,000 percent. International Monetary Fund, "World Economic Outlook Database" (April 2019).

151 **Tens of thousands of people:** According to the United Nations High Commissioner for Refugees, four million Venezuelans have fled the country. In the seven months since November 2018, one million additional Venezuelans fled the country. UNHCR, "Refugees and Migrants from Venezuela Top 4 Million."

151 **great strain on its neighbors:** According to the United Nations High Commissioner for Refugees, Colombia is hosting some 1.3 million Venezuelan refugees. UNHCR, "Refugees and Migrants from Venezuela Top 4 Million."

151 **Argentina has struggled:** Luigi Manzetti, "Accountability and Corruption in Argentina During the Kirchners' Era," *Latin America Research Review* 49, no. 2 (2014): 173–95.

151 **Murder rates in these countries:** International Crisis Group, "Mafia of the Poor: Gang Violence and Extortion in Central America," April 6, 2017.

151 **causes people to flee:** According to a recent report, "security concerns play a central role in individual motivation to migrate," and nearly 30 percent of adults in the Northern Triangle have considered migrating in the last year specifically due to insecurity. Ben Raderstorf et al., "Beneath the Violence: How Insecurity Shapes Daily Life and Emigration in Central America," *Dialogue*, October 2017, 8.

PART III: THE GLOBAL ERA

Globalization

159 **Globalization—the emergence:** For a defense of globalization, see Martin Wolf, *Why Globalization Works* (New Haven, Conn.: Yale University Press, 2004); and Jagdish Bhagwati, *In Defense of Globalization* (Oxford: Oxford University Press, 2007). For a more skeptical view, see Joseph Stiglitz, *Globalization and Its*

Discontents Revisited: Anti-globalization in the Era of Trump (New York: W. W. Norton, 2018).

159 **more than 1.5 billion departures:** World Bank Database, data.worldbank.org /indicator/ST.INT.DPRT.

159 **between twenty-five and thirty million refugees:** According to the United Nations High Commissioner for Refugees, as of June 2019 there were 25.9 million refugees worldwide. See www.unhcr.org/en-us/figures-at-a-glance.html.

159 **top $1 trillion a year:** Organisation for Economic Co-operation and Development, "OECD International Direct Investment Statistics 2018" (Paris: OECD Publishing, 2019).

159 **Trade in goods is valued:** World Trade Organization, *World Trade Statistical Review 2019*, 8.

159 **seven times what it was:** The World Trade Organization estimates that total merchandise trade stood at $2.5 trillion in 1987 and $2.9 trillion in 1988, roughly one-seventh of the current level. See www.data.wto.org.

159 **one hundred times what it was fifty years ago:** The World Trade Organization estimates that total merchandise trade stood at $218 billion in 1967 and $242 billion in 1968, roughly one-eightieth of the current level. See www.data.wto.org.

161 **less than 5 percent of the world's people:** The United States has a population of roughly 330 million people, which represents around 4.3 percent of the global population of 7.6 billion.

Terrorism and Counterterrorism

166 **Terrorism is best defined:** For those interested in learning more about terrorism, the standard work on this subject is Bruce Hoffman, *Inside Terrorism*, 3rd ed. (New York: Columbia University Press, 2017).

168 **Provisional Irish Republican Army:** For those interested in terrorism in Northern Ireland, see Richard English, *Armed Struggle: The History of the IRA* (Oxford: Oxford University Press, 2003).

168 **Palestine Liberation Organization:** For those interested in the Palestinian use of terrorism, see Barry Rubin, *Revolution Until Victory? The Politics and History of the PLO* (Cambridge, Mass.: Harvard University Press, 1996).

168 **The most recent wave of international terrorism:** There is an extensive literature on al-Qaeda and ISIS, but a few books I would recommend are Wright, *Looming Tower*; Daniel Byman, *Al Qaeda, the Islamic State, and the Global Jihadist Movement: What Everyone Needs to Know* (Oxford: Oxford University

Press, 2015); and Joby Warrick, *Black Flags: The Rise of ISIS* (New York: Anchor Books, 2016).

169 **nearly twenty thousand people:** The University of Maryland maintains the Global Terrorism Database, which tracks terrorist events around the world beginning in 1970 and includes information on more than 180,000 attacks. National Consortium for the Study of Terrorism and Responses to Terrorism (START), Global Terrorism Database, www.start.umd.edu/gtd.

169 **more than twenty-six thousand:** Erin Miller, "Global Terrorism in 2017" (College Park, Md.: START, 2018), www.start.umd.edu/pubs/START_GTD _Overview2017_July2018.pdf.

169 **Most terrorists are to be found:** National Consortium for the Study of Terrorism and Responses to Terrorism, Global Terrorism Database, www.start.umd .edu/gtd.

170 **Efforts to frustrate terrorists:** For more on the tools of counterterrorism and U.S. counterterrorism policy, see Paul R. Pillar, *Terrorism and U.S. Foreign Policy* (Washington, D.C.: Brookings Institution, 2001); and Peter L. Bergen, *The Longest War: The Enduring Conflict Between America and Al-Qaeda* (New York: Free Press, 2011).

Nuclear Proliferation

174 **Some prominent scholars:** The most famous proponent of this view is Kenneth Waltz, who argued that if more countries had nuclear weapons, the world would be more stable, because countries would not attack each other and risk nuclear retaliation. Waltz wrote, "I have found many reasons for believing that with more nuclear states the world will have a promising future." Kenneth Waltz, "The Spread of Nuclear Weapons: More May Better," *Adelphi Papers*, no. 171 (London: International Institute for Strategic Studies, 1981). For a debate on this proposition, see Scott D. Sagan and Kenneth N. Waltz, *The Spread of Nuclear Weapons: A Debate* (New York: W. W. Norton, 1995).

175 **cannot be deterred:** Such scholars often invoke historical precedents such as the Cuban Missile Crisis, when Fidel Castro urged the Soviet Union to attack the United States with nuclear weapons, accepting the fact that Cuba would be destroyed but willing to pay that price in order to further Communism. James G. Blight and Janet M. Lang, "How Castro Held the World Hostage," *New York Times*, October 25, 2012. Mao Zedong is reported to have told the Indian prime minister, Jawaharlal Nehru, "If the worst came to the worst [nuclear war] and half of mankind died, the other half would remain while imperialism would be razed to the ground and the whole world would become socialist." For Mao,

nuclear war would quicken the transition to socialism. Margaret MacMillan, *Nixon and Mao: The Week That Changed the World* (New York: Random House, 2007), 132.

175 **The NPT requires:** Article I of the NPT states, "Each nuclear-weapon State Party to the Treaty undertakes not to transfer to any recipient whatsoever nuclear weapons or other nuclear explosive devices or control over such weapons or explosive devices directly, or indirectly; and not in any way to assist, encourage, or induce any non-nuclear-weapon State to manufacture or otherwise acquire nuclear weapons or other nuclear explosive devices, or control over such weapons or explosive devices." NPT text is available at www.un.org/disarmament /wmd/nuclear/npt/text/.

176 **sets forth the principle:** Article VI of the NPT states, "Each of the Parties to the Treaty undertakes to pursue negotiations in good faith on effective measures relating to cessation of the nuclear arms race at an early date and to nuclear disarmament, and on a treaty on general and complete disarmament under strict and effective international control."

177 **States have used cyberattacks:** Most famously, the United States and Israel employed cyberattacks to slow Iran's nuclear weapons program. David E. Sanger, *Confront and Conceal: Obama's Secret Wars and Surprising Use of American Power* (New York: Crown, 2012), 141–225.

180 **1994 Budapest Memorandum:** The memorandum states, "The Russian Federation, the United Kingdom of Great Britain and Northern Ireland and the United States of America reaffirm their obligation to refrain from the threat or use of force against the territorial integrity or political independence of Ukraine, and that none of their weapons will ever be used against Ukraine except in self-defence or otherwise in accordance with the Charter of the United Nations." Full text available at www.securitycouncilreport.org/atf/cf/%7B65BFCF9B -6D27-4E9C-8CD3-CF6E4FF96FF9%7D/s_1994_1399.pdf.

180 **trying to establish deterrence:** There is an entire subfield on deterrence theory and nuclear strategy, but the best one-volume study is Lawrence Freedman, *The Evolution of Nuclear Strategy*, 3rd ed. (New York: Palgrave Macmillan, 2003).

182 **John F. Kennedy predicted:** In 1960, during the third presidential debate between candidates John F. Kennedy and Richard M. Nixon, Kennedy stated, "There are indications, because of new inventions, that ten, fifteen, or twenty nations will have a nuclear capacity—including Red China—by the end of the presidential office in 1964." Commission on Presidential Debates, "October 13, 1960 Debate Transcript," https://www.debates.org/voter-education/debate -transcripts/october-13-1960-debate-transcript/.

Climate Change

183 **Global climate change:** For those interested in learning more about climate change, a good start is Elizabeth Kolbert, *Field Notes from a Catastrophe: Man, Nature, and Climate Change* (New York: Bloomsbury, 2015). For more on the science behind climate change, see Jeffrey Bennett, *A Global Warming Primer: Answering Your Questions About Science, the Consequences, and the Solutions* (Boulder, Colo.: Big Kid Science, 2016).

184 **measures of average air temperature:** Since 1901, the planet's surface has warmed at an average of 0.7–0.9 degree Celsius per century, but this rate of change has nearly doubled since 1975 to 1.5–1.8 degrees Celsius per century. Jessica Blunden, Derek S. Arndt, and Gail Hartfield, eds., "State of the Climate in 2017," *Bulletin of the American Meteorological Society* 99, no. 8 (2018): 12.

184 **average temperature of the world's oceans:** A recent study found that oceans are heating up 40 percent faster than a United Nations panel estimated five years ago. Kendra Pierre-Louis, "Ocean Warming Is Accelerating Faster Than Thought, New Research Finds," *New York Times*, January 10, 2019.

184 **polar ice is melting away:** John Schwartz and Henry Fountain, "Warming in Arctic Raises Fears of a 'Rapid Unraveling' of the Region," *New York Times*, December 11, 2018.

184 **rising sea levels:** In 2017, the average sea level was three inches above the 1993 average—the highest annual average in the satellite record (1993–present). It was the sixth consecutive year, and the twenty-second out of the last twenty-four years in which the average sea level increased relative to the previous year. Rebecca Lindsey, "Climate Change: Global Sea Level," Climate.gov, August 1, 2018.

184 **increase in the concentrations:** For instance, carbon dioxide levels today are higher than at any point in at least the past 800,000 years, and this rise is due to the fossil fuels that people burn for energy. Rebecca Lindsey, "Climate Change: Atmospheric Carbon Dioxide," Climate.gov, August 1, 2018.

184 **the second decade:** Henry Fountain and Nadja Popovich, "2019 Was the Second-Hottest Year Ever, Closing Out the Warmest Decade," *New York Times*, January 15, 2020.

184 **has been accelerating:** Lindsey, "Climate Change: Global Sea Level."

184 **Rising sea levels and flooding:** Amy M. Jaffe, "UN Climate Report Highlights Extreme Risk to Many Regions," cfr.org, October 12, 2018.

184 **areas of countries become uninhabitable:** For this view, in a highly readable form, see David Wallace-Wells, *The Uninhabitable Earth: Life After Warming* (New York: Tim Duggan Books, 2019).

185 **Bangladesh may well be the first:** A rise in temperatures above 1.5 degrees Celsius could mean that by mid-century more than fifty million people in Bangladesh will have to flee their country. Amy M. Jaffe, "UN Climate Report Highlights Extreme Risk to Many Regions."

185 **food and water shortages:** Christopher Flavelle, "Climate Change Threatens the World's Food Supply, United Nations Warns," *New York Times*, August 8, 2019. A summary of the UN report can be found at www.ipcc.ch/site/assets /uploads/2019/08/4.-SPM_Approved_Microsite_FINAL.pdf.

185 **national security issue as well:** In his 2015 National Security Strategy (NSS), President Barack Obama listed climate change as a top strategic risk to U.S. interests. The NSS noted, "Climate change is an urgent and growing threat to our national security, contributing to increased natural disasters, refugee flows, and conflicts over basic resources like food and water." President Barack Obama, "National Security Strategy of the United States of America," February 2015, obamawhitehouse.archives.gov/sites/default/files/docs/2015_national_securi ty_strategy_2.pdf.

185 **consumption has nearly tripled:** British Petroleum, "BP Energy Outlook: 2019 Edition," 79.

186 **China and India in particular:** British Petroleum, "BP Energy Outlook: 2019 Edition," 67.

186 **Much of the use:** British Petroleum, "BP Energy Outlook: 2019 Edition," 29.

186 **Oil generates roughly one-third:** British Petroleum, "BP Energy Outlook: 2019 Edition," 79.

186 **Deforestation is a significant cause:** Frances Seymour, "Deforestation Is Accelerating, Despite Mounting Efforts to Protect Tropical Forests. What Are We Doing Wrong?," *World Resources Institute*, June 26, 2018, www.wri.org/blog/2018 /06/deforestation-accelerating-despite-mounting-efforts-protect-tropical-forests.

186 **responsible for a good deal of:** Estimates differ, but recognition of the problem of deforestation is widely shared. Intergovernmental Panel on Climate Change, *Climate Change 2007—Mitigation of Climate Change: Working Group III Contribution to the Fourth Assessment Report of the IPCC* (Cambridge: Cambridge University Press, 2007).

186 **widely accepted by scientists:** The Intergovernmental Panel on Climate Change special report on the impacts of global warming of 1.5 degrees Celsius above preindustrial levels contains references to twenty-five hundred scientific reviews and represents something of a consensus. Intergovernmental Panel on Climate Change, *Global Warming of 1.5°C: An IPCC Special Report on the Impacts of Global Warming of 1.5°C Above Pre-industrial Levels and Related Global*

Greenhouse Gas Emission Pathways, in the Context of Strengthening the Global Response to the Threat of Climate Change, Sustainable Development, and Efforts to Eradicate Poverty (Geneva: World Meteorological Organization, 2018). The full report can be accessed at www.ipcc.ch/sr15/.

186 **small minority questions:** The retired MIT professor Richard Lindzen, for instance, is an outspoken climate change skeptic who wrote an open letter to President Donald Trump in 2017 arguing, "Since 2009, the US and other governments have undertaken actions with respect to global climate that are not scientifically justified." Zahra Hirji, "Climate Contrarian Gets Fact-Checked by MIT Colleagues in Open Letter to Trump," *Inside Climate News*, March 6, 2017.

187 **fastest growing among all fuels:** British Petroleum, "BP Energy Outlook: 2019 Edition," 15.

188 **one-third of the 1.0 degree Celsius increase:** According to the International Energy Agency (IEA), "$CO2$ emitted from coal combustion was responsible for over $0.3°C$ of the $1°C$ increase in global average annual surface temperatures above pre-industrial levels. This makes coal the single largest source of global temperature increase." IEA, "Global Energy & $CO2$ Status Report: The Latest Trends in Energy and Emissions in 2018," www.iea.org/geco/emissions/.

188 **China now accounts for about half:** British Petroleum, "BP Energy Outlook: 2019 Edition," 103.

188 **energy use in 2040:** British Petroleum, "BP Energy Outlook: 2019 Edition," 79.

191 **Such steps, termed adaptation:** For more on adaptation strategies, see Alice C. Hill and Leonardo Martinez-Diaz, *Building a Resilient Tomorrow* (New York: Oxford University Press, 2019).

191 **Such actions (termed geo-engineering):** For more on geo-engineering, see Oliver Morton, *The Planet Remade: How Geoengineering Could Change the World* (Princeton, N.J.: Princeton University Press, 2016).

192 **1978 international convention:** This is formally known as the Convention on the Prohibition of Military or Any Other Hostile Use of Environmental Modification Techniques. The full text can be found at treaties.un.org/doc/Treaties /1978/10/19781005%2000-39%20AM/Ch_XXVI_01p.pdf.

Migration

193 **defines a migrant:** United Nations International Organization for Migration, "Who is a Migrant?," https://www.iom.int/who-is-a-migrant.

193 **"who live temporarily or permanently":** United Nations Educational, Scientific and Cultural Organization, "Information Kit: United Nations Convention on Migrants' Rights" (2005), unesdoc.unesco.org/ark:/48223/pf0000143557.

193 **some 250 million international migrants:** According to the UN, "The number of international migrants worldwide has continued to grow rapidly in recent years, reaching 258 million in 2017, up from 220 million in 2010 and 173 million in 2000." United Nations, Department of Economic and Social Affairs, Population Division, *International Migration Report 2017: Highlights*, www.un.org/en/development/desa/population/migration/publications/migrationreport/docs/MigrationReport2017_Highlights.pdf.

193 **The vast majority:** By the end of 2016, there were 25.9 million refugees and asylum seekers in the world, equivalent to 10.1 percent of all international migrants. United Nations, Department of Economic and Social Affairs, Population Division, *International Migration Report 2017: Highlights*, 7.

193 **They tend to settle in countries:** High-income countries host almost two-thirds of all international migrants and have absorbed 64 million of the 85 million migrants added worldwide between 2000 and 2017. United Nations, Department of Economic and Social Affairs, Population Division, *International Migration Report 2017: Highlights*, 4.

194 **just under 50 million immigrants:** United Nations, Department of Economic and Social Affairs, Population Division, *International Migration Report 2017: Highlights*, 6.

194 **71 million people:** According to the United Nations High Commissioner for Refugees, as of June 2019 there were 70.8 million forcibly displaced persons worldwide. See www.unhcr.org/en-us/figures-at-a-glance.html.

194 **26 million are refugees:** Of the 25.9 million refugees, 5.5 million are categorized as Palestinian refugees, while the remaining 20.4 million refugees come from other parts of the world. See www.unhcr.org/en-us/figures-at-a-glance.html.

194 **The United States:** For those interested in the history of U.S. immigration policy, see Daniel J. Tichenor, *Dividing Lines: The Politics of Immigration Control in America* (Princeton, N.J.: Princeton University Press, 2002); and Susan F. Martin, *A Nation of Immigrants* (Cambridge: Cambridge University Press, 2011).

194 **more immigrants than any other country:** The United States hosts 50 million migrants, equal to 19 percent of the world's total and more than any other country. United Nations, Department of Economic and Social Affairs, Population Division, *International Migration Report 2017: Highlights*, 6.

194–195 **one million people obtain permanent resident status:** The United States granted lawful permanent resident status to 1.13 million people in 2017 (578,000 were new arrivals, and 549,000 were the result of an adjustment in status), 1.18 million in 2016, and 1.05 million in 2015. From 2001 to 2017, at least 1 million people obtained lawful permanent resident status in the United States each year for fourteen out of the seventeen years. U.S. Department of Homeland Security, Office of Immigration Statistics, *2017 Yearbook of Immigration Statistics,* 5.

195   **grounds of family reunification:** Of the 1.13 million people granted lawful permanent resident status in the United States in 2017, 516,500 people were given that status based on being immediate relatives of U.S. citizens, while another 232,200 were given that status based on being sponsored by family members. U.S. Department of Homeland Security, Office of Immigration Statistics, *2017 Yearbook of Immigration Statistics,* 18.

195   **permits no more than 7 percent:** No more than 7 percent of the visas may be issued to natives of any one independent country in a fiscal year; no more than 2 percent may be issued to any one dependency of any independent country. See www.uscis.gov/tools/glossary/country-limit. For a full discussion on current U.S. immigration policy, see William A. Kandel, "A Primer on U.S. Immigration Policy," Congressional Research Service, June 22, 2018, fas.org/sgp/crs /homesec/R45020.pdf.

195   **enter on the basis of skills:** In 2017, 137,900 people were granted lawful permanent resident status in the United States due to employment-based preferences: priority workers, professionals with advanced degrees or exceptional ability, employment creation (investors and so on). U.S. Department of Homeland Security, Office of Immigration Statistics, *2017 Yearbook of Immigration Statistics,* 18.

195   **naturalized American citizens:** In 2017, 987,000 people filed a petition for naturalization. U.S. Department of Homeland Security, Office of Immigration Statistics, *2017 Yearbook of Immigration Statistics,* 52.

195   **major source of innovation and talent:** Jennifer Hunt and Marjolaine Gauthier-Loiselle, "How Much Does Immigration Boost Innovation?," National Bureau of Economic Research, NBER Working Paper 14312, September 2008; J. David Brown et al., "Immigrant Entrepreneurs and Innovation in the U.S. High-Tech Sector," IZA Institute of Labor Economics Discussion Paper No. 12190, February 2019.

195   **Almost 45 percent of companies:** New American Economy Research Fund, "New American Fortune 500 in 2019: Top American Companies and Their Immigrant Roots," July 22, 2019.

195   **compete with and replace workers:** The best exposition of this view can be found in George J. Borjas, *We Wanted Workers: Unraveling the Immigration Narrative* (New York: W. W. Norton, 2016).

196   **highest it has been since World War II:** United Nations High Commissioner for Refugees, *Global Trends: Forced Displacement in 2018,* www.unhcr.org /5d08d7ee7.pdf.

196 **nearly doubled over the past decade:** In 2008, there were 42 million forcibly displaced persons worldwide, which ballooned to 70.8 million in 2018. The refugee population—excluding Palestinians—has nearly doubled since 2012, from 10.5 million to 20.4 million. United Nations High Commissioner for Refugees, *Global Trends: Forced Displacement in 2018*; United Nations High Commissioner for Refugees, *2008 Global Trends: Refugees, Asylum-Seekers, Returnees, Internally Displaced and Stateless Persons*, www.unhcr.org/4a375c426.pdf.

196 **Eighty-five percent of the world's refugees:** United Nations High Commissioner for Refugees, *Global Trends: Forced Displacement in 2018*, 18.

196 **60 percent of all current refugees:** Excluding Palestinians, of the 20.4 million refugees around the world 6.7 million originated in Syria, 2.7 million in Afghanistan, and 2.3 million in South Sudan. United Nations High Commissioner for Refugees, *Global Trends: Forced Displacement in 2018*, 3.

197 **Refugees are defined:** 1951 Convention Relating to the Status of Refugees, Article I, Section A, Paragraph 2.

198–199 **Turkey, Pakistan, Uganda, and Sudan:** In 2018, Turkey hosted 3.7 million refugees, while Pakistan hosted 1.4 million, Uganda 1.2 million, and Sudan 1.1 million. United Nations High Commissioner for Refugees, *Global Trends: Forced Displacement in 2018*, 3.

199 **defined in a 1998 UN document:** Francis M. Deng, "Report of the Representative of the Secretary-General Mr. Francis M. Deng, Submitted Pursuant to Commission Resolution 1997/39, February 11, 1998," https://digitallibrary.un.org/record/251017.

The Internet, Cyberspace, and Cybersecurity

201 **Nearly 300 billion email messages:** Radicati Group, "Email Statistics Report, 2019–2023," February 2019.

202 **billions of sensors and devices:** Ericsson estimates that by 2022 there will be around twenty-nine billion connected devices, of which eighteen billion will be related to the Internet of Things. Ericsson, "Internet of Things Forecast," www.ericsson.com/en/mobility-report/internet-of-things-forecast.

203 **same human rights online as off:** In 2016, the UN Human Rights Council passed a resolution that "affirms that the same rights that people have offline must also be protected online, in particular freedom of expression." The full resolution is available at undocs.org/A/HRC/32/L.20.

203 **United States and China agreed:** The full clause reads, "The United States and China agree that neither country's government will conduct or knowingly support cyber-enabled theft of intellectual property, including trade secrets or other

confidential business information, with the intent of providing competitive advantages to companies or commercial sectors." White House, "Fact Sheet: President Xi Jinping's State Visit to the United States," September 25, 2015.

203 **prevailing view in the United States:** Dustin Volz, "China Violated Obama-Era Cybertheft Pact, U.S. Official Says," *Wall Street Journal*, November 8, 2018; David E. Sanger and Steven Lee Myers, "After a Hiatus, China Accelerates Cyberspying Efforts to Obtain U.S. Technology," *New York Times*, November 29, 2018; Ken Dilanian, "China's Hackers Are Stealing Secrets from U.S. Firms Again, Experts Say," NBC News, October 9, 2018.

203 **U.S. government in 2011 called for the internet:** White House, "International Strategy for Cyberspace: Prosperity, Security, and Openness in a Networked World," May 2011, 8, https://obamawhitehouse.archives.gov/sites/default/files/rss_viewer/internationalstrategy_cyberspace.pdf.

203 **internet already appears to be fragmenting:** Adam Segal, "When China Rules the Web: Technology in Service of the State," *Foreign Affairs*, September/October 2018.

203 **described as the "splinternet":** For more on the fragmentation of the internet and the creation of several distinct internets, see Scott Malcomson, *Splinternet: How Geopolitics and Commerce Are Fragmenting the World Wide Web* (New York: OR Books, 2016); "Lost in the Splinternet," *Economist*, November 5, 2016.

203 **all shut down social media:** Max Fisher, "Sri Lanka Blocks Social Media, Fearing More Violence," *New York Times*, April 21, 2019.

204 **Improving global governance:** For those interested in the challenges cyber threats pose to policy makers and approaches to responding to these threats, see Richard A. Clarke and Robert K. Knake, *The Fifth Domain: Defending Our Country, Our Companies, and Ourselves in the Age of Cyber Threats* (New York: Penguin Press, 2019).

204 **carried out such cyberattacks:** Sanger, *Confront and Conceal*, 141–225.

204 **disrupt North Korea's nuclear and missile programs:** David E. Sanger and William J. Broad, "Trump Inherits a Secret Cyberwar Against North Korean Missiles," *New York Times*, March 4, 2017.

204 **one of the most sophisticated cyber arsenals:** David E. Sanger, David D. Kirkpatrick, and Nicole Perlroth, "The World Once Laughed at North Korean Cyberpower. No More," *New York Times*, October 15, 2017.

205 **"digital Geneva Convention":** President Emmanuel Macron of France launched the Paris Call for Trust and Security in Cyberspace in November 2018, which called for the development of common principles for securing cyberspace. So far,

sixty-six countries have signed on to the document, but China, Russia, and the United States have not.

205 **international rules and norms:** For more on the attempt to craft global rules, see Adam Segal, *The Hacked World Order: How Nations Fight, Trade, Maneuver, and Manipulate in the Digital Age* (New York: PublicAffairs, 2017).

205 **strong disagreement on these issues:** Laurens Cerulus and Mark Scott, "Europe Seeks to Lead a New World Order on Data," *Politico*, June 7, 2019.

206 **Deterrence is often discussed:** For a discussion on cyberattacks, cyber warfare, and the difficulty in deterring or responding to such attacks, see David E. Sanger, *The Perfect Weapon: War, Sabotage, and Fear in the Cyber Age* (New York: Crown, 2018); Fred Kaplan, *Dark Territory: The Secret History of Cyber War* (New York: Simon & Schuster, 2016); and Jason Healey, ed., *A Fierce Domain: Conflict in Cyberspace, 1986–2012* (Washington, D.C.: Cyber Conflict Studies Association, 2013).

Global Health

208 **global health is considerably better:** For those interested in learning more about global health, I recommend Randall M. Packard, *A History of Global Health: Interventions into the Lives of Other Peoples* (Baltimore: Johns Hopkins University Press, 2016); and Angus Deaton, *The Great Escape: Health, Wealth, and the Origins of Inequality* (Princeton, N.J.: Princeton University Press, 2013).

208 **Health-related costs and crises:** Daniels and Donilon, *Emerging Global Health Crisis*, 15.

208 **close to 10 percent of global economic output:** Health spending globally reached $8 trillion in 2016, or 8.6 percent of the global economy. Global Burden of Disease Health Financing Collaborator Network, "Past, Present, and Future of Global Health Financing: A Review of Development Assistance, Government, Out-of-Pocket, and Other Private Spending on Health for 195 Countries, 1995–2050," *Lancet*, April 24, 2019.

208 **18 percent of its gross domestic product:** The U.S. Centers for Medicare & Medicaid Services reports that U.S. health-care spending reached $3.5 trillion in 2017, representing 17.9 percent of U.S. GDP. Centers for Medicare & Medicaid Services, "National Health Expenditures 2017 Highlights," www.cms.gov /Research-Statistics-Data-and-Systems/Statistics-Trends-and-Reports/Nation alHealthExpendData/Downloads/highlights.pdf.

209 **expect to reach his or her seventy-second birthday:** Life expectancy at birth for the world's population reached 72.6 years in 2019. United Nations, Department

of Economic and Social Affairs, Population Division, "World Population Prospects 2019: Highlights," 2.

209 **expect to reach his or her eightieth birthday:** For instance, life expectancy at birth is over 80 years in Chile, Costa Rica, Slovenia, Portugal, Germany, Greece, Finland, Belgium, Denmark, Austria, the United Kingdom, France, South Korea, Canada, Luxembourg, the Netherlands, New Zealand, Ireland, Australia, Israel, Spain, Italy, Sweden, Norway, Iceland, Japan, and Switzerland. Notably, it is only 78.6 years in the United States. OECD Health Statistics, "Life Expectancy at Birth," data.oecd.org/healthstat/life-expectancy-at-birth.htm.

209 **more than double what it was a century ago:** James C. Riley, "Estimates of Regional and Global Life Expectancy, 1800–2001," *Population and Development Review* 31, no. 3 (September 2005): 537–43.

209 **average woman lives several years longer:** Current female life expectancy is estimated at 75 years, compared with male life expectancy of 70.2 years. United Nations, Department of Economic and Social Affairs, Population Division, "World Population Prospects 2019: Highlights," 29.

209 **fifty million children's lives were saved:** World Bank, *Levels and Trends in Child Mortality: Estimates Developed by the UN Inter-agency Group for Child Mortality Estimation (IGME)—Report 2015* (Washington, D.C.: World Bank Group, 2015).

209 **Polio cases have decreased:** Polio cases have dropped from an estimated 350,000 cases in 1988 to 33 reported cases in 2018—a 99 percent drop. As a result, the World Health Organization estimates that more than 18 million people are able to walk today who would otherwise have been paralyzed. World Health Organization, "Fact Sheet: Poliomyelitis," July 22, 2019, www.who.int/en/news-room/fact-sheets/detail/poliomyelitis.

209 **people dying from AIDS-related causes:** UNAIDS, "Global HIV & AIDS Statistics—2019 Fact Sheet," www.unaids.org/en/resources/fact-sheet.

209 **Incidence of both malaria and measles:** Institute for Health Metrics and Evaluation, *Financing Global Health 2016: Development Assistance, Public and Private Health Spending for the Pursuit of Universal Health Coverage* (Seattle: IHME, 2017), 39.

210 **Life expectancy in several African countries:** Life expectancy is under fifty-five years in Sierra Leone, Central African Republic, Chad, Nigeria, and Côte d'Ivoire. World Bank Database, data.worldbank.org/indicator/SP.DYN.LE00.IN.

210 **average life expectancy for sub-Saharan Africa:** Life expectancy in sub-Saharan Africa as a whole is 61.1 years, over ten years below the global average of 72.6.

United Nations, Department of Economic and Social Affairs, Population Division, "World Population Prospects 2019: Highlights," 29.

210 **represents a sharp improvement:** In 1960, the region had a life expectancy of just over forty years. World Bank Database, data.worldbank.org/indicator/SP .DYN.LE00.IN?locations=ZG.

210 **much easier for diseases to spread:** Lance Saker et al., *Globalization and Infectious Diseases: A Review of the Linkages* (Geneva: UNICEF/UNDP/World Bank/ WHO Special Program for Research and Training in Tropical Diseases, 2004); Tong Wu et al., "Economic Growth, Urbanization, Globalization, and the Risks of Emerging Infectious Diseases in China: A Review," *Ambio* 46 (2017): 18–29; Douglas W. MacPherson et al., "Population Mobility, Globalization, and Antimicrobial Drug Resistance," *Emerging Infectious Diseases* 15, no. 11 (2009): 1727–32.

210 **refugee populations have also become vulnerable:** For instance, due to the ongoing war in Yemen and the displacement of its population, the UN reported nearly half a million cases of cholera in the country in the first six months of 2019. United Nations Office for the Coordination of Humanitarian Affairs, "Yemen: Over 460K Cases of Cholera Registered to Date This Year," July 8, 2019.

210 **drug-resistant organisms:** U.S. Department of Health and Human Services, Centers for Disease Control and Prevention, "Antibiotic Resistance Threats in the United States, 2013," www.cdc.gov/drugresistance/threat-report-2013/pdf /ar-threats-2013-508.pdf.

210 **at least fifty million people died:** Douglas Jordan, "The Deadliest Flu: The Complete Story of the Discovery and Reconstruction of the 1918 Pandemic Virus," U.S. Centers for Disease Control and Prevention, www.cdc.gov/flu/pan demic-resources/reconstruction-1918-virus.html.

211 **noninfectious or what are termed noncommunicable diseases:** For more on NCDs, see Thomas J. Bollyky, *Plagues and the Paradox of Progress: Why the World Is Getting Healthier in Worrisome Ways* (Cambridge, Mass.: MIT Press, 2018); Daniels and Donilon, *Emerging Global Health Crisis.*

211 **In 1990, three of the top seven causes:** Institute for Health Metrics and Evaluation, *Rethinking Development and Health: Findings from the Global Burden of Disease Study* (Seattle: IHME, 2016), 29.

211 **thirty-eight million—or 68 percent:** World Health Organization, *Global Status Report on Noncommunicable Diseases 2014* (Geneva: World Health Organization, 2014), xi.

211 **By 2030, NCDs are projected:** United Nations, "Report to the Secretary-General: Prevention and Control of Non-communicable Diseases," May 19, 2011.

212 **Global efforts in the health realm:** For an overview of this issue, see David P. Fidler, "The Challenges of Global Health Governance," Council on Foreign Relations Working Paper, May 2010, www.cfr.org/report/challenges-global-health-governance.

212 **it lacks the necessary authority:** For more on the shortcomings of the WHO, see Laurie Garrett, "Ebola's Lessons: How the WHO Mishandled the Crisis," *Foreign Affairs,* September/October 2015; Suerie Moon et al., "Will Ebola Change the Game? Ten Essential Reforms Before the Next Pandemic. The Report of the Harvard-LSHTM Independent Panel on the Global Response to Ebola," *Lancet* 386, no. 10009 (2015).

212–213 **"attainment by all peoples":** World Health Organization, "Constitution of the World Health Organization," Chapter 1, Article 1, apps.who.int/gb/bd/PDF/bd47/EN/constitution-en.pdf?ua=1.

213 **receive only a few cents on the dollar:** In 2018, just 2 percent (or $778.3 million) of development assistance for health was allocated to NCDs, even though NCDs represented 62.1 percent of the global disease burden. Institute for Health Metrics and Evaluation, *Financing Global Health 2018: Countries and Programs in Transition* (Seattle: IHME, 2019), 86.

213 **twice as many premature deaths:** Institute for Health Metrics and Evaluation, Global Burden of Disease Database (2017), ghdx.healthdata.org/gbd-results-tool.

Trade and Investment

215 **Trade at the international level:** For a history of trade, see William J. Bernstein, *A Splendid Exchange: How Trade Shaped the World* (New York: Atlantic Monthly Press, 2008). For a wide-ranging discussion of trade, see Wolf, *Why Globalization Works.* For an accessible discussion of U.S. trade policy, see Douglas A. Irwin, *Clashing over Commerce: A History of US Trade Policy* (Chicago: University of Chicago Press, 2019); and Craig VanGrasstek, *Trade and American Leadership: The Paradoxes of Power and Wealth from Alexander Hamilton to Donald Trump* (Cambridge, U.K.: Cambridge University Press, 2019).

215 **trade is a good thing:** For an accessible, cogent defense of trade, see Jason Furman, "Trade, Innovation, and Economic Growth" (remarks at the Brookings Institution, April 8, 2015); U.S. Council of Economic Advisers, "The Economic Benefits of U.S. Trade," May 2015.

215 **export-oriented jobs tend to be relatively high paying:** Andrew B. Bernard et al., "Firms in International Trade," *Journal of Economic Perspectives* 21, no. 3

(2007): 105–30; David Riker, "Do Jobs in Export Industries Still Pay More? And Why?," *Manufacturing and Services Economics Brief,* no. 2 (International Trade Administration, U.S. Department of Commerce, 2010).

217 **This phenomenon is known:** For more on how global supply chains or global value chains are reshaping trade, see Organisation for Economic Co-operation and Development, "Trade Policy Implications of Global Value Chains," November 2015; Organisation for Economic Co-operation and Development, "Making Trade Work for All," OECD Trade Policy Papers, no. 202 (Paris: OECD Publishing, 2017).

218 **There is research indicating:** Organisation for Economic Co-operation and Development, "Making Trade Work for All," 9.

223 **stolen valuable intellectual property:** Chuin-Wei Yap et al., "Huawei's Yearslong Rise Is Littered with Accusation of Theft and Dubious Ethics," *Wall Street Journal,* May 25, 2019; Aruna Viswanatha, Kate O'Keeffe, and Dustin Volz, "U.S. Accuses Chinese Firm, Partner of Stealing Trade Secrets from Micron," *Wall Street Journal,* November 21, 2018; Eric Rosenbaum, "1 in 5 Corporations Say China Has Stolen Their IP Within the Last Year: CNBC CFO Survey," CNBC, March 1, 2019; Office of the U.S. Trade Representative, "Findings of the Investigation into China's Acts, Policies, and Practices Related to Technology Transfer, Intellectual Property, and Innovation Under Section 301 of the Trade Act of 1974," March 22, 2018.

224 **falling from more than 20 percent:** A recent paper estimated that the average tariff level going into the first round of trade negotiations in 1947 was around 22 percent. Chad P. Brown and Douglas A. Irwin, "The GATT's Starting Point: Tariff Levels Circa 1947," NBER Working Paper 21782, December 2015. The World Trade Organization reported that the world average applied tariff in 2018 was 9 percent. World Trade Organization, *World Trade Statistical Review 2019* (Geneva: World Trade Organization, 2019), 73.

225 **the Doha Round:** For a discussion of the Doha negotiations, see Will Martin and Aaditya Mattoo, eds., *Unfinished Business? The WTO's Doha Agenda* (Washington, D.C.: World Bank, 2011).

225 **The volume of world trade:** World Bank Database, data.worldbank.org/topic /trade.

225 **International merchandise trade:** World Bank Database, data.worldbank.org /indicator/TG.VAL.TOTL.GD.ZS.

225 **World merchandise trade volume:** World Trade Organization, *World Trade Statistical Review 2019,* 8.

226 **The number of regional trade agreements:** World Trade Organization, "Regional Trade Agreements Database," rtais.wto.org/UI/PublicMaintainRTA Home.aspx.

226 **North American Free Trade Agreement:** For a comprehensive introduction to NAFTA, see M. Angeles Villarreal and Ian F. Fergusson, "The North American Free Trade Agreement (NAFTA)," *Congressional Research Service*, May 24, 2017, fas.org/sgp/crs/row/R42965.pdf.

226 **overall benefit of all three countries:** For a look back on NAFTA's first twenty years and the benefits it has brought to the United States, Canada, and Mexico, see Carla A. Hills, "NAFTA's Economic Upsides: The View from the United States," *Foreign Affairs*, January/February 2014.

226 **Eleven countries in the Americas and Asia:** The eleven members of the CPTPP are Australia, Brunei, Canada, Chile, Japan, Malaysia, Mexico, New Zealand, Peru, Singapore, and Vietnam.

227 **The arrival of artificial intelligence:** For more on how new technologies will alter the job landscape, see Edward Alden and Laura Taylor-Kale, *The Work Ahead: Machines, Skills, and U.S. Leadership in the Twenty-first Century* (New York: Council on Foreign Relations, 2018).

227 **Cross-border investment, like trade:** Philip R. Lane and Gian Maria Milesi-Feretti, "International Financial Integration in the Aftermath of the Global Financial Crisis," IMF Working Paper No. 17/115, May 10, 2017.

228 **increased more than one hundred times:** Foreign direct investment flows stood at $13.26 billion in 1970 and rose to $1.3 trillion in 2018. United Nations Conference on Trade and Development STAT, unctadstat.unctad.org/wds/TableViewer/tableView.aspx.

Currency and Monetary Policy

231 **known as monetary policy:** It is difficult to truly understand monetary policy without picking up a textbook and learning various equations and technical relationships. For a good overview of the monetary policy choices the world's leading central banks made during the global financial crisis, I would recommend Neil Irwin, *The Alchemists: Three Central Bankers and a World on Fire* (New York: New American Library, 2014). For a broader overview of the issues facing the global economy, I would recommend Martin Wolf, *The Shifts and the Shocks: What We've Learned—and Have Still to Learn—from the Financial Crisis* (New York: Penguin Books, 2015). For a discussion on what happens when monetary policy goes wrong, see Liaquat Ahamed's study of the Great Depression, *Lords of Finance: The Bankers Who Broke the World* (New York: Penguin Press, 2009).

232 **International Monetary Fund:** For a concise look at the ideas underpinning the IMF, see James M. Boughton, "The IMF and the Force of History: Ten Events and Ten Ideas That Have Shaped the Institution," IMF Working Paper, May 2004.

232 **Bretton Woods Conference:** For those interested in this pivotal conference that shaped the post–World War II economic order and the debates that occurred during the conference, see Benn Steil, *The Battle of Bretton Woods: John Maynard Keynes, Harry Dexter White, and the Making of a New World Order* (Princeton, N.J.: Princeton University Press, 2013).

233 **The dollar's role:** The literature on the dollar's role in the global economy is voluminous, but a few pieces to start with are Richard N. Cooper, "The Future of the Dollar," Peterson Institute for International Economics, September 2009; and Barry Eichengreen, "The Dollar Dilemma: The World's Top Currency Faces Competition," *Foreign Affairs*, September/October 2009.

233 **According to the IMF:** IMF Data, "Currency Composition of Official Foreign Exchange Reserves (COFER)," latest update on June 28, 2019.

236 **mostly good for the United States:** One study attempted to quantify the costs and benefits of being a global reserve currency and concluded that as a result of the dollar's status as the global reserve currency the United States gains between $40 billion and $70 billion per year—or roughly 0.3 to 0.5 percent of U.S. GDP. McKinsey Global Institute, "An Exorbitant Privilege? Implications of Reserve Currencies for Competitiveness," December 2009.

237 **a cryptocurrency, or some combination:** Mark Carney, "The Growing Challenges for Monetary Policy in the Current International Monetary and Financial System" (speech given at the Jackson Hole Symposium, August 23, 2019), www.bankofengland.co.uk/speech/2019/mark-carney-speech-at-jackson -hole-economic-symposium-wyoming.

238 **China obviously comes to mind here:** Periodically, scholars revisit the question of whether China's currency, the yuan or RMB, can or will replace the dollar as the international currency of choice. A few pieces worth reading on this prospect are Sebastian Mallaby and Olin Wethington, "The Future of the Yuan: China's Struggle to Internationalize Its Currency," *Foreign Affairs*, January/February 2012; Financial Times Special Report, "The Future of the Renminbi," *Financial Times*, November 29, 2015; Benn Steil and Emma Smith, "The Retreat of the Renminbi," *Project Syndicate*, June 22, 2017.

238 **European countries tried:** "Europe Struggles to Protect Iran Trade as US Reimposes Sanctions," *Financial Times*, November 5, 2018; "European Companies Will Struggle to Defy America on Iran," *Economist*, November 8, 2018.

Development

240 **Development is a widely used:** For an optimistic view of global development, see Charles Kenny, *Getting Better: Why Global Development Is Succeeding—and How We Can Improve the World Even More* (New York: Basic Books, 2011). For a more skeptical take, see William Easterly, *The White Man's Burden: Why the West's Efforts to Aid the Rest Have Done So Much Ill and So Little Good* (Oxford: Oxford University Press, 2006). For another overview of development, see Paul Collier, *The Bottom Billion: Why the Poorest Countries Are Failing and What Can Be Done About It* (Oxford: Oxford University Press, 2007).

240 **The World Bank has rejected the distinction:** The World Bank announced this decision in its 2016 *World Development Indicators* report and is phasing out use of the terms "developing world" and "developing countries." World Bank, *World Development Indicators 2016* (Washington, D.C.: World Bank, 2016), iii.

240 **Countries are then determined to be:** Low-income economies are those with a GNI per capita of $1,045 or less in 2014. Lower-middle-income economies are those with a GNI per capita of $1,046–$4,125. Upper-middle-income economies are those with a GNI per capita of $4,126–$12,735. High-income economies are those with a GNI per capita of $12,736 or more. World Bank, *World Development Indicators 2016*, xiii.

240 **GDP per capita ranges:** World Bank Database, data.worldbank.org/indicator/NY.GDP.PCAP.CD.

241 **range of social factors:** An important book that brought about this shift in thinking away from GDP as the primary measure of development and toward looking at "capabilities" was Amartya Sen, *Development as Freedom* (New York: Anchor Books, 1999). As the United Nations Development Programme puts it, "Human development is about enlarging freedoms so that all human beings can pursue choices that they value. Such freedoms have two fundamental aspects—freedom of well-being, represented by functionings and capabilities, and freedom of agency, represented by voice and autonomy." United Nations Development Programme, *Human Development Report 2016: Human Development for Everyone* (New York: United Nations, 2016), 1.

241 **According to the latest HDI rankings:** United Nations Development Programme, *Human Development Indices and Indicators: 2018 Statistical Update* (New York: United Nations, 2018).

243 **people living in extreme poverty:** World Bank, *Poverty and Shared Prosperity 2018: Piecing Together the Poverty Puzzle* (Washington, D.C.: World Bank, 2018), 1–2.

243 **plummeted from 66 percent in 1990:** World Bank Poverty & Equity Data Portal: povertydata.worldbank.org/poverty/country/CHN.

243 **world's people were literate:** Jan Luiten van Zanden et al., eds., *How Was Life? Global Well-Being Since 1820* (OECD Publishing, 2014), 20.

243 **more than 85 percent of the world's people:** UNESCO Institute for Statistics Data, data.uis.unesco.org/index.aspx?queryid=166&lang=en.

244 **has improved by some twenty-five years:** Riley, "Estimates of Regional and Global Life Expectancy, 1800–2001."

244 **more than tripled between 1950 and 2010:** From 1950 to 2010, the average person in the developing world increased his or her years of education from 2.0 to 7.2. World Bank, *World Development Report 2018: Learning to Realize Education's Promise* (Washington, D.C.: World Bank, 2018), 4–5.

244 **Access to improved sanitation:** United Nations Development Programme, *Human Development Report 2016: Human Development for Everyone*, 3.

244 **more than 7.5 billion mobile cellular subscriptions:** International Telecommunication Union, 2018 Global and Regional Information and Communication Technologies (ICTs) Dataset, www.itu.int/en/ITU-D/Statistics/Pages/stat/default .aspx.

244 **3.9 billion, or just over half the people on the planet:** International Telecommunication Union, "ITU Releases 2018 Global and Regional ICT Estimates: For the First Time, More than Half of the World's Population Is Using the Internet," December 7, 2018; International Telecommunication Union, 2018 Global and Regional Information and Communication Technologies (ICTs) Dataset.

244 **two in five African adults cannot:** Beegle et al., "Poverty in a Rising Africa," 86.

244 **Nearly 900 million people:** World Health Organization and the United Nations Children's Fund, *Progress on Drinking Water, Sanitation, and Hygiene: 2017 Update and SDG Baselines* (Geneva: World Health Organization and the United Nations Children's Fund, 2017), 4.

245 **nearly one billion people:** United Nations Development Programme, *Human Development Indices and Indicators: 2018 Statistical Update* (New York: United Nations, 2018).

245 **top 10 percent holds 85 percent:** Kathleen Elkins, "How Much Money You Need to Be Among the Richest 10 percent of People Worldwide," CNBC.com, November 7, 2018.

248 **Development aid or assistance:** Nicholas D. Kristof, "Aid: Can It Work?," *New York Review of Books*, October 5, 2006.

248 **Companies need to feel confident:** This emphasis on building the proper institutions is termed the institutionalist approach to development. The best exposition of this approach—and one of the best books on development anywhere—is Daron Acemoglu and James Robinson, *Why Nations Fail: The Origins of Power, Prosperity, and Poverty* (New York: Crown Business, 2012).

249 **the record was mixed:** United Nations, "The Millennium Development Goals Report 2015," available at https://www.un.org/millenniumgoals/2015_MDG _Report/pdf/MDG%202015%20rev%20(July%201).pdf.

PART IV: ORDER AND DISORDER

254 *The Anarchical Society:* Hedley Bull, *The Anarchical Society: A Study of Order in World Politics,* 4th ed. (New York: Columbia University Press, 2012).

Sovereignty, Self-Determination, and Balance of Power

257 **respect for sovereignty:** For a fuller treatment of the concept of sovereignty, see Robert Jackson, *Sovereignty: The Evolution of an Idea* (Cambridge, U.K.: Polity Press, 2007); and Stephen D. Krasner, *Sovereignty: Organized Hypocrisy* (Princeton, N.J.: Princeton University Press, 1999). For a discussion of sovereignty debates in the United States since the country's founding and how these play out in several policy realms, see Stewart Patrick, *The Sovereignty Wars: Reconciling America with the World* (Washington, D.C: Brookings Institution, 2018).

258 **An ongoing debate:** On this debate, which largely revolves around the responsibility to protect, see Power, *"Problem from Hell"*; and Kofi Annan, "Two Concepts of Sovereignty," *Economist,* September 16, 1999.

258 **genocide, defined as:** Article II of the 1948 Convention on the Prevention and Punishment of the Crime of Genocide defines genocide as "any of the following acts committed with intent to destroy, in whole or in part, a national, ethnical, racial or religious group, as such: (a) Killing members of the group; (b) Causing serious bodily or mental harm to members of the group; (c) Deliberately inflicting on the group conditions of life calculated to bring about its physical destruction in whole or in part; (d) Imposing measures intended to prevent births within the group; (e) Forcibly transferring children of the group to another group." The text of the Genocide Convention is available at: https://www.un.org/en/genocide prevention/documents/atrocity-crimes/Doc.1_Convention%20on%20the%20 Prevention%20and%20Punishment%20of%20the%20Crime%20of%20 Genocide.pdf.

259 **Responsibility to Protect doctrine:** United Nations General Assembly, "Resolution Adopted by the General Assembly on 16 September 2005" (A/RES/60/1), undocs.org/A/RES/60/1.

259 **some 500,000 Syrians lost their lives:** Specia, "How Syria's Death Toll Is Lost in the Fog of War."

260 **influence the outcome of the 2016 presidential election:** Office of the Director of National Intelligence, "Assessing Russian Activities and Intentions in Recent US Elections."

261 **self-determination, or the notion:** For an excellent treatment of the concept of self-determination, see Margaret Moore, ed., *National Self-Determination and Secession* (Oxford: Oxford University Press, 1998); and Alfred Cobban, *The Nation State and National Self-Determination* (New York: Crowell, 1970). For a riveting discussion of the post–World War I debates on self-determination, see Margaret MacMillan, *Paris 1919: Six Months That Changed the World* (New York: Random House, 2002).

261 **"respect for the principle":** The charter's full text can be found at www.un.org /en/sections/un-charter/un-charter-full-text/.

262 **1978 Camp David Accords:** The full text can be found at avalon.law.yale.edu /20th_century/campdav.asp.

Alliances and Coalitions

264 **strengthened or undermined by alliances:** For a treatment of alliances, see Stephen M. Walt, *The Origins of Alliances* (Ithaca, N.Y.: Cornell University Press, 1987).

264 **"There is only one thing":** Churchill made this comment at Chequers on April 1, 1945: winstonchurchill.org/uncategorised/quotes-slider/2014-11-3-16-25-06/.

265 **"appeasement" was the term:** Bouverie, *Appeasement.*

267 **America's alliances with countries:** For more on the makings of America's alliance system in Asia, see Victor D. Cha, *Powerplay: The Origins of the American Alliance System in Asia* (Princeton, N.J.: Princeton University Press, 2016).

267 **voiced his skepticism:** Drew Middleton, "The de Gaulle Nuclear Doctrine Is Alive in Paris," *New York Times*, May 6, 1981.

267 **Article 5 of its charter:** Article 5 of the North Atlantic Treaty reads, "The Parties agree that an armed attack against one or more of them in Europe or North America shall be considered an attack against them all and consequently they agree that, if such an armed attack occurs, each of them, in exercise of the right of individual or collective self-defence recognised by Article 51 of the Charter of the United Nations, will assist the Party or Parties so attacked by taking forthwith, individually and in concert with the other Parties, such action as it deems necessary, including the use of armed force, to restore and maintain the security of the North Atlantic area."

International Society

271 **More than 40 percent of the world's countries:** Freedom House, *Freedom in the World 2018: Democracy in Crisis*, 2.

271 **"democratic peace" theory:** Michael E. Brown, Sean M. Lynn-Jones, and Steven E. Miller, eds., *Debating the Democratic Peace* (Cambridge, Mass.: MIT Press, 1996).

271 **immature or illiberal democracies:** Fareed Zakaria, *The Future of Freedom: Illiberal Democracy at Home and Abroad*, rev. ed. (New York: W. W. Norton, 2007).

272 **The argument is:** Just before World War I, Norman Angell popularized this argument in his book *The Great Illusion*. Norman Angell, *The Great Illusion: A Study of the Relation of Military Power to National Advantage* (New York: G.P. Putnam's Sons, 1910).

274 **"Meeting jaw to jaw":** Churchill's biographer, Sir Martin Gilbert, notes that during a trip to Washington in 1954, Churchill made this statement when trying to persuade the U.S. Congress to pursue high-level meetings with the Soviet Union. International Churchill Society, *Finest Hour 122* (Spring 2004), 12, https://winstonchurchill.org/publications/finest-hour/finest-hour-122/around-and-about-26/.

277 **large body of law:** On international law and the use of force, see Louis Henkin et al., *Right v. Might* (New York: Council on Foreign Relations Press, 1991).

277 **when a war can be justified:** On just war theory, see Michael Walzer, *Just and Unjust Wars* (New York: Basic Books, 1977).

278 *jus post bellum*: Gary J. Bass, "Jus Post Bellum," *Philosophy and Public Affairs* 32, no. 4 (Autumn 2004): 384–412.

War Between Countries

280 **"the growth of Athenian power":** Thucydides, *The Peloponnesian War* (Rex Warner, trans.), (New York: Penguin Books, 1954), 49.

280 **Some observers would argue:** Graham Allison, *Destined for War: Can America and China Escape Thucydides's Trap?* (New York: Houghton Mifflin Harcourt, 2017).

281 **violence must claim at least one thousand lives:** For instance, this is the metric used by the Correlates of War Project, which compiles data sets on war. The data are available at www.correlatesofwar.org/data-sets.

282 **Some nine million soldiers:** Merriman, *History of Modern Europe*, 923, 1102.

282 **continuation of politics by other means:** Carl von Clausewitz, *On War*, ed. and trans. Michael Howard and Peter Paret (Princeton, N.J.: Princeton University Press, 1976).

282 **common trigger for interstate war:** Bryan A. Frederick, Paul R. Hensel, and Christopher Macaulay, "The Issue Correlates of War Territorial Claims Data, 1816–2001," *Journal of Peace Research* 54, no. 1 (2017): 99–108; Monica Duffy Toft, "Territory and War," *Journal of Peace Research* 51, no. 2 (2014): 185–98.

285 **has claimed some 500,000 lives:** Specia, "How Syria's Death Toll Is Lost in the Fog of War."

286 **military spending continues to increase:** Stockholm International Peace Research Institute, "SIPRI Military Expenditure Database 2019," www.sipri.org /databases/milex.

286 **enduring trend or something of an aberration:** For a debate on this proposition, see Nils Petter Gleditsch et al., "The Decline of War," *International Studies Review* 15, no. 3 (2013): 396–419.

286 **Some judge this trend:** Steven Pinker, "Violence Vanquished," *Wall Street Journal*, September 24, 2011.

287 **I am less sanguine:** For a longer rebuttal of Pinker's thesis, see Lawrence Freedman, "Stephen Pinker and the Long Peace: Alliance, Deterrence, and Decline," *Cold War History* 14, no. 4 (2014): 657–72.

Internal Instability and War Within Countries

288 **There is no evidence:** David Armitage, *Civil Wars: A History of Ideas* (New York: Alfred A. Knopf, 2017).

289 **1.5 billion—live in fragile states:** OECD, *International Engagement in Fragile States: Can't We Do Better?* (Paris: OECD Publishing, 2011), doi.org/10.1787 /9789264086128-en.

289 **weak state from a failed state:** Gerald B. Helman and Steven R. Ratner, "Saving Failed States," *Foreign Policy* (Winter 1992–1993): 3–20.

290 **Vulnerable countries:** For further elaboration on these themes, see Acemoglu and Robinson, *Why Nations Fail*.

292 **civil wars are more frequent:** Jeffrey Dixon, "What Causes Civil Wars? Integrating Quantitative Research Findings," *International Studies Review* 11, no. 4 (December 2009): 707–35.

292 **Other traits that suggest:** Dixon, "What Causes Civil Wars?"

293 **civil wars ended by negotiation:** Monica Duffy Toft, "Ending Civil Wars: A Case for Rebel Victory?," *International Security* 34, no. 4 (Spring 2010): 7–36.

293 **sow the seeds of stability:** Edward N. Luttwak, "Give War a Chance," *Foreign Affairs*, July/August 1999, 36–44.

The Liberal World Order

296 **Much has been said and written:** For a defense of the liberal world order, see Daniel Deudney and G. John Ikenberry, "Liberal World: The Resilient Order," *Foreign Affairs*, July/August 2018; and G. John Ikenberry, *Liberal Leviathan: The Origins, Crisis, and Transformation of the American World Order* (Princeton, N.J.: Princeton University Press, 2011). For a more skeptical take, see Graham Allison, "The Myth of the Liberal Order: From Historical Accident to Conventional Wisdom," *Foreign Affairs*, July/August 2018. This final chapter draws on my essay "How a World Order Ends: And What Comes in Its Wake," *Foreign Affairs*, January/February 2019.

301 **United States get its own house in order:** I wrote about this at length in my book *Foreign Policy Begins at Home: The Case for Putting America's House in Order* (New York: Basic Books, 2013).

302 **Far higher percentage of GDP:** The Stockholm International Peace Research Institute (SIPRI) tracks military expenditure as a percentage of GDP from 1949 to the present. During the Cold War (1949–1991), the U.S. defense budget averaged approximately 7.3 percent of its GDP. In 1952 and 1953, defense spending topped 13 percent of U.S. GDP. In 2018, U.S. defense spending stood at 3.2 percent of GDP, or less than half the Cold War average. See SIPRI, "SIPRI Military Expenditure Database," https://www.sipri.org/databases/milex.

INDEX

Note: Page numbers in *italics* indicate illustrations and maps.

Abyssinia (Ethiopia), 23
Acheson, Dean, 34
Adams, John Quincy, 14
Afghanistan, 41, 47, 55–56, 62, 106–10, 124, 166, 196, 259, 281, 291, 295
Africa (sub-Saharan), 131–42, *132*
  development, 136–37, 241, 244–45
  economics, 136–38
  geopolitics, 136, 161
  and global health issues, 138, 210
  historical background, 133–36
  people and society, 138–39, *139*
  politics, 139–41
  regional institutions, 141
  terrorism, 169
  and UN Security Council, *275*
  See also specific countries
African Continental Free Trade Area, 138
African National Congress (ANC), 135, 140
African Union (AU), 141
Alawites, 113, 126
Albania, 32–33, 44
Algeria, 134
alliances, 12, 14, 36, 44, 67, 70, 72, 77–78, 89, 105, 219, 264–69, 287, 300
al-Qaeda, 47, 108–9, 130, 168–69, 259
America First movement, 26
American Civil War, 291
American War of Independence, 10
Americas, 143–53, *144*
  contemporary issues, 150–51
  geopolitics, 154
  historical background, 147
  overview, 143–47
  politics, 146–47
  violence and crime, 146, *146*, 151
  See also specific countries
Amnesty International, 260
Anarchical Society, The (Bull), 254–55

Anti-Ballistic Missile Treaty, 37
Antidumping Code, 223
apartheid, 134–35
appeasement, 23–24, 27, 265
Arabian Gulf, 112
Arabian Peninsula, 112
Arab League, 128
Arab nationalism, 117
Arab Spring, 54, 125–29
Arctic region, 63
Argentina, 55, 146, 150–51
arms control agreements, 37, 49, 72, 177, 255, 279, 296, 300
"Asian Tigers," 88–89, *89*
Asia-Pacific Economic Cooperation (APEC), 84
Assad, Bashar al-, 126
Association of Southeast Asian Nations (ASEAN), 84
Australia, 82, 89, 91, 109–10, 194
Austria, 7–8, 22, 24
Austria-Hungary, 11–12, 14, 280
authoritarianism and autocracy, 22–23, 39, 45–46, 54–56, 82, 87, 90, 99, 102, 113–14, 122, 125, 146–48, 297, 300, 302

Bahrain, 112, 125
balance of power, 8, 12, 26–27, 72, 130, 253, 255, 262–63, 270, 296
Balkans, 12, 67, 78
Bangladesh, 62, 97, 102, 104–5, 110, 185, 196
  population density, *103*
Basel Committee on Banking Supervision, 238
Bay of Pigs invasion, 148–49
Belgium, 19, 24, 71, 133–34
Belt and Road Initiative, 91, 110
Berlin blockade and airlift, 33, 40
Berlin Wall, 38, 41–43, 45
Bharatiya Janata Party (BJP), 101

bin Laden, Osama, 170–71. *See also* al-Qaeda
biological weapons, 170, 173, 283
bipolar/bipolarity, 39, 263
Bismarck, Otto von, 8, 13, 303
Boko Haram, 141, 168
Bosnia, 73
Brazil, 55, 145–46, 151, 153, 186
Bretton Woods Conference, 232
Brexit, 54–55, 75, 81
Brezhnev, Leonid, 38
Brezhnev Doctrine, 38
Britain. *See* Great Britain and the United Kingdom
Bulgaria, 32–33, 44
Bull, Hedley, 254–55
Bush, George H. W., 42, 45–46, 94, 123
Bush, George W., 109, 124

Camp David Accords, 262
Canada, 143, 145, 151–53, 194, 199, 226, 276, 302
cap and trade agreements, 51–52, 189
carbon dioxide emissions, 51–52, 183–84, 186–89
carbon tax, 189
Carter, Jimmy, 38–39
Castro, Fidel, 148
Catalonia, 289
Centers for Disease Control and Prevention (CDC), 213
Central African Republic, 140, 294
Central America, 146, 150, 198, 295. *See also specific countries*
Central Asia, 44, 55, 63, 99, *100*
Central Intelligence Agency (CIA), 148
chemical weapons, 16, 123, 126, 170, 173, 267, 283
Chiang Kai-shek, 85
Chile, 146
China
    and the Americas, 145–46
    and Asian geopolitics, 91–96
    and Asian regional history, 82, 84–87
    Civil War, 85
    and climate change, 186, 188, 190
    Cultural Revolution, 90
    and cyber policy, 203
    and development, 240–41, 243, 246–47
    early twentieth century history, 23
    and economic interdependence theory, 273
    economic reform and growth, 90–91
    and global governance, 274, *275*, 276
    Great Leap Forward, 90
    and Korean War, 34, 40, 85–86
    and liberal world order, 296–97, 299, 300–301, 302
    and migration, 195
    and monetary policy, 232, 234, *234*, 237–38
    nineteenth century history, 9
    and nuclear program, 174–77, *179*, 180
    and responsibility to protect (R2P) doctrine, 47, 259
    Sino-American relations, 49–51, 57, 93–94, 203, 218–19
    and South Asian geopolitics, 106, 109–10
    and sub-Saharan Africa, 136
    and Taiwan, 92–93, 261, 273
    and trade relations, *216*, 218, 220, 222–23

and Vietnam War, 34–35, 86–87
    and World War II, 28
Churchill, Winston, 16, 24, 30, 33, 264, 274
civil wars, *286*, 288, 291–94
Clausewitz, Carl von, 282
Clemenceau, Georges, 18
climate change, 51–52, 56–58, 183–92, *185, 191,* 198, 245, 301. *See also* global warming
Clinton, Bill, 77
coal power, 183, 186, 188
Cold War, 29–42
    alliances, 266, 268 (*see also* North Atlantic Treaty Organization (NATO); Warsaw Pact)
    and the Americas, 145–46, 148, 150
    and Asian regional history, 85, 86
    and development, 243, 245
    end of, 41–42
    and European regional history, 72
    major tests of, 33–35
    managing superpower rivalry, 36–40
    and Middle East regional history, 117–18
    and nuclear proliferation, 173–74, 176
    origins of, 18, 28–33
    and South Asia, 105
    and sub-Saharan Africa, 133–36
Colombia, 55, 151, 169, 295
colonialism, 8, 33, 114, 133, 136, 148, 168, 241
communication technology, 56, 160, *160*
Communism, 29–30, 70
Communist Party of China, 9, 88, 95
comparative advantage, 216–17
Comprehensive and Progressive Agreement for Trans-Pacific Partnership (CPTPP), 226, 279
conflict prevention, 198, 248
Congress of Vienna (Concert of Europe), 7–8, 300
containment doctrine, 32, 34
corruption, 113, 137, 140–41, 228, 246–49, 290
Crimea, 8, 49, 69, 79–80, 180, 260, 281, 294, 300. *See also* Ukraine
Crimean War, 8, 69, 300
cryptocurrency, 237
Cuba, 39, 148–49
Cuban missile crisis, 35, 148–49
currency manipulation, 219, 222–23, 225, 297
cyber security and warfare, 52–53, 129, 176, 201–7, 282
Cyprus, 67, 293
Czechoslovakia, 19, 24, 32–33, 38, 44
Czech Republic, 78

Dayton Accords, 73
decolonization, 33, 136, 262, 299
deforestation, 186
De Gaulle, Charles, 267
De Klerk, F. W., 135
democracy and democratization, 28, 29–31, 44, 54–56, 72–73, 81, 88–90, 124, 139–40, 146, 270–72, *271, 272,* 292
Democratic People's Republic of Korea. *See* North Korea
Democratic Republic of the Congo, 134, 140, 294
demographic shifts
    and challenges of post–Cold War Europe, 76
    and climate change, 185
    and development, 244–45

and East Asia, 95
impact on regions of the world, 63–64
and the Middle East, 112–14
population density in South Asia, *103*
and South Asian regional dynamics, 101
and sub-Saharan Africa, *139*
Deng Xiaoping, 50, 90
d'Estaing, Valéry Giscard, 237
détente, 40
deterrence, 37, 175, 180, 206, 262–63, 287, 296
developing countries, 39–40, 50, 189–90, 196, 209, 211, 240, 244
development, 240–50, *242*
Diaoyu Islands, 91. *See also* Senkaku Islands
Dien Bien Phu, 34, 86
diplomacy, 135, 254–55, 258, 278, 292–93
Doctors Without Borders, 260
Doha Round of trade negotiations, 225
dumping, 223, 225

East Asia and the Pacific, 53, 82–96, *83*
and Asian economic miracle, 88–90
geopolitics of, 91–95
historical background, 85–88
prospects for, 95–96
See also specific countries
East China Sea, 91–92
Eastern Europe, 19, 31–33, 42, 70, *275*, 297.
See also specific countries
East Germany, 32–33, 38, 43–44
East Pakistan, 104–5, 196
Ebola, 138, 161, 210
economic interdependence, 21–22, 161, 219–20, 272–73, 286–87
education, 88, 113, 228–29, 241, *242*, 244, 248–49, 290, 292
Egypt, 40, 111–12, 117–20, 125, 130, 262, 284–85
Eisenhower, Dwight, 117–18
El Salvador, 55, 150–51
embargo, 25, 282
"end of history" thesis, 81
Estonia, 33, 44
Ethiopia, 23. *See also* Abyssinia
euro (currency), 54, 74, *75*, 233, *234*, 236–37
Europe, 54–55, 67–81, *68*
alliances and coalitions, 265
economic and political challenges, 75–76
and emergence on modern international system, 5–6, 9–10
and geopolitical challenges, 77–81
historical background, 69–75
and Middle East regional history, 117
and migration challenge, 196–97
See also Eastern Europe; Western Europe; *specific countries*
European Central Bank, 54, 76
European Coal and Steel Community (ECSC), 71–72, 241
European Community (EC), 71–72, 74, 241
European Union (EU), 54, 61–62, 69, 72–76, *75*, 81
and cybersecurity issues, 205
and development, 241
and global governance, 275
and liberal world order, 298–99

and migration challenge, 197, 199
and sovereignty, 260
Euskadi Ta Askatasuna (ETA), 169
exclusive economic zone, 278
export controls, 223–24

failed states, 288–92, 294
fair trade, 220
Falkland Islands (Malvinas), 150
fascism, 22–23
fiat currency, 234–35
Financial Stability Board, 238
"Finlandization," 265
fiscal policy, 76, 231–32
5G technology, 50, 218–19
foreign aid, 105, 243, 247–48, 250
foreign direct investment, 159, 228
fossil fuels, *116*, 183, 185–88
Fourteen Points, 17
France
    and Cold War, 33–34, 39, 71, 86, 111, 117–18, 134, 267
    and global governance, 274, *275*, 276
    and interwar period, 18, 20
    and nineteenth century history, 7
    and nuclear proliferation, 129, 175–77, *179*, 267
    and post–Cold War era, 47, 54, 75, 109–10
    and World War I, 11, 14
    and World War II, 28
Franco-Prussian War, 19
Franz Ferdinand, Archduke of Austria, 12, 168
free trade, 88–89, 152–53, 220, 224, 226, 296, 298
French Revolution, 7
Fukuyama, Francis, 81

Gallipoli campaign, 16
Gandhi, Mahatma, 104
Gates Foundation, 213
Gaza Strip, 118, *119*, 120–21
General Agreement on Tariffs and Trade (GATT), *216*, 223–25, 296
General Data Protection Regulation, 205
Geneva Peace Conference, 86
genocide, 28, 35, 46, 56, 140, 258–59, 297
geoeconomics, 118
geo-engineering, 191–92
geopolitics, 77–81, 91–95, 105–6, 121–30, 136, 145, 161
Georgia, 33, 44, 67, 79, 281
Germany
    and Cold War, 31, 33, 43–44, 69–71
    and global governance, *275*, 276
    and interwar period, 18–19
    and monetary policy, 230–32, 236
    and nineteenth century history, 8–9, 69
    and nuclear proliferation, 129, 177
    and post–Cold War era, 76
    and World War I, 11–18
    and World War II, 21–28, 115, 265, 280
global financial crisis (2008-2009), 48, 161, *216*, 237–38, 299
global governance, 163–64, 189, 204, 273–76
global health, 208–14, *212*
globalization, 157–58, 159–65, *160*, 208, 217–18, 239, 273, 297–99, 301

global supply chain, 217–20, *219*
global warming, 186, *191*, 210. *See also* climate change
Golan Heights, 118, *119*
gold standard, 234–35
Gorbachev, Mikhail, 42
Great Britain and the United Kingdom
  and Afghanistan, 107
  and Cold War, 30–31, 33, 39
  colonialism and decolonization, 8–10, 33, 97, 104, 133
  and European regional history, 7, 74–75
  Falkland War, 150
  and global governance, 274, *275*
  and interwar period, 19–20
  and the Middle East, 117–18, 129
  and monetary policy, *234*
  and nuclear proliferation, 129, 175–77, *179*, 180
  and post–Cold War era, 47
  rise of, 11
  and South Asian regional history, 104
  and sub-Saharan Africa, 133–34, 140–41
  and World War I, 11, 14–15
  and World War II, 22–24, 27–28
Great Depression, 21–23, 31
"Great Firewall," 52
Great Leap Forward, 90
Greece, 19, 31, 54
Greenpeace, 260
Group of Eight (G8), 80, 276, 297
Group of Seven (G7), 151, 276
Group of Twenty (G20), 151, 276, 297
Guam, 148
Guatemala, 55, 151
Gulf Cooperation Council (GCC), 128–29
Gulf War, 45–46, 111, 123–24, 274, 281
gunboat diplomacy, 282

Hart, Liddell, 12
Helsinki Conference on Security and Cooperation in Europe, 72
Hezbollah, 128, 130
Hindus, 55–56, 63, 97, 101, 104
Hiroshima, Japan, 27, 182
Hitler, Adolf, 22–26, 71, 231, 303
HIV/AIDS, 138, 140–41, 209, *212*, 213, 249
Ho Chi Minh, 86
Holocaust, 28, 115
Honduras, 55, 150–51
Hong Kong, 51, 88, *89*
Human Development Index (HDI), 240–41, *242*, 248
humanitarianism and human rights, 38–39, 46, 50–51, 70, 89, 108, 110, 196–200, 203, 259, 297. *See also* development
Hungary, 32–33, 38, 44, 54, 78, 118, 272
Hussein, Saddam, 45–46, 54, 122–24

import substitution, 246
India
  and climate change, 185–86, 188, 190
  and Cold War, 105
  and cybersecurity issues, 203
  and democratization, 101–2, 271
  economic development, 99–101, 245
  and geopolitics, 92, 104–6, 109–10, 294, 302
  and global governance, 275
  and human development, 101, 245
  independence, 33, 104
  and migration, 195–96
  and nuclear program, 176, 178, *179*
  population density, *103*
  and post–Cold War era, 55–56, 62
  and view on sovereignty, 259
Indian National Congress (INC), 101, 104
Indonesia, 62, 84, 97, 186
infectious disease, 138, 161–62, 208–14, *212*, 243
intellectual property, 50, 201, 203–4, 223–26, 228–29, 297
internal instability and war within countries, 288–95
internally displaced persons (IDPs), 193–94, *194*, 196, 199–200
International Atomic Energy Agency (IAEA), 176
International Bank for Reconstruction and Development. *See* World Bank
International Court of Justice, 276–77
International Criminal Court, 277
International Health Regulations, 213
international law, 193, 197, 276–79
International Monetary Fund (IMF), 232–33, 237, 296–97
internet, 160–61, 201–7, *202*
Internet Corporation for Assigned Names and Numbers (ICANN), 202–3
investment, 227–30
Iran, 54, 113–14, 121–30, 168
  nuclear program, 52, 106, 115, 129–30, 177–78, 204, 284
  and sanction regimes, 129–30, 238
Iran-Iraq War, 111, 123
Iraq, 121–24
  and Arab Spring, 127–28
  and intrastate conflict, 293
  and nation-building efforts, 124, 295
  and nuclear weapons program, 129, 179–80, 284
  and post–Cold War era, 45–46, 53–54, 56, 128
Iraq War, 124, 285, 299–300
Islam, 63, 97, 107–8, 112–15, 122–29, 131, 141
Islamic State (ISIS), 126–27, 130, 168–69, 171
isolationism, 14, 20, 24–26, 32
Israel, 40, 54, 111–13, 115, 117–21, *119*, 128–30, 262
  and cyber issues, 52, 204
  and nuclear program, 129–30, 176, 178, *179*
  and preventive/preemptive war, 181, 284–85
Italy, 9, 14, 19, 21–24, 27–28, 54, 69, 71, 133, 268, 276

Japan
  alliances, 89, 176, 267
  and Asian economic miracle, 88–91
  and Asian geopolitics, 91–93, 95, 302
  and Asian regional history, 82, 85–86, 90
  and Cold War, 30–31, 33–34
  and global governance, 275–76
  and global health, 209
  and monetary policy, 232–33, *234*, 237
  nineteenth century history, 8–10
  and prevalence of war, 286

and South Asian regional dynamics, 109–10
and World War II, 21–28
Jerusalem, 115, 118, *119,* 120
Jinnah, Mohammed Ali, 104
Joint Comprehensive Plan of Action (JCPOA), 129–30, 177–78, 279
Jordan, 112, 118–21, 127
Judaism, 63, 113, 115

Kashmir, *98,* 104–6, 110
Kazakhstan, 44, 99, *100*
Kellogg-Briand Pact, 21
Kennan, George, 32
Kennedy, John F., 35, 148–49, 182
Kennedy, Paul, 41
Keynes, John Maynard, 25–26
Khan, A. Q., 106
Khomeini, Ruhollah, 122
Kissinger, Henry, 87
Korea. *See* North Korea; South Korea
Korean War, 34, 40, 85–86, 94
Kosovo, 73, 261
Kosovo War, 73, 78
Kurds, 46, 113, 123–24, 127, 130, 293
Kuwait, 45–46, 53–54, 112, 123–24, 127, 274, 281

Lashkar-e-Taiba, 168
Latin America, 39, 55, 63–64, 241, *275. See also specific countries*
Latvia, 44
League of Nations, 17–20, 23–24, 26, 274
least developed countries, 240
lend-lease program, 24
Lenin, Vladimir, 18, 22
liberal world order, 296–303
Libya, 47, 106, 125, 179–80, 248, 259, 285, 291, 299–300
life expectancy, 55–56, 77, 88, 95, 101, 138, 209–10, 241, *242,* 244
Lima Group, 152
Lindbergh, Charles, 26
Lithuania, 44
Luxembourg, 71

Maastricht Treaty, 74
MacArthur, Douglas, 85
malaria, 138, 209, *212,* 213, 249
Maldives, 110
Malvinas (Falkland Islands), 150
Manchuria, 23
Mandela, Nelson, 135–36
Mao Zedong, 9, 85, 90
Marshall, George, 31, 71. *See also* Marshall Plan
Marshall Plan, 31–32, 71–73, 241
Meiji Restoration, 10
mercantilism, 220
Mexico, 12, 55, 102, 145–47, 151–53, 195, 226, 271, 290, 295
Middle East, 53–54, 111–30, *112*
and Arab Spring, 125–29
and Cold War, 40
and development, 241
energy resources, 114–15, *116,* 185–88
historical background, 117–21
and intrastate conflict, 289, 291

and Iran-Iraq dynamics, 121–24
and nation-building efforts, 295
and nuclear proliferation, 129–30, 178
overview, 111–15, *112*
and post–Cold War era, 53
and refugees, 197
sources of instability, 129–30
and terrorism, 115, 169
See also specific countries
Middle East respiratory syndrome, 210
migrants and migration, 76, 193–200, *194*
Millennium Development Goals, 249
Minsk Agreement, 80
monetary policy, 54, 230–39, *234*
monetary unions, 74–75
Monroe, James, 147
Monroe Doctrine, 39, 147–48
Morocco, 127
mujahideen, 107
multilateralism, 163–64, 269
multipolar/multipolarity, 263, 269
Muslim Brotherhood, 125
Mussolini, Benito, 23
Myanmar (Burma), 83–84, 102

Nagasaki, Japan, 27, 182
Napoleon I, Emperor of the French, 7, 25, 69, 147–48, 303
Napoleonic Wars, 147
nationalism
and interwar period, 19–20
and liberal world order, 298–99, 302
and post–Cold War era, 44, 54–56, 70, 73–74, 81
and World War I, 12–13, 255
and World War II, 26, 255
nation-building, 124, 294. *See also* Marshall Plan
Nauru, 82
Netherlands, 24, 71, 75, 134
New Zealand, 82, 84, 194
Nicaragua, 39, 150
Nigeria, 134, 138, 140–41, 169
Nixon, Richard, 87, 94
Non-Aligned Movement, 39–40
noncommunicable diseases (NCDs), 138, 211–14, *212*
non-state actors, 130, 166, 169–70, 260–61, 289, 299. *See also* terrorism and counterterrorism
nontariff barriers, 221–22, 225–26, 297, 301
North American Free Trade Agreement (NAFTA), *152,* 152–53, 226
North Atlantic Treaty Organization (NATO)
and Afghanistan, 109
and Cold War, 32, 36, 42, 67, 70, 72, 255
general background, 266–68
geographical depiction of, *30*
and global governance, 276
and post–Cold War era, 44, 47, 49–53, 69, 73, 77–80, 298
and responsibility to protect doctrine, 47, 259
and Yugoslavia conflict, 46, 73, 78, 276, 293
Northern Ireland, 108, 168, 293–94
Northern Triangle, 55, 151
North Korea
and Asian geopolitics, 93
and Asian regional history, 82, 85–86

North Korea (*cont.*)
   and Cold War, 34, 40
   and cyber issues, 52, 204
   and globalization, 163
   and nuclear weapons program and proliferation,
      53, 106, 176, 178–80, *179,* 204, 279, 284
North Vietnam, 35, 86–87
nuclear power, 176–77, 186–88
nuclear weapons and proliferation, 173–82, *174, 179*
   and Asian geopolitics, 92
   and Cold War, 36–37, 72
   cyberattacks on nuclear programs, 204
   and Middle East instability, 129–30
   and mutually assured destruction (MAD), 36
   and post–Cold War era, 45, 51, 52
   and regional dynamics of the Americas, 145
   and South Asia, 106
   and terrorism, 169–70
   and types of war, 283
   and World War II, 27

Obama, Barack, 126, 130, 226
oil and gas resources, *116,* 151, 183, 186, 292
Opium Wars, 9
order and disorder, 253–56
Organization of African Unity (OAU), 141
Organization of American States (OAS), 152
Organization of Petroleum Exporting Countries
   (OPEC), 114–15
Oslo accords, 120
Ottoman Empire, 8, 11–12, 16, 19, 117, 122, 280
outer space, 52–53, 278, 301
Outer Space Treaty, 53
Owen, Wilfred, 16

Pahlavi, Mohammed Reza, Shah of Iran, 122
Pakistan
   and Asian geopolitics, 92
   modern history of, 104–5
   and nuclear program and proliferation, 176,
      178, *179*
   population density, *103*
   and post–Cold War era, 55–56, 290
   and refugees, 196, 198–99
   and South Asian regional dynamics, 55, 62, 97,
      99–103, 105–10, 294
   and terrorism, 169–71
Palestine and Israeli-Palestinian conflict, 33, 54,
   104, 112, 115, *119,* 120–21, 168, 262
Palestine Liberation Organization (PLO), 168
Panama Canal, 148
Paris Agreement, 51–52, 190, *191,* 279
Paris Peace Accords, 87
Paris Peace Conference, 18
peacekeeping, 46, 73, 281, 292–93
Pearl Harbor attack, 27
Persian Gulf, 112, *113*
Philippines, 33, 82–84, 89, 148, 195, 271–72, 297
Poland, 19, 24–25, 31–33, 38, 44, 54, 78, 272
populism, 48, 54–55, 76, 81, 147, 197, 299, 302
Portugal, 133, 147
post–Cold War era, 4, 43–57, 255
poverty, 55, 90, 101, 131, 136–37, *137,* 169, 215,
   243–45, 249–50
Powell, Colin, 108, 228

preemption and preemptive war, 181, 284–85
prevention and preventive war, 175, 181,
   283–85, 292
privatization, 246–47
protectionism, 21–22, 26, 162–63, 220, 224, 227,
   246, 255, 302
Provisional Irish Republican Army, 168
Prussia, 7–8, 11, 18
Puerto Rico, 148
Putin, Vladimir, 49, 78–79

Qaddafi, Muammar al-, 125
Qatar, 112, 114

Reagan, Ronald, 38–39
refugees, 56, 70, 102, 104–5, 110, 120, 136, 159,
   161, 185, 193–99, 210, 243, 248, 285, 294
religious identity and conflict, 5, 63, 101–2,
   175, 294
renewable energy resources, 186–88
reparations, 18–19, 21–22, 26
Republic of Korea. *See* South Korea
reserve currencies, 233–39, *234*
Responsibility to Protect (R2P), 46–47, 258–59,
   297–98
Revolutionary Armed Forces of Colombia
   (FARC), 169
Ricardo, David, 216–17
Rohingya refugees, 102
Romania, 19, 32–33, 44
Roosevelt, Franklin Delano, 24, 26–27, 30, 148
Roosevelt, Theodore, 148
Roosevelt Corollary, 148
Russia
   and Arab Spring, 126
   and Asian geopolitics, 91
   civil war, 18
   and collapse of Soviet Union, 44
   election interference, 49, 53, 81, 204, 260
   and Georgia, 281
   and global governance, 274, *275,* 276
   and interwar period, 18
   and liberal world order, 49, 79, 296–97, 298,
      300–301
   and nuclear proliferation, 129–30, 176–78,
      179, 180
   and post–Cold War era, 49, 77, 79–80, 266,
      285, 294
   and responsibility to protect doctrine, 47, 259
   Russia-U.S. relations, 49, 71, 79–81, 279
   and Ukraine, 54, 79–81, 281, 298
   and views on sovereignty, 260
   and World War I, 11–12, 14, 18
   and World War II, 25, 27, 30–31
   See also Soviet Union
Russo-Japanese War, 10
Rwandan civil war and genocide, 46, 140, 259

Sadat, Anwar, 119
sanctions, 23, 46, 49, 73, 80, 123, 129–30, 135,
   166, 170, 177–80, 206, 211, 238, 259, 282,
   284, 292–93, 297, 301
Santayana, George, 3
Saudi Arabia, 112, 114, 127–30, 286, 300
Schengen Area, 74

Schuman, Robert, 71
secession, 140, 288, 291
Second Boer War, 134
self-determination, 17–19, 127, 261–62
Senkaku Islands, 91. *See also* Diaoyu Islands
September 11, 2001 terrorist attacks (9/11), 47–48,
    108–9, 166–69, 171, 259–60
Serbia, 12, 73, 78, 261, 293
severe acute respiratory syndrome (SARS), 210
Sharia law, 108, 141
Shia Islam, 113, 122–24, 126, 128
Sinai Peninsula, 118
Singapore, 84, 88, *89*
Sino-Indian War, 84, 106
Six-Day War, 118, 120, 281, 285
slavery, 133
Smoot-Hawley Tariff Act, 21, 221
Somalia, 131, 240, 290, 294
South Africa, 134–36, 138, 140, 178–79, 182
South Asia, 55–56, 97–111, *98*
    and China, 109–10
    and development, 244–45
    history and geopolitics of, 104–6
    India-Pakistan relations, 99–106, 196
    ongoing challenges, 109–10
    population density, *103*
    See also specific countries
South Asian Association for Regional Cooperation
    (SAARC), 97
South China Sea, 50, 91, 297
Southeast Asia, 33–34, 84. *See also specific*
    countries
South Korea
    alliances, 267
    and Asian economic miracle, 88–91, *89*
    and Asian geopolitics, 91, 93
    and Asian regional history, 86
    and Cold War, 34, 40
    and development, 247
    and post–Cold War era, 77
South Sudan, 196, 240, 288–89, 294
South Vietnam, 34–35, 86–87
sovereignty, 6–7, 47, 61, 74, 203, 255, 257–61
Soviet Union
    alliances and coalitions, 265–66
    and Asian geopolitics, 94
    and Cold War, 29–42, 133–34, 148–50,
        203, 243
    collapse of, 43–44, 73
    and European regional history, 69–70
    and nuclear proliferation, 173–79, 283–84
    origins of, 18, 22
    and preventive/preemptive war, 283–84
    Soviet-Afghan War, 107
    and Vietnam, 34–35, 86–87
    and World War II, 25, 27–28, 30–31
    See also Russia
Space Command, 53
Spain, 133, 147–48, 169, 289
Spanish-American War, 148
Spanish flu, 210
sphere of influence, 38–39, 69–70, 117, 302
Sri Lanka, 110, 203
Stalin, Joseph, 22, 25, 30–31, 34
state-owned enterprises, 222, 246

Strait of Hormuz, 130
Straits of Tiran, 118
Strategic Arms Limitation Talks (SALT), 36
Strategic Arms Reduction Treaty (START), 36
sub-Saharan Africa. *See* Africa (sub-Saharan)
subsidies, 39, 50, 162, 222–23, 225, 246, 297, 301
Sudan, 131, 140, 199, 285, 288–89
Sudetenland, 24
Suez Crisis, 117–18
Sunni Islam, 55, 107–8, 113, 122–24, 126–29
Sustainable Development Goals, 213, 250
Sykes-Picot Agreement, 117
Syria, 40, 49, 80–81, 112–113, 118, 120, 125–29,
    181, 196, 198, 248, 259, 284–85, 290–91,
    294, 300

Taiwan, 82, 85, 88–89, *89*, 92–93, 95, 182, 261, 273
Taliban, 55, 107–9, 166–68, 259, 291
tariffs, 21, 162, 218, 220–21, 223–25, 226–27, 247,
    282, 297, 301
technology and technological advance
    and development, 244, 246, 248–49
    and globalization, 159–61
    and the internet and cyberspace, 201–7
    Internet of Things, 202
    and liberal world order, 299, 301
    and trade relations, 216, 223–24, 228–29
    and World War I, 16
terrorism and counterterrorism, 12, 36, 47–48, 51,
    55, 56, 62, 102, 105–6, 108–10, 115, 121,
    126, 136, 141, 146, 166–72, *167*, 175, 181,
    201, 203–4, 206, 243, 259–60, 281, 288–89,
    294–95, 299, 300
Thailand, 82–84, 89
Thatcher, Margaret, 150
Thirty Years' War, 3, 5–6, 69, 257, 281
Thucydides, 280
Tiananmen Square protests, 94
total war, 283
trade, 88–89, 152, 159–62, 215–29, *216*, 246–47,
    296, 298–99, 301
trade adjustment assistance, 227
trade balance (surplus/deficit), 76, 217–18, 220,
    232, 234–36
treaties, 278–79. *See also* alliances; *specific treaty*
    names
Treaty of Versailles, 18–19, 22, 24, 26, 71
Treaty of Westphalia, 3–4, *6*, 6–8, 257
Treaty on the Non-Proliferation of Nuclear
    Weapons (NPT), 175–76, 178, 279, 298
Truman, Harry, 27, 31, 42, 85
Truman Doctrine, 31
Trump, Donald, 52, 126–27, 129–30, 153, 190,
    197–98, 221, 279, 300
Tuchman, Barbara, 25
Tunisia, 125
Turkey, 31, 35, 117, 127, 129–30, 149, 198–99, 272,
    293, 297

Uganda, 198–99
Uighurs, 50–51
Ukraine
    and the Cold War, 33
    and nuclear weapons, 178–80, 182
    and post–Cold War era, 44, 49, 79–81

Ukraine (*cont.*)
  and Russian military intervention, 49, 79–81,
    260, 281, 285, 300
  See also Crimea
unconventional war, 283
underdeveloped countries, 240
ungoverned spaces, 289–90
unipolar/unipolarity, 263
United Arab Emirates, 112, 127
United Kingdom. *See* Great Britain and the United
    Kingdom
United Nations (UN), 30–31, 273–75
  alliances and coalitions, 34, 46, 85, 268–69
  Convention on the Law of the Sea (UNCLOS),
    278–79
  and cyberspace, 203
  and development, 249
  General Assembly, 115, 258, 275
  High Commissioner for Refugees
    (UNHCR), 197
  and liberal world order, 296
  and migration, 193
  and principle of self-defense, 277
  and refugees and internally displaced persons,
    197–99
  and responsibility to protect, 46–47
  Security Council, 46–47, 77, 85, 120, 178,
    274–76, 275, 297, 299
  and self-determination, 261–62
United States
  and Afghanistan, 107–9, 124, 166–68, 295, 299
  alliance system, 89, 266–67
  and the Americas, 143, 145, 151, 153
  and Asian geopolitics, 94–95
  and climate change, 185–86
  and Cold War, 29–33, 36–42, 263
  and cyber issues, 203–5
  and decolonization, 33
  and development, 240–41, 243
  and global governance, 274, 275
  and global health issues, 208
  and globalization, 161
  and interwar period, 20
  and liberal world order, 296–303
  and migration, 193–96
  and monetary policy, 233–39, 234
  and nuclear proliferation, 173–78, 179, 180–82
  and post–Cold War era, 47, 49–53, 56–57
  and preventive/preemptive war, 284–85
  and responsibility to protect doctrine, 47, 259
  Sino-American relations, 49–51, 57, 93–94, 203,
    218–19
  and South Asia, 99, 105, 109–10
  and trade relations, 215–20, 226
  U.S.-Russia relations, 49, 71, 79–81, 279
  and World War I, 14–16
United States-Mexico-Canada Agreement
    (USMCA), 153, 226
U.S. Federal Reserve, 236–37

Venezuela, 55, 114, 145, 150–52, 198, 231, 290
Vietnam, 34–35, 84, 86–88, 302
Vietnam War, 34–35, 82, 86–88, 94

war and warfare, 280–87, 283, 286
Warsaw Pact, 36, 44, 72, 266, 268
  geographical depiction of, 30
Washington, George, 14
weak states, 55, 63, 146, 243, 288–90,
    294, 300
wealth inequality, 48, 56, 69, 76, 81, 101, 140, 147,
    169, 245, 249–50, 291, 299
weapons of mass destruction (WMD), 53, 173,
    175, 204. *See also* nuclear weapons and
    proliferation
Weber, Max, 258
Weimar Republic, 21–22
West Bank, 118, 119, 120–21
West Berlin, 33, 38, 41, 43, 149
Western Europe, 7, 64, 72–73
West Germany, 33, 43–44, 70, 73
Wilson, Woodrow, 17, 20
World Bank, 50, 213, 232, 240–41, 296–97
World Health Organization (WHO), 212–13
World Trade Organization (WTO), 50, 216,
    223–26, 228, 260, 296–97, 301
World War I
  American entry, 15–16
  casualties of, 16, 282
  causes of and paths to, 11–13, 168
  Central and Allied powers, 15
  end of, 18–20
  and Kurds, 127
  and Middle East regional history, 117
  and origins of World War II, 26
  outbreak of, 14
World War II
  and African regional history, 134
  American entry, 27
  and Asian geopolitics, 91, 94
  and Asian regional history, 82, 85–86
  casualties of, 27–28, 282
  causes and outcomes of, 21–28
  and European regional history, 69
  and nation-building efforts, 295
  and refugees, 196
  and South Asian regional history, 104

Xi Jinping, 50–51

Yalta conference, 30–31
Yemen, 112, 125, 128, 285, 290–91,
    294, 300
Yom Kippur War (October War), 40, 118–19
Yugoslavia, 19, 46, 73, 78, 276, 280, 291

Zika, 210
Zimbabwe, 231
Zimmermann Telegram, 15